Enhancing Children's Cognition With Physical Activity Games

Phillip D. Tomporowski
Bryan A. McCullick
Caterina Pesce

Human Kinetics

Library of Congress Cataloging-in-Publication Data

Tomporowski, Phillip D., 1948-
  Enhancing children's cognition with physical activity games / Phillip D. Tomporowski, Bryan A. McCullick, Caterina Pesce.
    pages cm
  Includes bibliographical references and index.
  1. Exercise for children--Psychological aspects. 2. Cognition--Effect of exercise on. I. McCullick, Bryan A. II. Pesce, Caterina, 1963- III. Title.
  GV443.T64 2015
  613.7'042--dc23
                    2014025420

ISBN: 978-1-4504-4142-1 (print)

The web addresses cited in this text were current as of October 2014, unless otherwise noted.

Acquisitions Editors: Cheri Scott and Ray Vallese; **Developmental Editor:** Ragen E. Sanner; **Managing Editors:** Tyler Wolpert, Coree Clark, and Karla Walsh; **Copyeditor:** Patsy Fortney; **Indexer:** Alisha Jeddeloh; **Permissions Manager:** Dalene Reeder; **Graphic Designer:** Denise Lowry; **Cover Designer:** Keith Blomberg; **Photograph (cover):** © Human Kinetics; **Photographs (interior):** © Human Kinetics, unless otherwise noted; **Photo Asset Manager:** Laura Fitch; **Photo Production Manager:** Jason Allen; **Art Manager:** Kelly Hendren; **Associate Art Manager:** Alan L. Wilborn; **Illustrations:** © Human Kinetics, unless otherwise noted; **Printer:** Sheridan Books

Printed in the United States of America   10 9 8 7 6 5 4 3 2 1

The paper in this book is certified under a sustainable forestry program.

Human Kinetics
Website: www.HumanKinetics.com

United States: Human Kinetics, P.O. Box 5076, Champaign, IL 61825-5076
800-747-4457
e-mail: humank@hkusa.com

Canada: Human Kinetics, 475 Devonshire Road Unit 100, Windsor, ON N8Y 2L5
800-465-7301 (in Canada only)
e-mail: info@hkcanada.com

Europe: Human Kinetics, 107 Bradford Road, Stanningley, Leeds LS28 6AT, United Kingdom
+44 (0) 113 255 5665
e-mail: hk@hkeurope.com

Australia: Human Kinetics, 57A Price Avenue, Lower Mitcham, South Australia 5062
08 8372 0999
e-mail: info@hkaustralia.com

New Zealand: Human Kinetics, P.O. Box 80, Torrens Park, South Australia 5062
0800 222 062
e-mail: info@hknewzealand.com

E5818

Contents

Part I *Physical Activity and Mental Development. . 1*

Foreword

The relationship between physical activity and cognition has been well established in adult and older adult populations. Phillip Tomporowski, Bryan McCullick, and Caterina Pesce present evidence-based information that addresses the same relationship among children. The collective expertise of the authors is maximized in *Enhancing Children's Cognition With Physical Activity Games.* The authors present a synthesis of basic research and ways of applying and translating it. This book will intrigue both scientists and nonscientists with information about children's movement patterns and motor development, implications of physical activity on cognition, how movement games can help children learn, how to motivate and engage children to learn through physical activity, teaching cognitive games, assessing children at play, and specific examples of games for various settings.

There is a strong need for this book, particularly among school health professionals, physical education teachers, and public health professionals who recognize the link between physical activity and learning. While many studies have been published indicating the relationship between physical activity and some aspects of learning (e.g., concentration, attention, time on task), many professionals have not had an authoritative resource on the science, practical strategies, and actual games that can be integrated into homes, preschools, and schools. This book meets that need.

The games presented align with SHAPE America's national standards for K-12 physical education. They are user friendly, enabling teachers of many abilities to integrate games in a variety of settings. Researchers, physical education teachers, classroom teachers, parents, and public health professionals will benefit from the accessibility of the scientific content. By encouraging multiple sectors of society to help young people engage in more physical activity games, we might just see a serious advancement in our education system.

Sarah M. Lee

Team lead, research application and evaluation team

School Health Branch

Division of Population Health

National Center for Chronic Disease Prevention and Health Promotion

Disclaimer: The findings and conclusions in this presentation are those of the authors and do not necessarily represent the views of the Centers for Disease Control and Prevention.

Preface

Our purpose in writing this book was to introduce practitioners to methods of teaching that can enhance children's physical and mental development. Our hope is that *Enhancing Children's Cognition With Physical Activity Games* will help educators apply concepts drawn from recent research in child development, cognitive science, physical education, and teacher training to create movement-based learning experiences that benefit children in both body and mind. The book is for anyone directly involved in engaging children in physical activity.

Regardless of background and preparation, this book provides insight into new ways to teach children. It not only provides examples of age-appropriate games that can be easily performed in real-world settings, but also explains why these games are so successful. It puts the teacher in the driver's seat by explaining how to structure games in a way that facilitates making those on-the-spot modifications so critical when teaching children.

This book is for teachers who instruct children in many contexts; for instance, preschools, after-school and in-school programs, and recreation and community centers. Our central theme is that teachers can create physical activity games that benefit children's cognitive development, learning, socialization, and academic performance. Our goal is to help teachers develop physical activity games that foster mental engagement and thoughtful decision making. At the heart of these instructional models is cross-disciplinary evidence that games that combine moderate-to-vigorous physical activity with appropriate instruction and feedback develop children's cognition, particularly those that underlie the capacity to think before acting, to remain focused and attentive, and to plan and reflect on the consequences of actions. The book is both an academic resource and an instructional model to help educators develop and implement physical activity games that motivate children to learn. To link academic information to authentic teaching conditions, we conclude each chapter with a section titled Implications for Educators.

Preschools, in-school, and after-school programs provide unique opportunities to develop programs that enhance children's physical and mental development. Over the past decade, after-school programs in the United States have played an increasingly important role in providing physical activity opportunities for children. Approximately 8.4 million American children were enrolled in after-school programs in 2009. Federal support for the 21st-Century Community Learning Centers began in 1998, and this program now targets $1 billion in annual funds to low-performing schools in disadvantaged areas serving approximately 1.2 million children. Although most after-school programs include time for free play and exercise, lacking is access to quality physical activity interventions that can be used by teachers and paraprofessionals. Numerous programs focus on children's physical fitness development; the physical activity games in this book are unique because they focus on both the physical health and mental development of children.

This book presents instructional methods from preparation and design, to implementation and evaluation. It was written by three authorities in the fields of teacher education, exercise psychology, and sport science. Each author has multidisciplinary training and experiences that link research and application. Thus, the physical activity games presented are based on research evidence and sound educational theory.

Scope of the Book

Physical activity plays an important role in many aspects of our lives. As such, the topics we address in this book range widely. However, the central focus of the book is on methods of teaching physical activity games in ways that promote learning. Our teaching methods and games are firmly rooted in theory and research drawn from many disciplines: child development, neurobiology, psychology, and teacher education. As a result, you can be confident in offering these games to the children entrusted to you.

Developmental psychology helps us understand how children's mental abilities emerge and how these capacities can be enhanced by teaching conditions that promote mental engagement and problem solving. In this book we offer evidence that games provide a natural context in which to learn and develop foundational executive functions. Successful programming requires developmentally appropriate games that are introduced at teachable moments.

The neurobiology of learning reveals the importance of games and conditions that keep children on the learning curve. Problem-solving games have been found to be intrinsically motivating for children. Games that increase excitement and mental engagement promote the development of cognitive skills that can be used to overcome challenges in daily activities and academic classes. New views of learning explain why games that involve responding to unexpected changes result in gains in mental ability, but that games that are routine, repetitive, and lacking in mental engagement do not.

Information drawn from theories of motivation is provided to help teachers arrange games that energize and motivate children to be physically active. Lessons learned from research on the attraction of computer games have provided insights into how to create games that promote healthy levels of physical activity. This is important because children's participation in physical activity games provides long-term benefits and establishes lifelong patterns of positive health activities.

Information drawn from the teacher effectiveness, sport pedagogy, and teacher training body of literature provides the basis for our discussion on how to select and implement physical activity games to produce favorable outcomes.

Unique Features of the Book

This book describes how specific games can be used and modified to meet the wide variety in children's abilities, backgrounds, and experiences. It is specifically for teachers working with children between the ages of 3 and 11. Glossary terms are provided with definitions in both a running glossary throughout the chapters and a complete glossary at the end of the book. Glossary terms within the text are highlighted in **bold** for easy identification.

How the Book Is Organized

This book is presented in three parts. Part I focuses on foundational information about children's physical and mental development. Chapter 1 draws primarily from the field of developmental psychology to describe the emergence of children's mental abilities and how they can be enhanced by physical activity experiences that promote mental engagement and problem solving. Chapter 2 presents neurodevelopmental research findings that explain how changes in children's developing brains provide windows of opportunity for movement-based game experiences that can directly affect the neural networks that are critical to the control of thought and action. Chapter 3 introduces a theory that will help teachers understand how children learn from their actions, how to use teachable moments, and how to address the wide differences in physical and mental development that exist among children. Chapter 4 makes the case that games can create motivational climates for learning and enjoyment. You will see that when physical activity games are presented in specific ways, they capture children's attention and engage them mentally. The energizing aspects of game play set the stage for children to learn mental skills that are used not only in game activities but also in daily activities and academic classes.

Part II focuses on translating research into practice to help teachers put into action the material presented in part I. We discuss the challenges involved in developing, implementing, and assessing the effectiveness of physical activity games. Chapter 5 describes the benefits children derive from being physically active early in life and how such activity can profoundly influence their physical and mental health throughout life. Clearly, physical activity teachers are very influential in promoting the health and wellness of the whole child. Chapter 6 addresses physical activity game development and describes the many options available when creating physical activity games that enhance children's cognition. Drawing from research on children's mental development, we outline three central principles that simplify game development. Chapter 7 focuses on the challenges of implementing physical activity games and offers guidance in being prepared to meet those challenges. Teaching is partly science and partly art. Chapter 8 describes ways to assess the impact of physical activity games on pupils' behaviors both in and out of the classroom. Ecological models that emphasize the important roles physical activity teachers play and their effects on children's health, wellness, and learning are introduced in chapter 9. Physical activity teachers are uniquely positioned to address the numerous health and educational problems challenging societies worldwide.

Part III provides games for preschool- and kindergarten-age children between 3 and 6 years of age (chapter 10) and for elementary school–age children between 7 and 11 years of age (chapter 11). Links are made between the foundational materials introduced in part I and the application of those materials presented in part II. Preschool games emphasize instructional methods that capitalize on children's natural inclination to engage in exploration, fantasy, and make-believe. Elementary school games emphasize direct instructional methods to bolster fundamental movement skills and encourage their use in complex situations. Each game reflects basic principles of learning, and examples show how they can be modified to meet teachers' specific needs.

Although we provide examples of games for children, we consider them prototypes based on principles of child development and learning. Attentive reading of this book will provide insights into how teachers can create and implement games of their own design.

Children learn much about themselves and the world they live in through experience. Physical activity games provide opportunities to learn how to solve problems and to acquire physical and mental skills that can be used throughout life. This book will start physical educators on the path to preparing their students to succeed physically, mentally, and emotionally.

Acknowledgments

To my wife, Regina Smith, who has been the source of my motivation, and my daughter, Ellis, who continues to be the light of my life.

Phil Tomporowski

To Alison and Adaline, Grá mo chroí sibh (You are the love of my heart).

Bryan McCullick

To my parents and to my children, who inspired insight for this book. My parents let me enjoy playing movement games when I was a child. My children, Sofia, Luca, and Matthias, did not let me stop enjoying movement games when I became an adult.

Caterina Pesce

In memory of Dr. Cliff Baile for his support of the development of our physical activity games as part of the University of Georgia Obesity Initiative.

Part I

Physical Activity and Mental Development

The importance of physical activity on children's developing minds was voiced by ancient Greek philosophers and echoed in the writings of many educators over the past 2,500 years. Only recently, however, has the link between physical activity and mental development been established. New research findings provide teachers with novel ways to organize and instruct classes that can profoundly influence the way children think and behave.

Chapters 1 through 4 describe why physical activity is essential for children to achieve maximal efficiency of their bodies and minds. Information is drawn from many academic disciplines to explain how children develop physically and mentally. An appreciation of how physical activity influences the developing brain will help physical educators understand how specific types of game interventions, presented in a precise way, can affect the way children think and act. These chapters explain how the subtle arrangement of instructional conditions increases children's motivation to be physically active and optimizes their mental development. Part I makes a clear case for the assertion that physical education teachers are uniquely positioned to guide children's physical and mental development in ways that can benefit them for the remainder of their lives.

Understanding Children's Mental Development

Without the need to move, there really is not much of a need to have a brain. For example, consider the life cycle of a very different, but evolutionary successful species, the sea squirt. This simple multicellular sea plant spends its adult life rooted to the bottom of the ocean and filter-feeds. When it is time to reproduce, it does so by budding and casting off larvae. The larval form is briefly free-swimming and is equipped with a brainlike ganglion containing approximately 300 cells. This primitive nervous system receives sensory information about the surrounding environment through an organ of balance, a rudimentary patch of skin that serves as a simple eye, and a primitive spinal cord. These features allow the tadpole-like creature to move and negotiate the ever-changing world within which it swims. Upon finding a suitable location, the larva proceeds to bury its head into a selected crevasse. Once reattached to a stationary object, the larva

absorbs and digests most of its own brain, including its tail musculature, thereupon regressing to the rather primitive adult stage: sessile and lacking a true nervous system. Because it no longer needs to move, it remains in this position for the remainder of its life. The lesson here is that the evolutionary development of a nervous system is an exclusive property of moving creatures. A nervous system is required to orchestrate and express active, goal-directed movement—a biological property known as **motricity**.

To understand how children's physical activity helps advance mental function, we need to know how children develop. For thousands of years, parents

> **motricity**—A biological property of the nervous system that oversees goal-directed actions.

3

and teachers have observed children and how they change. Scientists have systematically studied children for over a century. Much has been learned from developmental psychologists, pediatric physicians, exercise scientists, and other specialists that teachers can use to create innovative instructional approaches to engage children in meaningful play and problem solving. Advances in neuroscience and the psychology of learning, for example, have revealed important evidence about developing children that has still not been fully integrated into the curricula of teacher preparation programs.

Some of this information provides support for the insight of experienced teachers who have developed excellent instructional methods in which students do more than just sit at a desk or stand in line awaiting a chance to participate. Other information may seem to have little to do with educational techniques and is therefore less well known by many teacher educators and therefore not introduced to those learning to teach, yet it explains how children learn (and why they sometimes don't learn) from their classroom experiences. Teacher educators, for example, recognize that child development is a holistic process that involves an interplay among biological, cognitive, and social factors, which are further molded by a child's unique history, culture, and family environment. Less well known by many teacher educators, however, are the conditions during development that influence the emergence of the brain systems and neuronal networks that are central to learning.

Advances in technology have revealed how environmental experiences modify the brain. The view that the brain displays an element of plasticity, or mutability, has emerged over the past few decades. This chapter describes how children develop mentally, particularly in the preschool, kindergarten, and elementary school years—the age span targeted by the physical activity games presented in part III. We believe that information about the developing brain and individual differences will be increasingly important for the next generation of physical activity teachers.

Mental Development

Children benefit when teachers recognize that their mental growth is the result of a blending of genetic and environmental factors. **Maturation** reflects a timetable of events that are genetically arranged and influenced little by environmental factors. **Development**, on the other hand, reflects changes

in physical or mental processes that are influenced by experience. Thus, although genetics provides the basic structures of the developing brain, the way those structures emerge can be influenced by what a child does.

The Child's Emerging Brain

Biological changes begin at the moment of conception and continue at a phenomenal pace over the first two decades of life. The brain, for example, grows initially at a rate of 250,000 neurons per minute, and it reaches its full complement of over 100 billion neurons by birth. Developmental neuroscientists have begun to trace the sequence of neurological events that ultimately lead to adult brain development. Early in development, some cells specialize into neurons and move to assigned areas of the expanding brain. Once neurons reach genetically coded locations, they begin to develop networks and strengthen their connections. Although the major areas of the brain and spinal cord are set at birth, networks of cells continue to form and emerge at various times throughout childhood and adolescence and into adulthood.

Specific areas located in the outer layers of the brain, the neocortex (shown in figure 1.1), are associated with particular functions; for example, vision with the occipital lobes and language with the temporal lobes. The prefrontal lobes are the most relevant and of special interest to educators because they are linked to children's problem solving, reasoning, and planning functions. The circuitry of the prefrontal cortex undergoes one of the longest periods of development of any brain region; it takes over two decades to reach full maturity.

The Child's Emerging Mind: Classical Views of Cognition

Children's cognitive growth has fascinated parents and teachers for thousands of years. **Cognition** is a

maturation—A timetable of events related to growth and development that are genetically arranged and influenced little by environmental factors.

development—Changes influenced by heredity, maturation, and experience.

cognition—Any process that allows an organism to know and be aware.

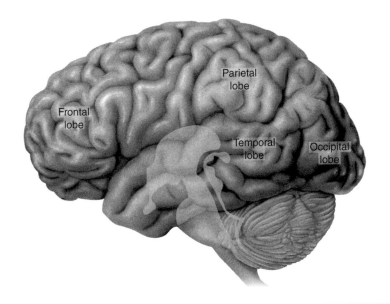

Figure 1.1 The neocortex.

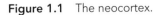

general term for any process that allows an organism to know and be aware. It includes perceiving, reasoning, conceiving, and judging. At the heart of cognition is the way people think and solve problems. Close observation of children's cognition reveals that it develops in a uniform fashion; that is, over time, virtually all children show similar changes in the way they think and solve problems.

Scientific understanding of the progressive development of children's cognition was pioneered by Jean Piaget (1896-1980). In the middle decades of the 20th century, he proposed that children's mental development, like physical development, is characterized by a progression of distinct stages all children go through before reaching maturity. His theory of children's mental development has served as a prototype for many modern educators and researchers. Trained as a zoologist, Piaget believed that the primary developmental task of childhood was one of adaptation—that is, learning how to overcome challenges.

Piaget's Stages of Cognitive Development

Piaget's theory was based on detailed observations of individual children and how they solved various types of mental problems. He concluded that children's experiences drive their cognitive development and proposed that, when challenged by new problems, children are forced to reorganize their thoughts. Piaget described a fixed sequence of four stages of cognitive development, each of which is characterized by specific patterns of thinking and problem solving.

Stage 1: Sensorimotor (Birth to 2 Years) Piaget's theory focuses considerable attention on the first two years of life. An infant faces multiple developmental challenges. Central to the sensorimotor stage of cognitive development is the building of relationships between the infant's actions, which are almost exclusively in the form of motor movements, and internal sensory experiences, which result from those actions.

Making physical movements and repeating them comprise the bulk of the infant's day. These movements, which are initially elicited reflexively, come to be initiated voluntarily. Through practice, the child begins to understand the effects of movements on the environment. Patterns of mental and behavioral action set the stage for play behaviors, through which the child develops rudimentary concepts of causality, spatial orientation, and the permanence of objects. The maturation and refinement of locomotor skills provides even more opportunities to experience and experiment with the world. The capacity for intelligent reasoning rapidly propels the child toward the next stage of cognitive development.

Stage 2: Preoperational (2 to 7 Years) Mental operations reflect the ability to organize and reorganize knowledge. The child in the preoperational stage of development is capable of representing objects mentally that are not physically present.

Children of this age can imagine all sorts of things. They often employ **animistic thinking**, which involves conferring human characteristics on physical, inanimate objects. A child's favorite teddy bear, for example, does indeed come alive for her. However, although she may have the ability to imagine the existence of objects, she has yet to be able to understand how objects can change their appearance and still keep, or conserve, their basic attributes. The mental process of **conservation** emerges when a child understands that an object remains the same even when its shape changes; for instance, when a ball of clay is rolled into a tube.

It is also true that children within this age range tend to be **egocentric**; that is, they are often unable to view events from the perspective of other people. Children in this stage have only one perspective: their own. Language, play, and social interactions, however, provide experiences that force the developing child to abandon this self-centered view and move toward the next stage of cognitive development.

Stage 3: Concrete Operational (7 to 11 Years)

The concrete operational stage is characterized by the display of logical reasoning skills. Children in this stage employ reasoning skills to understand the world in which they live. They become increasingly aware of the rules that govern both nature and their own lives.

Stage 4: Formal Operational (11 and Older)

The final stage in Piaget's theory is characterized by the ability to perform the type of logical problem solving performed by scientists. Advanced **deductive logic**, in particular, is the ability to generate and test hypotheses about events. This form of reasoning requires the capacity to develop and manipulate knowledge in symbolic form. These newly developed cognitive skills provide the opportunity to see linkages among environmental events or objects that appear, on the surface, to have little in common. The capacity to use mental operations to manipulate knowledge also permits children to view the world from multiple perspectives and points of view (Tomporowski, 2003b, pp. 190-191).

Push and Pull of Learning: Assimilation and Accommodation

Over several decades, Piaget developed a theory of cognitive development that explained children's thinking as a way to adapt to environmental demands. He held that two opposing processes push and pull children from one level of understanding of how the natural world works to the next level of understanding. One is the process of assimilation,

© Eyewire

Animistic thinking is a sign that a child has a healthy amount of creativity.

which reflects children's conception of the world at a particular moment in time. **Assimilation** is a process that directs children to establish an equilibrium, or balance, between their physical and mental worlds. The other process that moves children to new levels of understanding is **accommodation**, which is an attempt to modify what they know to reflect how the world really is. A child's world is not static; it is constantly changing. The changing world provides new experiences and new information that must be incorporated into previously learned knowledge and organized into patterns, or schemas, that match the world as it is. Schemas, for Piaget, emerge as a result of the processes of assimilation and accommodation. **Schemas** are conceptual rules that children use to link previously learned ways of viewing the world with potentially new ways of viewing it. The ongoing dynamics of the real world create a **disequilibrium**, or imbalance, that forces children to reorganize and restructure their perceptions of nature. Assimilation and accommodation simultaneously push and pull on the child's cognitive schemas of the world. To Piaget, childhood is characterized by constant mental activity that is directed toward restructuring and modifying children's views of their place in nature.

Piaget suggested that children's experiences, rather than maturation, are the key to their cognitive development. Only when faced with the challenges imposed by the real world do they experience cognitive disequilibrium and a state of tension that motivates them to regain equilibrium by reorganizing their thoughts. The processes of mental organization that occur as children attempt to obtain a sense of equilibrium push them toward more complex levels of cognitive organization. Adults may experience similar cognitive tension when facing difficult mental challenges. Persistence and mental effort can lead to success, a decrease in tension, and the pleasant feeling that everything fits. This is called **equilibrium**, which is a steady state or balance between opposing forces.

animistic thinking—Conferring human characteristics on physical, inanimate objects.

conservation—The understanding that the amount or area of an object remains the same even though its shape is altered.

egocentric—The characteristic of being unable to view events from the perspective of other people.

deductive logic—The ability to generate and test hypotheses about events.

assimilation—A process that directs children to establish an equilibrium, or balance, between their physical and mental worlds.

accommodation—A process by which children attempt to modify what they know to reflect how the world really is.

schemas—Conceptual rules that children use to link previously learned ways of viewing the world with potentially new ways of viewing it.

disequilibrium—A sense of imbalance that forces children to reorganize and restructure their perceptions of nature.

equilibrium—A steady state or balance between opposing forces.

executive function—The capacity to think before acting, retain and manipulate information, reflect on the possible consequences of specific actions, and self-regulate behavior.

response inhibition—The ability to withhold actions or modify ongoing behaviors.

Later chapters reveal that views held by contemporary theorists are not dissimilar to those expressed by Piaget many decades ago. Each stage of Piaget's theory is characterized by patterns of thinking about nature and how it works that change in complexity. The movement from one stage to the next is discontinuous, however. Children's cognitive growth leads them to a threshold that, when crossed, enables them to view nature in a qualitatively different way than they did during the previous stage. The transition from one stage of cognitive development to the next depends greatly on a child's experiences. Problem-solving experiences push them to search for new and more complex ways of understanding and adapting to the world. Piaget believed that progression comes about as children attempt to balance what they know with what they are presently experiencing.

Piaget's views sparked considerable debate among developmental researchers that continues to the present day. Although not all of Piaget's hypotheses have been supported, his theory of cognitive development is considered a classic by many contemporary researchers. Piaget's approach to examining individual children and how they perform specific types of mental tasks is similar to the approach that many educators use to assess students' classroom performances and develop teaching interventions.

The Child's Emerging Mind: Contemporary Views

Modern views of children's mental development have been influenced greatly by advances in the neuropsychological study of the brain and by laboratory-based research. As described previously, cognition is a general term that reflects a number of relatively separate mental processes. Presently, many researchers focus on an aspect of cognition called **executive function**, which is the capacity to think before acting, retain and manipulate information, reflect on the possible consequences of specific actions, and self-regulate behavior. Most researchers believe that there are three core executive functions (Diamond, 2013):

- **Response inhibition** is the ability to withhold actions or modify ongoing behaviors. Children who act before they think often make mistakes (e.g., a boy who reaches for a hot cookie just out of the oven). Success in school and in life depends on the ability to wait and to think through consequences before acting. Adaptive thinking is reflected in an awareness that long-term benefits may be gained by withholding actions. The game Simon Says taxes children's developing response inhibition.

- **Working memory** is the capacity to hold and manipulate information in consciousness. Children face situations daily that require them to attend and remember what they are experiencing to solve problems and plan actions. Mathematic problems, for example, tax children's working memory because they require remembering steps to achieve a correct answer.

- **Mental shifting** is the ability to recognize changes in conditions that require a change in strategy and different behaviors. Ball games that require children to switch quickly from playing offense to playing defense require mental flexibility, a trademark of mental shifting.

Children's executive functions develop rapidly during the preschool, kindergarten, and elementary school years and then emerge continuously, but at a slower pace, during adolescence and into young adulthood. Like the stages of cognitive development described by Piaget, the three core executive functions come online at different times to help the developing child overcome challenges. Response inhibition is the first executive function to develop and can be seen in the behaviors of infants and preschool children; the executive functions of working memory and mental shifting follow and play increasingly important roles in children's behaviors during the elementary school years. Improvement in planning and strategic thinking, which rely on core executive functions, has been linked to the development of neuronal networks in the prefrontal lobes and their connections to structures deep in the brain.

A key to brain growth is physical and mental activity, which guide the connection and strengthening of neural connections (Curlik & Shors, 2012). During brain development an initial wave of massive neuron production is followed by a period of neuronal death. This process, referred to as pruning, leads to the weeding out of neurons that fail to make synaptic connections. Neurons communicate with one another via transmitter substances that flow from one neuron to the next at junctions called synapses. Neurons that make connections with other cells live and become part of the network, whereas those that fail to make connections die. The experiences that children have during periods of neuronal expansion and contraction help select which neurons live.

The initial neural expansion that creates the neural networks important for inhibition processes may be influenced by physical activity games that challenge the child's ability to withhold one response in favor of another. The later neural expansion that creates networks for working memory and mental shifting may likewise be influenced by learning experiences that challenge the child's ability to maintain information in consciousness, plan actions, and shift strategies. However, the impact of physical activity games on the development of brain networks is not as simple as described here. In reality, it is not possible to identify games that challenge one specific executive function, because the functions are interrelated. In all likelihood, all core executive functions are affected by games and experiences that challenge children's ability to inhibit behaviors when necessary, think through problems and plan actions before moving, and exhibit mental flexibility and the ability to shift strategies when needed.

Physical activity games and experiences can be designed and structured in ways that promote the development of each aspect of executive function. The games presented in part III of this book have been developed specifically to develop children's executive functions. They challenge children's problem-solving and decision-making skills and emphasize creative solutions to novel conditions. Why is participating in these problem-solving games important? The evidence suggests that when children learn skills that rely on executive functions, they can apply them in a wide variety of real-world conditions including many areas of academics (e.g., mathematics, science, reading).

It is important to remember that the age-related changes in the developing brain mentioned earlier have been described in terms of typical, or average, development. Children actually exhibit large differences in terms of brain growth and physical

---

working memory—The capacity to hold and manipulate information in consciousness.

mental shifting—The ability to recognize changes in conditions that require a change in strategy and different behaviors.

skill—The ability to use knowledge effectively and readily in the execution of performance.

abilities—Genetically linked physical and mental attributes that determine how quickly and how well particular skills can be learned.

Problem-solving games develop executive functions that can help children down the road in academia.

development. The emergence of brain structure and changes in their functions do not explain all behavior. Researchers agree that a one-to-one relation between brain structure and behavior does not exist. Indeed, studies of people with developmental disorders, neurological impairments, and brain injury show patterns of brain organization that may be quite different from typical and yet these people behave quite normally. Although our knowledge of brain development has increased greatly over the past two decades, there is much to learn about the brain-cognition-behavior relationship.

Skill and the Trajectory of Cognitive Development

Skill is the ability to use knowledge effectively and readily in the execution of performance. Almost everyone learns motor skills (tying shoelaces),

cognitive skills (playing chess), and psychomotor skills (riding a bicycle). Skills differ from **abilities**, which are genetically linked physical and mental attributes that determine how quickly and how well particular skills can be learned. For example, one child may have exceptional vision, which can help her track the flight of a ball and catch it. Another child may have exceptional muscular strength, which can help him jump higher than others in basketball. However, having exceptional vision or exceptional strength alone will not make a child a good catcher or basketball player. A characteristic of all skills is that they are learned with practice. Skills are learned most rapidly and to maximal levels when teachers provide appropriate learning environments, instruction, guidance, and feedback. Later chapters discuss skills in depth and describe how they are learned. At this point, however, it is important to understand that the cognitive skills children learn help them make the most of their mental abilities and shape the direction of cognitive development.

The core components of executive function—response inhibition, working memory, and mental shifting—emerge at different points of brain growth. Consider, however, that learning mental skills that rely on these executive functions may alter the connectivity of the networks of the brain and its control of the body. The notion that children's experiences can fundamentally influence the course of their physical and mental development has been held and discussed for many decades. Most of the dialogue and research focuses on the notions of critical periods and environmental enrichment.

Critical Period Concepts

Even to the casual observer, it is clear that the first few years of life are characterized by tremendous physical and mental change. The acquisition of many skills seems to occur almost without conscious effort. The development of language, for example, begins slowly about the second year and then accelerates rapidly. Children can learn multiple languages and the control of muscles in the face and mouth needed for speaking like natives by the time they are 10 years old. However, children introduced to a second language after the age of 14 or so appear to have more difficulty with learning. In extreme cases of being deprived the opportunity to develop language at all, a child may never acquire the ability to communicate orally. These types of observations have led some to suggest that there are critical periods of development that are linked to experiences.

Critical periods are optimal times for the emergence of specific developmental processes and behaviors. However, they emerge only if a specific event or condition is experienced. The concept of the critical period suggests that maturational processes can be influenced markedly, either positively or negatively, by the presence or absence of particular events.

Early scientific support for the role of physical activity on the development of brain networks important for adaptive mental function can be traced back to classic studies of body movement and vision by Held and Hein (Held, 1965). Their experiments were conducted under laboratory conditions with newborn kittens whose eyes had not yet opened. While vision was not available to the kittens prior to their eyes opening, critical brain networks required for taking in and interpreting visual information were being formed. Upon the kittens' eyes opening, some were assigned to a condition in which they actively walked in a corridor that had distinctively painted walls. Other kittens were placed on a platform that carried them passively and individually through the same corridor; they did not walk. Although all of the kittens were exposed to the same visual experiences, the neural organization and visual functions differed. The act of walking led to changes in the neural pathways of the kittens' brain.

Other studies support the existence of critical periods, most clearly during neonatal development when the circuitry of brain networks is in the process of being laid down prior to and soon after birth. Under some conditions, the brain appears to have only one chance for normal development. If not stimulated in a specific fashion at a specific point in the developmental sequence, the developing structures are permanently affected. Even if the needed environmental experience is given at a later point in development, brain networks are atypical.

Although the evidence for critical periods during the development of basic sensory processes, such as vision, is strong, there has been debate as to how far the concept can be applied to higher-level cognitive development during childhood and adolescence. Consider that cognitive development continues for decades after birth and that children's mental progress is continuous rather than "all or none." Some researchers have proposed an alternative **sensitive period**, in which children are particularly receptive to certain environmental experiences.

Enrichment Concept

Normal brain development depends on both genetic and environmental factors. Considerable evidence indicates that the lack of proper parental contact, guidance, and support at a particular point of development can result in atypical development that can impede the trajectory of a child's progress across the life span. But is it possible that specific types of experiences can enhance children's brain development and accelerate the trajectory? The notion that early **enriching environments**, defined as any situation or condition that maximizes or enhances the development of a person's abilities, can affect learning has caught the attention of many parents who want to hasten their children's academic and sport progress. An entire market of infant and child enrichment products intended to advance children's mental and physical development has emerged. Indeed, some parents have gone as far as exposing their children to music and language programs while they are still in the womb to accelerate learning. Further, mothers and fathers often introduce sport training to very young children to promote skill development.

Although enrichment products and training programs abound, few have been tested to verify their impact on mental or physical development. As a result, the benefits of enrichment programs are based primarily on testimonials. Given the premise that the physical activity games we describe in later chapters can enhance developing children's cognition, it is important to understand why physical activity, which is only one of many possible enrichment programs, is unique.

critical periods—Optimal times for the emergence of specific developmental processes and behaviors.

sensitive period—A period during which children are particularly receptive to certain environmental experiences.

enriching environment—Any situation or condition that maximizes or enhances the development of a person's abilities.

generalization—The transfer of learning from one task or situation to other tasks or situations.

mnemonics—Strategies to improve memory and information recall.

neurogenic reserve hypothesis—A hypothesis that states that combinations of physical activity and cognitive engagement are particularly important early in the life span because the reserve provides resources in later life.

Enrichment programs for children are considered effective when they meet two basic criteria. First, the effects of the intervention must be relatively long lasting. It must be determined whether changes produced by a given intervention are temporary or relatively permanent. Many factors can temporarily change behavior (e.g., drugs). Stimulant medication, for example, may increase children's attention; however, the effects disappear when the drug is metabolized. Many enrichment programs change behavior simply because they are novel and people expect them to work. The power of expecting something to alter behavior is well documented. However, the motivation that drives the expectancy is short lived and decreases over time. If physical activity games truly enrich cognition, the effects of games played in preschool should influence behaviors in elementary and middle school and, perhaps, into adulthood. Second, improvements in cognitive skills used to solve problems during the intervention must generalize and be used to solve other types of problems. **Generalization** is the transfer of learning from one task or situation to other tasks or situations. For example, aspects of baseball batting skills may be applied to the game of cricket. The movements learned in one game make it easier to learn and perform in a new game.

Methods of improving human performance have been used for thousands of years. The memory skills of orators in ancient Greece, for example, were improved with the use of **mnemonics**, which are strategies to improve memory and information recall. For example, consciously linking words with mental images helps actors learn their lines. The memory skills of adults and children alike can be improved greatly through the application of mnemonic methods. However, although performance improvements displayed following training and practice are impressive, do they promote changes in cognitive abilities that can be used in other situations? This question is critical for any enrichment intervention. The fact is, mnemonic memory training interventions fail to demonstrate generalization. Improvements in memory are restricted to specific types of information—a memory "expert" may be superior in remembering peoples' names, but be only average in remembering items on a shopping list. If physical activity games truly enrich cognition, children should be able to take what they learn from solving problems during games and use that knowledge to solve problems in the classroom and outside of school.

Recent comprehensive reviews of enrichment programs for older adults note that the vast majority do not promote long-lasting changes in cognitive abilities; nor do they generalize across conditions (Hertzog et al., 2009). However, the interventions that show the greatest evidence for cognition enhancement are those that involve physical exercise and those that provide structured experience in games that demand the use of the core executive functions—response inhibition, working memory, and mental shifting. Although the focus of the Hertzog review was on the maintenance of older adults' mental functions, the conclusions drawn are applicable to cognition across the life span and specifically to the importance of physical activity during childhood.

Several researchers have attempted to explain why, of all the interventions, exercise shows the greatest benefits for mental function. Studies conducted with animals provide evidence that exercise increases the number of neurons in brain areas that are critical for learning. Exercise, particularly conducted under mentally challenging conditions, is hypothesized to lead to a "neurogenic reserve" that enables people to respond adaptively to real-world challenges (Kempermann, 2008). The **neurogenic reserve hypothesis** states that combinations of physical activity and cognitive engagement are particularly important early in the life span because the reserve provides resources in later life. As proposed by Kempermann (2008), "Broad ranges of physical activity early in life would not only help build a highly optimized hippocampal network adapted to a complex life . . . [but] would also contribute to a neurogenic reserve by keeping precursor cells in cycle" (p. 167). This suggests that what happens to the brain during childhood can influence greatly the capacity to learn, make good choices, and achieve goals throughout life.

Studies providing evidence of the uniqueness of physical activity enrichment programs are reviewed in chapter 2. At this point, however, it is important to recognize that the topic of children's physical activity and its effects on academic achievement and mental function has drawn the interest of educators, parents, physicians, and more recently, policy makers. In the near future, physical education teachers may well be called on to go beyond classes designed to teach sport skills to develop instructional programs designed to maximize children's physical, mental, and social development. Rising to this task will require the next generation of physical educators to broaden their areas of expertise and recognize the merits of cross-disciplinary methods of instruction and training.

Understanding Children's Development From Multiple Points of View

Historically, teachers in universities and colleges have focused on specialized areas of research—arts, science, medicine, and history. This practice has created domains of knowledge. The advantage of specialization is that researchers can focus extensively on one topic. The disadvantage is that information tends to stay within a domain and is not readily available to researchers in other domains. Called the silo effect, this tendency has had pronounced consequences on the information provided to educators. Our goal in this book is to increase the cross-talk across academic domains and to provide a multidomain model that can be used to prepare teachers to play important roles in 21st-century educational settings.

Presently, three types of researchers study topics that are of particular relevance to teacher education.

Biological scientists tend to focus on the structures of the body related to behavior. Cognitive scientists tend to focus on the processes of thinking and problem solving. Social scientists often focus on the environmental, cultural, and familial conditions that motivate children's behavior. Throughout this book information is drawn from these three areas to help teachers and teacher educators understand children holistically, in terms of body, mind, and spirit.

Biological Domain

Adults' physiological responses to physical activity have been studied for over a century, and the processes involved are relatively well known. Children's responses to exercise, until relatively recently, were less well understood; however, over the past two decades, much has been learned. Pediatric exercise physiologists have expanded our understanding of the complex interrelationships among systems of the body that control how children behave. As described previously, advances

Photo courtesy of Mammadù Nonprofit Organization. agnes@mammadu.org

Kids should play to get their physical activity! These kids are playing as part of the Mammadù Nonprofit Organization in Namibia. This organization works with some of the 200,000 kids living in poverty in Namibia to, among other things, see that their basic needs for nutrition, health, and hygiene are met. For more information on the important work of this organization and to learn how you can help, go to www.mammadu.org/no_profit_africa/index.html.

in neuroscience provide insights into the development of the brain. In addition, progress has also been made in the study of the development of the cardiovascular, skeletal, endocrine, and muscular systems. This knowledge has begun to revolutionize our understanding of how children respond and adapt to exercise training.

Until the 1960s the consensus among many pediatricians and educators was that children were not able to withstand the physical stress of long-duration physical exertion, and that doing so was dangerous. The basis for restricting children's level of physical activity has been traced to misinterpretations of children's cardiovascular development. It was believed that strenuous physical activity could interfere with the development of children's heart muscles and blood vessels. Although these conclusions were later found to be erroneous, members of the medical community continued to be wary of prescribing vigorous physical activity for children. Today, children are encouraged to be physically active. However, the evidence is clear that children are not small adults and that they may not enjoy exercise routines that attract adults. Throughout the day, the activity patterns of children differ greatly from those of adults. Because these age-related differences can influence children's motivations to be physical active, the topic of developmentally appropriate activity programs is addressed in detail in later chapters.

Cognitive Domain

Humans display the capacity to think, use language, manipulate symbols to solve problems, and plan for the future. Cognitive scientists focus on these processes and have developed methods for studying them. Psychological tests, such as those of intelligence, academic achievement, and problem solving, measure a variety of mental processes. Developmental psychologists have been extremely interested in how children learn, and they have found differences between children's and adults' mental processing.

Perhaps the most robust finding is that young children's speed of processing is slower than older children's. Even on simple reaction time tests, children take longer to respond than do adults. There are several reasons for this age-related difference in response time. Young children have more difficulty than older children in organizing information. A young child dealing with a complex problem has more difficulty focusing on the elements of the problem than does an older child.

Younger children also take more time inspecting individual elements of complex problems than do older children. Until age 5 or 6, children often display overexclusiveness, which is the tendency to focus on only a few cues that may or may not be related to the task at hand. Between the ages of about 6 and 12 years, however, children tend to show overinclusiveness; that is, attending to both relevant and irrelevant cues. It is during this period that children are most likely to be easily distracted from the task at hand. Taken together, the developmental differences in organizing and storing information suggest that physical activity programs need to be adjusted to match children's cognitive capacities.

Social-Affective Domain

Motivation and emotion play import roles in children's development. Human activity is dynamic; it is more than a series of behavioral actions. It reflects an internal driving force that sparks people to move. Much of human activity is goal directed; that is, there is a purpose for behavior. Some motivating forces have a biological basis, such as hunger and thirst. Other motivating forces are learned, such as fame and monetary reward. Still others are tied to emotional experiences, such as play, challenge, and exhilaration.

Social scientists are interested in explaining not only how the human body functions, but also why we behave as we do. Some children may desire to become skilled in games but lose their motivation when the demands are too great for them to overcome. Central to social science research are methods for understanding how children muster their resolve and attack the task at hand. Their willingness to act and show "spirit" is vital to the development of their real-world intelligence.

Some have suggested that early in life children possess an innate drive to master their world. Children at play seek out problems to be solved and in doing so acquire the skills necessary for success. Children are inquisitive and drawn to games that involve a challenge and a problem to be solved. Indeed, children can become so engrossed in games that they dominate their daily activities. The popularity of video games provides a clear example of the link between total engagement and pleasure. Physical activity games can also provide children with challenges and rewards similar to those of video games. Later chapters introduce instructional methods that capitalize on children's innate internal motivation.

Children are motivated to meet their needs. A **motive** is a psychological state or physiological disposition that energizes behavior A **need** is the object of a motive; it is the specific object (e.g., food, water, money), event (e.g., praise), or psychological state (e.g., well-being, happiness) that a person desires. Social scientists are particularly interested in the interplay among children, their families, and social networks and how this dynamic relationship enables them to acquire their needs.

Abraham Maslow (1908-1970) developed an early influential theory of motivation that is based on need fulfillment, commonly referred to as Maslow's hierarchy of needs. He proposed that we are all naturally motivated to become self-actualized; that is, to become the best that we can be. **Self-actualization** is a psychological state experienced when we attain our full potential, personal growth, and creative fulfillment. This state is attained, however, only after we meet a series of needs, which are arranged in a hierarchy. Maslow's **hierarchy of needs** theory states that basic needs must be met before progress can be made toward self-actualization. All humans are motivated to secure the physiological needs necessary for survival; that is, food, water, shelter, and clothing. When our basic needs are met, we are then driven by a need for security—an environment that is safe and stable. Next, we seek social acceptance, love, and affiliation. If all of these basic needs are met, we are driven to seek the esteem of others and to experience autonomy, competence, and relatedness. It is only then that we begin to experience the psychological state of self-actualization, which is characterized by feelings of inner peace and harmony.

Normal development throughout childhood requires that many needs, both physical and psychological, be met. Children who possess the requisite skills are best able to achieve their goals and meet their needs. As described in later chapters, children's beliefs about their competency and self-efficacy can be enhanced through play and games. These beliefs can also play central roles in their motivation to meet and overcome the challenges they face in a complex social world.

Interdisciplinary Progress

Children benefit from educators who are receptive to interdisciplinary methods of teaching. Historically, physical education teachers have defined their role as teachers who help children refine psychomotor abilities and develop skills that can be used in games. National organizations in the United States, such as the Society of Health and Physical Educators (SHAPE America), have outlined skills that are needed for the profession. These skills are important because they help educators prepare children to engage in lifelong sport and recreation activities. However, physical educators have the potential to affect children more broadly. Today's physical educators are in a unique position to develop interventions that improve children's physical health, help them avoid negative lifestyle choice, and improve their real-world intelligence. A goal of this book is to help educators understand how children learn in terms of a dynamic interaction of body, mind, and spirit.

Implications for Educators

We hope that, by this point, it is quite apparent that the more teachers and child care specialists know about brain development and the importance of early childhood experiences, the better equipped they will be to advance children's development. The study of typical brain development from the point of conception to adulthood provides insights into the interrelations between genetics and experiences that mold the functioning of the central nervous system. Recent advances in neuropsychology have helped us understand the biological sequences that unfold based on biological programming and how the trajectories of cell growth and organization may be altered as the developing child interacts and adapts to an ever-changing environment. It is clear that childhood experiences can influence the rapid and dramatic physical, mental, and behavioral transformations that occur from infancy to childhood and

---

motive—A psychological state or physiological disposition that energizes behavior.

need—The object of a motive; it is the specific object (e.g., food, water, money), event (e.g., praise), or psychological state (e.g., well-being, happiness) that a person desires.

self-actualization—A psychological state characterized by feelings of inner peace and harmony that is experienced when we attain our full potential, personal growth, and creative fulfillment.

hierarchy of needs—Maslow's theory of motivation that states that basic needs must be met before progress can be made toward self-actualization.

adolescence, and into adulthood. Experiences can either impair or promote brain development and alter behavior.

The challenge for parents and educators is to maximize children's physical and mental development. Given that most children spend seven or more hours a day with teachers in a learning environment for most of the year, it should be no surprise how instrumental teachers can be and how essential the information about brain development is to a teacher who hopes to enhance children's learning.

The scientific evidence on how the brain develops through early movement experiences and how the environment can be enriched to promote brain development has guided the descriptions of the movement games presented in part III of this book. In fact, these games represent a form of environmental enrichment to jointly promote children's physical and mental development. Furthermore, we have used scientific evidence on the developmental trajectories of the core executive functions during infancy and childhood to provide an in-depth analysis of the involvement of executive functions in the games in part III. This is what makes these games unique. They show how specific components of executive function can be challenged at different developmental ages by applying specific teaching principles.

© Marzanna Syncerz

How Movement Influences Children's Mental Development

Children are full of energy. Throughout their waking moments, they run, play, and socialize. Physical activity encompasses all of these actions and many, many more. Indeed, **physical activity** is defined as bodily movement produced by skeletal muscle contraction that requires energy expenditure (Dishman, Heath, & Lee, 2012). Humans are physically active from soon after conception to the end of life. As will be described here and in the chapters to follow, physical activity provides each of us with a way to interact with our world, to learn the consequences of our actions, and to make our plans for the future.

Most people tend to use the terms *physical activity* and *exercise* interchangeably. However, there are important distinctions between the two. Researchers restrict the word **exercise** to mean a subset of physical activity consisting of planned, structured, repetitive bodily movements with the purpose of improving or maintaining one or more components of physical fitness or health (Dishman, Heath, & Lee, 2012). Often, when adults think about getting children physically active, they typically visualize exercise training activities described using such terms as frequency, time, intensity, and type.

physical activity—Bodily movement produced by skeletal muscle contraction that requires energy expenditure.

exercise—A subset of physical activity consisting of planned, structured, repetitive bodily movements with the purpose of improving or maintaining one or more components of physical fitness or health.

The physical activity games described in this book are not intended to be performed as exercise, which involves training regimens constrained to timing and scheduling. Rather, they focus on behaviors that children do naturally—play games. Games differ widely in the level of physical activity needed for participating. Some require minimal levels of physical activity, whereas others require much more and can even improve or maintain physical fitness or health. Games performed under the right circumstances provide natural learning experiences that have the potential to promote both physical and mental health. In the chapters to come, we describe how to construct game environments that give children opportunities to explore and understand their worlds, and how to enhance their movement-based learning.

The notion that children learn through game participation is not new; several researchers have discussed at length the merits of action-based programs (Kirk & MacPhail, 2002). A generation of physical education teachers has been introduced to instructional methods that promote children's motor development and link those experiences to sport performance. Like all scientists, we strive to extend the work of others and to introduce new research findings to maximize teachers' influence not only on children's sport skills, but also on their cognitive skills. Evidence that has accumulated over the past decade shows that children's actions can lead to the acquisition of fundamental knowledge that underlies academic achievement, problem solving, and "thoughtful behavior" (Diamond & Lee, 2011).

This chapter examines how physical activity performed in natural contexts, such as play and games, has the potential to shape cognitive development. Evidence from studies focused on exercise-related improvements in children's cognition and academic performance are summarized. Finally, the implications for maintaining physical activity programs in schools and at home are discussed.

Children's Physical Activity

It is clear to virtually everyone that children are born to be physically active. Indeed, it seems that children's job is to explore and get into everything; throughout their waking moments, typical children crawl, climb, run, and fall. It's what they are designed to do. As we will see, these behaviors help in the development of not only muscles and physical abilities, but also the brain and mental abilities.

Activity Patterns

Physical activity occurs throughout life—humans are continuously moving. However, several important differences exist between children's and adults' physical activity. Children are not very efficient in moving; they expend more energy than adults do when they run and jump. This is due to several anatomical factors: leg stride length, the regulation of muscles that need to work together to control limbs, and muscle force (Rowland, 2005). Movement efficiency improves throughout adolescence and young adulthood as the skeletal muscles mature and movement becomes more controlled as a result of learning motor skills.

Because children are built differently than adults, it should not be surprising that they also show a different pattern of physical activity (Welk, Corbin, & Dale, 2000). Young children exhibit high levels of short-burst activity. In a classic study of children's activities, Bailey and associates rated the intensity and timed the duration of 6- to 10-year-old children's activity (Bailey et al., 1995). Observations taken over a 12-hour period revealed that children's physical activity is spontaneous and brief. As shown in figure 2.1, most high-intensity activity lasted only three to nine seconds. Consider that not one child engaged in vigorous activity longer than 10 consecutive minutes. It is not until adolescence and adulthood that the length of physical activity bouts becomes longer.

Clearly, children are not little adults; their activity patterns are driven by both developmental forces and the environments in which they live. Given a choice and opportunity, the vast majority of children spend their free time climbing, sprinting, jumping, swinging, and sliding. Seldom do children choose to go on long-distance runs, as might be preferred by adults. Given that short bursts of physical activity are children's natural movement patterns, some researchers have suggested that they should be encouraged to do so in the form of games and sport. Daily routines that involve games and sports empasizing short bursts of activity promote bone health, maintain muscle development, and increase caloric expenditure (Gutin, 2013).

Children's Response to Exercise Training

Recall that exercise is a subset of physical activity. Exercise is defined as a constrained period of time in which a person moves in a prescribed way to improve one or more of the components of physi-

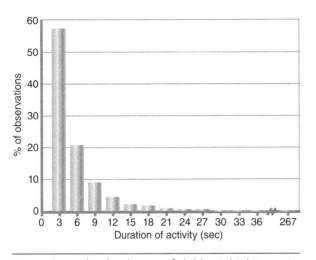

Figure 2.1 The distribution of children's high-intensity activities by the duration of the activity in seconds. The median duration was 3 seconds, and 95 percent of high-intensity activities lasted less than 15 seconds.

Adapted, by permission, from R.C. Bailey et al., 1995, "The level and tempo of children's physical activities: an observational study," *Medicine and Science in Sports and Exercise* 27(7): 1033-1041.

cal fitness: muscular strength or endurance, flexibility, and aerobic capacity. **Trainability** reflects how children respond to an exercise intervention at various stages of growth. Similar to the critical periods notion described in chapter 1, the premise of exercise training is that there may be periods during which children are susceptible to the beneficial effects of specific experiences. Pediatric exercise scientists who studied closely the impact of fitness training on children's developing bodies discovered that the following aspects of children's physical fitness improve with training:

- *Aerobic fitness.* Endurance training produces relatively little improvement in the cardiorespiratory efficiency of children compared to adults. Gains, at best, are a third of those seen in adults. Changes in aerobic capacity during childhood appear to be guided primarily by maturation and influenced little by habitual levels of physical activity. Although many assume that children who are physically active attain higher levels of aerobic fitness, the data do not support this. Physical activity levels are only weakly associated with aerobic fitness.

> **trainability**—How children respond to an exercise intervention at various stages of growth.

- *Muscular strength and endurance.* Children who participate in training programs show increases in strength; however, the increases are not due to changes in the muscle fibers. Similar to adult females, gains in strength are explained mostly by improved muscle control that comes about through learning. Without specific growth hormones, muscle fiber size and fiber type are not altered by training.

- *Body size and stature.* At one time many believed that participation in some sports could slow children's growth patterns. However, participation in physical training programs has little influnce on children's terminal height. Regular activity does not stunt or have a negative impact on height.

- *Skeletal tissue.* Regular physical activity during childhood affects bone mineral content. This finding is important because the bone mineral levels established early in life set the levels in adulthood. Routine physical activity, particularly weight-bearing activity, appears to be especially important in establishing bone mineral levels.

- *Body weight and body composition.* Components of body weight, particularly fat mass, can be influenced by regular physical activity (Malina, Bouchard, & Bar-Or, 2004, pp. 467-468).

It should be remembered, however, that trainability can be influenced by a number of conditions and may depend on a multitude of factors (e.g., age, sex, culture).

Some aspects of children's physical fitness can be enhanced through systematic exercise training programs. These findings have led some physical educators to develop training activities similar to those typically used by adults. Specialized sport-specific training programs for children have become popular over the past decade. Training camps and sport schools focus on adapting children's bodies and developing skills that are required for elite levels of performance. Recall, however, that children are not small adults. The exercise training programs used by adults may not meet children's developmental needs. Teachers need to consider carefully the goals of their physical activity interventions. If the goal is to improve sport performance or to reduce obesity, then specialized training programs have merit. However, if the goal is to improve children's physical and cognitive function, developmentally appropriate games may be more fitting.

Physical Activity in Natural, Educational, and Recreational Settings

Play, games, and sports serve important roles in normal development and enhance children's cognitive processes and socialization. Educators have long recognized that children need free time to move and explore their world. Through the consequences of their explorations, they learn to control their thoughts and actions, which, as previously discussed, are the cornerstones of executive function. Importantly, the greatest gains in cognitive functions are achieved when children are mentally engaged and involved in play, games, and sport. Activities that require only repetitive actions with minimal mental involvement lead to reactive, mindless behaviors that do little to promote the advancement of executive functions.

Children's Play

Spontaneous **play** is activity that is freely chosen and intrinsically motivating and pleasurable. Children can play by themselves (solitary play), adjacent to others, but not trying to influence others' behavior (parallel play), or by interacting with others (cooperative play). During play, children are often engaged in make-believe and distortions of reality. There are no exterior rules of play; children construct their own forms of reality. Play provides the opportunity to exercise and practice ways of physically and mentally altering the world. Children can construct, deconstruct, and reconstruct goal-directed activities. When in play, children appear to be deeply engrossed in their actions and oblivious of what is going on around them. When children are absorbed in play, their physical and mental arousal is high; the pleasurable experiences they get from play motivate continued engagement.

Arousal modulation theorists propose that children are innately driven to attain an optimal level of arousal. To a child, a predictable and unchanging world is a boring and monotonous world. Play provides a way to alter the world so that it becomes unpredictable and uncertain. The physical and mental tension created by uncertainty and novelty motivates children to action; they are driven to reestablish a state of organization and predictability. Drawing on Piaget's beliefs outlined in chapter 1, play first creates disequilibrium and then the child restores equilibrium. The act of attaining equilibrium produces powerful positive psychological feelings.

Of course, attaining harmony and order results in an environment that is unchanging and predictable, which are the precise conditions that once again bring on feelings of boredom and monotony, which, in turn, motivate the child to renew the play cycle.

As addressed in later chapters, teachers can draw children into games by using instructional methods based on the **optimal challenge point** hypothesis (Guadagnoli & Lee, 2004). This hypothesis states that skill learning is facilitated when the skill level of the performer, the complexity of the task, and the task environment are taken into consideration. In this case, the teacher, rather than the child, modifies game conditions based on the child's skill level and the difficulty of the game.

Psychologists have emphasized that play serves as a way to learn problem-solving skills. It provides a relatively safe opportunity for children to use emerging cognitive capacities to solve problems in the natural environment in a variety of ways (Csikszentmihalyi, 2000). Through play, children learn how movement and action change the surrounding world. Instead of passively receiving information in a classroom setting, they learn to interact, modify, and manipulate their environments. Parents often accuse their children of having short attention spans because they stay with one activity for brief amounts of time. Engaging and reengaging in many activities may well establish lifelong behavioral

play—Activity that is freely chosen and intrinsically motivating and pleasurable. Children can play by themselves (solitary play), adjacent to others (parallel play), or by interacting with others (cooperative play).

arousal modulation—A theory that children are innately driven to attain an optimal level of arousal.

optimal challenge point—The hypothesis that skill learning is facilitated when the skill level of the performer, the complexity of the task, and the task environment are taken into consideration.

cooperative play—Organized play that involves acting out roles.

creativity—The ability to produce work that is novel and useful as defined within a given social context.

rough-and-tumble play—A social activity in which two or more children engage in pretend fighting, hitting, and wrestling.

patterns. Children learn to actively modify the world to produce pleasurable experiences. During these experiences, they use their developing mental imagery and problem-solving skills to find novel ways to take virtually any object or situation and turn it into a play activity. Parents often find that their children have more fun playing with the box that enclosed an expensive toy than the toy itself. The capacity to change one's environment to attain positive outcomes is central not only to theories of play, but also to theories of intelligence. One of the components of adult intelligence is the ability to modify the environment to maximize learned skills (Sternberg, 2005). Thus, the instinctual patterns of play serve as a cornerstone for the development of intelligence and patterns of behavior that are used throughout life.

There are also social components to play. **Cooperative play** is organized and involves acting out roles. Relationships with peers and social skills often develop in the context of social play. Through cooperative interactions, children learn to inhibit antisocial behavior and form friendships. These social skills, or competencies, are important for children as they enter primary school. Worldwide, young children are given time to rest or access to recess, or break time, as it is called in the United Kingdom. Typically, recess periods are interspersed during the academic day, and are typically longer for younger children. Learning to cooperate and work with others helps children develop feelings of competence and leads to successful relationships with schoolmates and teachers.

There is also an element of creativity in children's play. **Creativity** is the ability to produce work that is novel and useful as defined within a given social context. Creativity can be expressed both in thought and movement. When children play, they develop ways to approach and solve problems that are new to them. Producing creative movements requires the integration of multiple mental processes; children must take what they know, visualize new actions and their final outcomes, and then reorganize known movement patterns into new series of movements. Some researchers consider the high-order thinking that leads to creativity to be an element of general intelligence (Sternberg, 2005).

Vigorous play serves as an outlet for energy expenditure. **Rough-and-tumble play** is a social activity in which two or more children engage in pretend fighting, hitting, and wrestling. This form of play differs from true aggression in a number

© Felix Mizioznikov

Play stretches the mental abilities of children to new heights.

of ways. Real fighting is usually limited to two children who show serious threatening gestures and use their strength to the maximum. Rough-and-tumble play can involve many children who restrain their strength and are more likely to smile and laugh while they are being active. This type of play provides a way for children to compare their skills with those of others. Children typically engage in rough-and-tumble play only with those whose level of play fighting skill is similar to theirs. They typically avoid contact play with those whose strength is considerably higher or lower than their own. Play fighting that is evenly matched provides a safe opportunity to learn their limitations, and it also helps establish a position within a social hierarchy that is based on skill and competence (Huges, 2010).

Children's Games

Games are forms of competitive play characterized by established rules and set goals. At the heart of every game are challenges and obstacles to overcome. Whether video games, chess, or soccer, games are contrived environments that require very specific actions to be successful. When beginning a game, the player agrees to limit actions to those that are dictated by a set of rules. Sociologists and anthropologists suggest that games introduce children to a culture's social rules. The ways they are played teach children the values that are attributable to success. Some societies present games as highly competitive activities in which individual success leads to rewards and social status. Other societies use games to teach cooperation and the value of group decisions. Some games reward players for working together to overcome a challenge.

Games provide parents and teachers with ways of introducing fair play to children. Cultural knowledge and beliefs are transferred from one generation to the next. As described in later chapters, teachers and parents can have a powerful influence on children's developing self-confidence by structuring games that match their abilities and developmental readiness to learn.

To draw children in, people must introduce games at the right time and in the right way. Often, children see brothers, sisters, or friends playing games and want to learn. The movement from play, which has no rules, to games, which are defined by rules, is an important developmental step. Young children tend to learn game rules from adults rather than from peers. In most cases, they place their faith in the norms that adults provide

(Rakoczy, Hamann, Warneken, & Tomasello, 2010). Thus, the way games are introduced to young children can have profound and long-term effects on their views of how games should be played and how rules should be followed. The memory of a specific game, the people with whom the game was played, and the emotions experienced during the game may be retained throughout a person's lifetime. When parents and children experience similar game-play emotions, long-lasting bonds may result (Ginsburg, 2007). The games played early in life often establish the stories that are shared with others later in life.

Children and Sports

Sports are forms of competitive physical activity. People participate in sports to develop, maintain, or improve physical fitness and to be entertained. Sports are seen in many cultures as a way to teach children proper ways to behave according to social expectations. It has long been thought that sport develops character and promotes strong moral values. In the early 20th century, with the growth of cities and the rise of industrialization, organized sports were supported by social welfare agencies as a way to instill values in children and adolescents. Over time, however, children's programs focused more and more on competition. Participating in sports may expose children to conditions in which they can learn skills they can transfer to nonsport settings, but only when content and delivery are tailored to facilitate personal development (Danish, Fomeris, Hodge, & Heke, 2004).

Proponents of organized competitive sports for children have stressed that they increase physical skills, enhance social competence and teamwork skills, and build character. Sport training conducted appropriately can promote health and physical fitness. Under normal conditions there is little reason to believe that sports will be detrimental to a child's physiological development and function. Only when extreme training demands are placed on a child can normal development be negatively affected. Some studies have found that sports that involve repetitive actions, such as swimming, tennis, and baseball, can compromise children's

> **games**—Forms of competitive play characterized by established rules and set goals.
>
> **sports**—Forms of competitive physical activity.

skeletal growth and integrity (Malina, Bouchard, & Bar-Or, 2004).

Children's perceptions of their abilities and competence can be affected greatly by their involvement in sports. Confidence is a general belief in one's ability to perform particular activities. Children's perceptions of their abilities and skills play an important role in the feelings generated prior to, during, and following sport activities. Children who view themselves as competent typically describe challenging situations as enjoyable and fun; those who doubt their competence often report negative feelings toward challenging situations. Children's perceptions of competence can carry through adolescence and into adulthood. People who rate their skill level as high typically believe that they have control over game conditions and can influence the outcomes of the event. Those who perceive themselves as less competent are more likely to believe that they are controlled by outside conditions and have less autonomy. Factors that establish children's beliefs about their abilities are discussed in some detail in later chapters.

Historically, participation in competitive sport at a young age has been seen as character building and a way to prepare children for the challenges they will encounter as adults. Success in sport demands an element of emotional control so that good decision making can occur. The young baseball player who is batting with the bases loaded in the final inning is more likely to play well when he is in control of his emotions. Those who promote sports typically believe that such emotional control can help children deal with competitive situations both on and off the playing field.

How Physical Activity and Exercise Enhance Children's Cognition

To understand how physical activity might affect cognition, it is important to have a general understanding of the structures and functions of the human brain and how those structures evolved. Many reflexive functions are controlled by brain systems that are evolutionarily very old; the brain structures involved in higher mental functions emerged relatively recently. The study of human evolution reveals that the physical activity of our early ancestors essentially guided the development of the modern human body and mind.

Our ancient ancestors faced life-threatening situations. To survive, they had to seek food, water, and shelter. Those who lacked the physical and mental skills essential to obtain these necessities perished. Brain size has been implicated as a crucial factor in the evolution of humans. The modern human brain consumes considerable energy—about 20 percent of the body's total energy production. Supplying the brain with the energy necessary to function efficiently led our ancestors to gradually alter their dietary intake and their behaviors. A hallmark accomplishment about 2.5 million years ago was the creation of tools that could be used to hunt and survive. The capacity to create and use tools requires complex cognitive and motor skills. Tools were made for specific tasks, and over time tool production became more sophisticated. As early humans migrated out of Africa, they learned not only how to deal with the immediate challenges of the environment, but also how to plan for future events. Survival depended on the ability to acquire and use knowledge about changes in terrain, weather patterns, sources of food and water, and shelter.

Over hundreds of thousands of years, the physical and mental characteristics seen in modern humans slowly changed. About 60,000 years ago, rapid changes in human cognition occurred. With language and the ability to think and reason, humans came to dominate the globe. Civilization emerged only 10,000 to 12,000 years ago, but within a short period of time, humans adapted to virtually every geographical area on the planet. In summary, the study of human evolution highlights the evolutionary role of physical activity and movement in the emergence of the brain structures responsible for complex cognitive and motor skills. The sections that follow address the link between physical activity and the development of brain and cognition across the life span and particularly during childhood.

Linking Physical Activity to Changes in the Brain

Although the brain is the center of thought and reasoning, relatively little was known about its structures until quite recently. Advances in technology and new tools over the past few decades revolutionized scientists' understanding of the brain and how it develops. Chapter 1 provided a brief description of brain development. Research conducted by neuroscientists over the past two decades has shed light on how physical activity and exercise may modify particular parts of the brain, which, in turn, alters the way children think and behave.

Four brain structures are likely to be influenced by physical activity—the **cerebellum**, **motor cortex**, **prefrontal cortex**, and **hippocampus**. As seen in figure 2.2, the cerebellum is a large brain structure that plays a key role in reflexive movement control and the fine-tuning of precise motor movement patterns. Recent research has shown that the cerebellum connects with every major brain structure and plays an important role in the control of movement and learning new skills. Studies conducted with animals have revealed that complex physical activity produces long-lasting structural adaptations in the cerebellum (Iacoboni, 2001).

Research conducted with laboratory animals, typically rats and mice, provides information about the effects of exercise that is not possible to obtain from humans. There is considerable support for the benefits of routine exercise on brain function in animals. Exercise leads to changes in neurons that control arousal and attention, increased levels of proteins that maintain brain health, the growth of new neurons in brain networks involved in learning and memory, and increased brain blood distribution (Hillman, Erickson, & Kramer, 2008).

Researchers who first showed that exercise causes improved cognition in humans were studying human aging. A number of studies conducted by Kramer and associates at the University of Illinois in the United States provided the first solid evidence that routine aerobic exercise increases older adults' executive functions (Kramer et al., 2002). Since then, experiments have linked exercise to alterations in brain structures and functions (Erickson & Kramer, 2009). More recently, these positive findings have been extended to younger adults and children (Krafft et al., 2014; Voss, Nagamatsu, Liu-Ambrose, & Kramer, 2011).

Linking Physical Activity to Children's Cognition

The ancient Greek philosopher Plato considered routine physical activity critical for children's education. His views have been supported by physicians and educators for centuries. However, until quite recently, relatively few studies considered whether and how physical activity influences children's thinking. Two general approaches have been used to study the effects of physical activity: one examines the effects of single bouts of acute exercise; the other examines chronic exercise training, which involves repeated bouts of exercise over several weeks, months, or years (Audiffren, 2009). **Acute exercise** produces temporary changes in children's physical arousal that affect thinking processes. **Chronic exercise training** produces structural changes in the brain and improvements in physical fitness. An understanding of the differences between the two approaches is important for appreciating the methods central to the physical activity games presented in later chapters.

Both acute exercise and chronic exercise training benefit children's mental functioning—but in different ways. As children start moving, their heart and respiration rates increase; they become more aroused. Several studies have found that children's attention and learning improve immediately following physical activity that produces moderate levels of arousal (Tomporowski, 2003a). Studies highlight the importance of the nature of children's physical activity. Budde and colleagues (2008) found that a 10-minute bout of activity characterized by high demands on motor coordination control to mentally engage children improved their executive functions more than less demanding activity did. Similarly, Pesce and colleagues (Pesce et al., 2009) found that a 40-minute bout of a sport game led to better classroom learning than less mentally engaging aerobic exercise did. Although the type of activity and the duration of the bouts were quite different in the two studies, both showed that movement task complexity is an important factor. These findings are in direct

cerebellum—An area of the brain that connects with every major brain structure and plays an important role in movement control and learning new skills.

motor cortex—A strip of brain tissue that sends commands to control muscles involved in movements.

prefrontal cortex—An area of the brain that consists of neural networks that make up the executive of the brain. It is involved in an awareness of current conditions, the retrieval of stored memories, and the formulation of action plans.

hippocampus—A structure located deep in the brain that plays a role in memory and learning.

acute exercise—Physical activity that produces temporary changes in children's physical arousal that affect thinking processes.

chronic exercise training—Repeated bouts of exercise over several weeks, months, or years that produce structural changes in the brain and improvements in physical fitness.

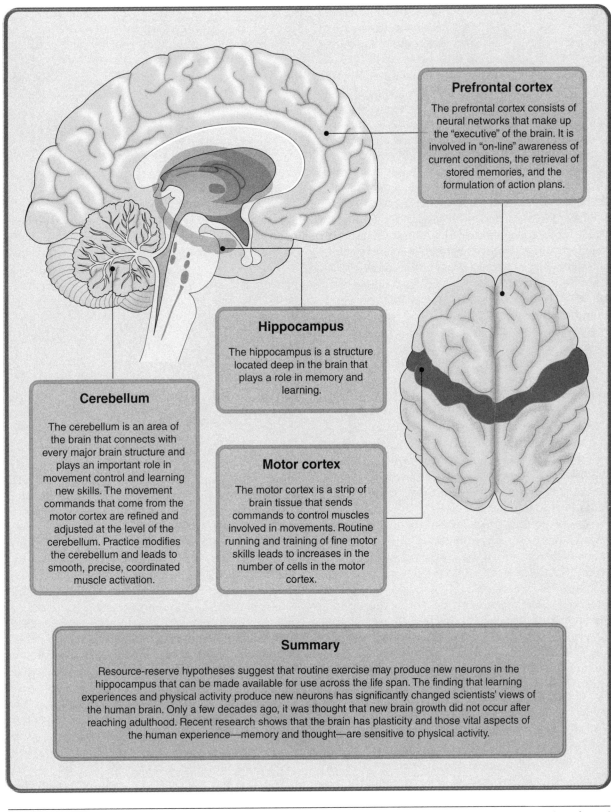

Prefrontal cortex

The prefrontal cortex consists of neural networks that make up the "executive" of the brain. It is involved in "on-line" awareness of current conditions, the retrieval of stored memories, and the formulation of action plans.

Hippocampus

The hippocampus is a structure located deep in the brain that plays a role in memory and learning.

Cerebellum

The cerebellum is an area of the brain that connects with every major brain structure and plays an important role in movement control and learning new skills. The movement commands that come from the motor cortex are refined and adjusted at the level of the cerebellum. Practice modifies the cerebellum and leads to smooth, precise, coordinated muscle activation.

Motor cortex

The motor cortex is a strip of brain tissue that sends commands to control muscles involved in movements. Routine running and training of fine motor skills leads to increases in the number of cells in the motor cortex.

Summary

Resource-reserve hypotheses suggest that routine exercise may produce new neurons in the hippocampus that can be made available for use across the life span. The finding that learning experiences and physical activity produce new neurons has significantly changed scientists' views of the human brain. Only a few decades ago, it was thought that new brain growth did not occur after reaching adulthood. Recent research shows that the brain has plasticity and those vital aspects of the human experience—memory and thought—are sensitive to physical activity.

Figure 2.2 Brain areas that change with physical activity: cerebellum, hippocampus, motor cortex, and prefrontal cortex.

opposition to the long-held view of many teachers that increases in children's arousal generated by recess and games interfere with academic classroom behavior and learning. In fact, the opposite is true. Physical activity, performed in the right way, may prepare, or prime, children to learn.

Also, physical fitness derived from habitual participation in physical activity seems to provide long-lasting benefits to cognitive functioning. Studies that compare physically fit and less physically fit children consistently show differences in brain structure and processing speed, which highlights the benefits of routine physical activity (Chaddock, Pontifex, Hillman, & Kramer, 2011).

The first experiment to clearly show that chronic exercise training improves children's mental function and alters brain function was conducted by Davis and colleagues (2011) at the Medical College of Georgia in the United States. They assigned overweight children randomly to a 20-minute or 40-minute exercise session, or to a nonintervention control group. Children in the exercise groups attended a 13-week after-school program in which they played games designed to maximize intermittent vigorous activity and to elicit high heart rate levels. The effects of the exercise programs on cognition were measured with a comprehensive test that provided measures of executive function, attention, spatial organization, and memory, and included a standardized test of academic achievement. The researchers discovered that exercise influenced specific measures of cognition and academic achievement.

As seen in figure 2.3, a dose–response effect was noted: gains in executive function performance and academic achievement in mathematics increased with more exercise (i.e., a greater dose). The dose–response effect is important because it addresses concerns about the amount of exercise needed to improve children's mental function. As part of this experiment, children were selected for a neuroimaging study. The results suggest that, as in adults, exercise training in children alters the neural brain networks important for information processing and executive function.

The games used in the Davis study served as prototypes for those described in this book for elementary school–age children (chapter 11). These games have been developed to take advantage of the benefits that can be obtained from both acute bouts of physical activity and chronic training interventions. As will be discussed later in more detail, acute periods of physical activity help a child to attend and learn, whereas repeated bouts of physical activity alter both body and mind.

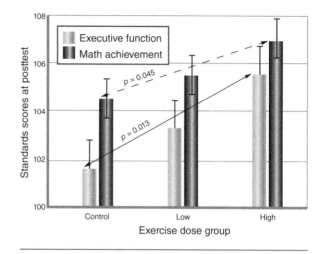

Figure 2.3 Overweight children's executive function and math achievement test performance showing dose–response effects of 20-minute and 40-minute exercise sessions.

Adapted, by permission, from C.L. Davis, P.D. Tomporowski et al., 2011, "Exercise improves executive function and achievement and alters brain activation in overweight children: A randomized, controlled trial," *Health Psychology* Vol. 30(1): 91-98.

Linking Physical Activity to Children's School Performance

The really important question is, therefore, can the gains seen in research studies be achieved in traditional school, after-school, and home environments? Researchers note that the amount of time children are involved in physical education, physical activity, and sports is consistently proportional to their academic performance—that is, more time spent being active benefits children's and adolescents' academic performance. Several large studies have shown linkages between children's time in physical education and their academic and classroom performance (California Department of Education, 2005; Carlson et al., 2008; Chomitz et al., 2009).

Donnelly and colleagues at the University of Kansas (2009) provided a clear demonstration of how to integrate physical activity programs into the school day and benefit academic performance. Over a three-year period, a physical activity intervention based on Take10!, a program developed by the U.S. Centers for Disease Control, was incorporated into second- and third-grade classrooms. Children were given break times during the school day during which teachers led programs of moderate-to-vigorous physical activity (MVPA). Children in schools that incorporated the activity programs performed significantly better on tests of academic achievement than did children in schools that did not offer the program. Over the past few years, the administrators of several school systems in the United States have changed their academic programs to include enhanced physical education and physical activity programs. The initial reports from these schools are positive and provide additional support for the benefits of physical activity programs on children's and adolescents' academics and behavior.

Translating research into practice is challenging. The data obtained by researchers have shown that exercise works, but teachers and educators have little information on how to use physical activity programs to enhance children's mental functions and academic performance. The methods used in research studies are typically quite different from those available in school and out-of-school programs. Often, researchers select children based on a set of criteria, provide extensive teacher training, and enjoy low teacher-to-student ratios. One way to ensure the successful, long-term translation from research into practice is to understand just how physical activity interventions work. Once that is known, effective teacher training programs focused on physical activity can be developed.

Contemporary Explanations for the Mental Benefits of Physical Activity

Is it simply the case that all it takes to enhance children's mental function is to increase the activation of their muscles? Or is it more complex than just running and jumping? Presently, there are three main explanations for how physical activity improves children's mental functions—biological, cognitive, and social-affective. Chapter 1 explained that scientists often work within specific domains of research. So it should not be surprising that these explanations have come from these three domains.

Biological Explanations

Perhaps the most enduring explanation for the beneficial effect of physical activity on the brain

> **cognitive immaturity hypothesis**—The notion that the less developed state of children's nervous systems and their lack of experience make it difficult for them to perform higher-level cognitive tasks with the same efficiency as adolescents and adults.

is blood flow. Although the brain comprises only about 3 percent of total body weight, it requires 20 to 25 percent of the body's oxygen supply to meet its needs. Oxygen is not stored in the brain; it must be supplied continuously, and even a few minutes of deprivation can result in brain damage. Given that exercise improves the cardiovascular system, aerobic fitness and its associated capacity to circulate blood and oxygen has been used to explain improvements in brain function and cognition (Dustman & White, 2006). More recently, neuropsychologists have found that exercise has many effects on the brain that may help mental processing. With exercise, capillary growth increases and improves the routing and distribution of the blood and oxygen in the brain. Further, exercise increases neurotransmitter substances that aid communication between brain neurons and improve the strength of neural networks. Recently, exercise has been linked to increases in brain proteins (brain-derived neurotropic factors) that play an important role in brain health and protection from injury. Perhaps most important for the developing child is evidence that exercise promotes the creation of new neurons in areas of the brain that are critical for learning and memory, such as the hippocampus (Chaddock et al., 2010). See figure 2.4.

Cognition and Learning Explanations

Providing children recess or breaks during the academic school day have been seen as a way to improve mental function and academic performance. Teachers involve children in tasks that demand attention and memory. Over the course of a class or a series of classes, the amount of information children need to retain increases. At some point, bits of knowledge begin to interfere with others. The buildup of interference makes it difficult for children to organize their thoughts. The **cognitive immaturity hypothesis** developed by Bjorklund and Green (1992) proposes that the less developed state of children's nervous systems and their lack of experience make it difficult for them to perform higher-level cognitive tasks with the same efficiency as adolescents and adults. Recess and breaks from mental demands are thought to allow the buildup of interference to dissipate and to improve learning. From this point of view, unstructured play and self-directed mental and physical activity are the critical elements.

An alternative explanation is that games are mentally engaging and challenging and therefore

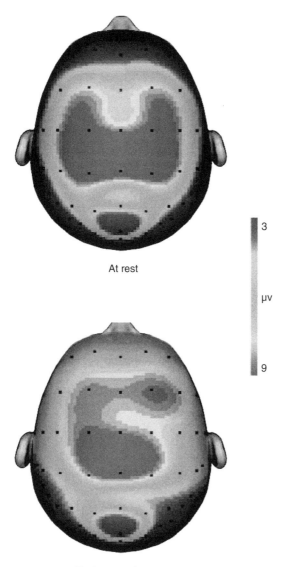

At rest

3

μv

9

During exercise

Figure 2.4 A brain scan of participants after sitting and a brain scan after walking for 20 minutes.

Reprinted from *Neuroscience*, Vol. 159, C.H. Hillman et al., "The effect of acute treadmill walking on cognitive control and academic achievement in preadolescent children," pgs. 1044-1054, Copyright 2009, with permission from Elsevier.

provide opportunities to learn sets of mental skills (Diamond & Lee, 2011). The executive functions of response inhibition, working memory, and mental shifting have been viewed as sets of mental skills that emerge gradually with continued practice and refinement. As children learn problem-solving strategies during play and games, they also learn how to use those strategies in other situations (e.g., academics). The **mental skill hypothesis** advocated by Diamond and colleagues views executive function as a group of mental skills that are acquired

gradually and influenced by practice. Mental skill learning highlights the importance of teacher-led interventions. The modification of specific foundational executive functions in children is believed to have far-reaching consequences across the life span.

Social-Affective Explanations

Social responsibility, which is the ability to interact cooperatively with others, inhibit antisocial behavior, and form close relationships, such as friendships, is considered a foundational skill in early elementary school. Social bonds and social skills often form in the context of games such as tag, soccer, and jump rope. Interactions with other children and teachers provide the basis for developing the social competence that is vital for adjusting to the demands of school. Friendships developed during play, games, and sports provide the emotional support needed for meeting and overcoming the challenges faced in school (Solmon & Lee, 2008).

Diamond's and Lee's (2011) inspection of the research suggests that the effectiveness of interventions aiding executive function development can differ. Focusing narrowly on either cognitive stimulation or physical activity in isolation seems not to be as effective as addressing cognitive, physical, emotional, and social development jointly. The advantage of the mentally challenging movement games proposed in this book is that they differ from computerized training or repetitive forms of physical training by embedding cognitive challenges into physically and socially engaging playful activities.

Human behavior is complex, and it can be influenced at a number of levels—biological, cognitive, and social-affective. In all likelihood, physical activity influences mental function through multiple interacting paths. Understanding how physical activity affects children's development can help teachers provide optimal educational experiences.

mental skill hypothesis—A hypothesis that views executive function as a group of mental skills that are acquired gradually and influenced by practice.

social responsibility—The ability to interact cooperatively with others, inhibit antisocial behavior, and form close relationships, such as friendships.

Learning how to play with others positively affects a child's ability to interact in a social world.

As described in detail in part III, specific instructional conditions can maximize the cognitive benefits of games.

Implications for Educators

Physical educators have debated the goals of teaching since the late 1800s. On one side of the debate, some have asserted that the aim of physical education is to teach students *about the physical.* That is, the content and curriculum ought to focus on becoming and remaining physically strong and healthy. Today, those who champion the education-of-the-physical philosophy strive to increase children's physical fitness and sport skills by focusing on exercise frequency, intensity, time, and type. Those who subscribed to an exercise-is-medicine perspective focus predominantly on physical fitness and its measurement (Rowland, 2005).

On the other side of the debate are those who believe that physical education should focus on teaching children how to participate in physical activities that provide learning, socialization opportunities, and enhanced well-being. For these people, the aim of physical education is to teach students *through the physical.* The education-through-the-physical philosophy is the belief that physical edu-

cators should strive to not only enhance children's physical health, but also contribute to their social, emotional, and intellectual development (Pesce, 2012).

Majority support for education of the physical and education through the physical fluctuated throughout the 20th century. Shifts in focus in the United States were often the result of national priorities initiated by policy makers. Events leading to the world wars and other military and political conflicts led policy makers to address the perceived lack of physical fitness of American citizens who volunteered for or were recruited into service. Presently, the worldwide obesity epidemic, particularly in children, is becoming a priority because it is a major health issue. The prevalence of children and adolescents classified as overweight or obese has profoundly affected the physical education profession. Parents, health providers, and the general public look to schools to provide the necessary regimen of physical activity and skills to help children be active for a lifetime. Media programs and magazines have featured physical education programs that resemble for-profit fitness centers that employ sophisticated training equipment and exercise activities designed primarily for adults. In response to federal and state initiatives, the focus of many physical educators has been primarily to reduce the prevalence of childhood obesity via exercise programs that increase and maintain children's levels of physical activity. Less emphasis is being placed on interventions that promote children's overall physical and mental development. As a result, there has been a shift away from the philosophy of education through the physical that has been the focus of teacher educators in North America since the mid-1980s toward the philosophy of education of the physical and weight reduction and obesity prevention programs.

Although children's bodies do respond to exercise training, there has been some concern that exercise programs developed for adults are not well suited for children. Given the normal activity patterns of children, it may be that exercise routines such as treadmill running, stationary cycling, and circuit training, which adults perform, are not the best way to engage children in physical activity. Also, emerging evidence suggests that motor skill proficiencies developed in childhood, rather than physical fitness, have a strong influence on subsequent fitness during adolescence (Barnett et al., 2008). This is probably because activities promoting motor skill development are more enjoyable for children and increase feelings of motor competence,

thus contributing to their present and future adherence to physical activity. Therefore, experts are beginning to call for developmentally appropriate exercise interventions. Missing from these recommendations, however, is information concerning the adaptation of interventions for children who are at different levels of physical and mental development and who may differ greatly in their basic abilities.

Teachers should remember that children are in a developmentally sensitive period of life in which they are receptive to experiences that promote fundamental executive mental skills, which they can use to control their actions and solve real-world problems. Teachers can capitalize on this sensitive period by creating physical activity and exercise–based learning experiences that are meaningful to them. In other words, teachers matter! The physical activity teaching model presented in this book addresses how preschool-, kindergarten- and elementary school–age children learn mental skills and develop cognitive abilities that they can use in many situations and across the life span. Physical activity games that take advantage of children's natural motives to play and engage in games may, in the long term, meet both the goal of education *about* the physical and the goal of education *through* the physical.

How Movement Games
Help Children Think and Learn

Children, like adults, learn from their experiences. When we think about learning, the first thing that usually comes to mind is education—what we learn from books and teachers. However, there are different forms of learning. Some is acquired with little effort or even awareness, whereas other forms require focused attention and effort. The study of memory and learning can be traced at least as far back as the ancient Greeks. Many of the early explanations of learning have persisted, and they have guided teachers' instructional plans for over 2,000 years. Modern researchers have a good understanding of the learning process; however, the challenge is to translate what is known about learning into the teaching environment.

Children can and will learn on their own without teachers through trial and error. As we will see in this chapter, not only is trial-and-error learning slow and difficult and therefore inefficient, but also, children who learn without teachers can develop bad habits and poor techniques. Further, children who are not provided proper guidance may lack the awareness of how they can apply the skills they are learning to solving problems. Efficient learning occurs under specific conditions, and teachers play a critical role in how quickly and how well children learn skills and behaviors. Teachers' instructions can not only affect children's academic success but also prepare them to meet the challenges of adulthood.

Learning

The primary role of educators is to help students learn. On the surface, this goal seems to be relatively simple and straightforward. However, the conditions that promote children's learning are complex, and subtle changes in instructional methods, student motivation, and presentation styles can have considerable effects on what children retain from their experiences. **Learning** is a process that results in a relatively permanent and consistent change in behavior and is based on experience. This relatively simple definition conveys several very important characteristics.

Learning takes place within the child and cannot be seen directly. When children learn, their experiences are captured in the form of memories that are stored in areas of the brain. As a child who does not know how to throw a ball is taught the basics of throwing, changes take place in the brain. Teachers cannot see what is happening in the networks in the brain, but these changes are taking place, nonetheless. Consider how computers work. When you press the keyboard keys, changes take place within the computer. You cannot see what is happening within the components of the computer, but you are pretty sure that the circuitry is changing. Teachers cannot see what is happening inside children's heads, but they can conclude, or infer, that some mental changes have taken place.

Learning is relatively permanent; that is, when experiences are learned, memories remain for some time. Memories differ in how long they are stored and can be used to guide actions. As all of us have found, we do not remember all of our experiences. Most of what we experience is forgotten quite rapidly, whereas the memories of other experiences can last a lifetime. When we are introduced to someone, it is not unusual to forget the person's name within a matter of minutes. The memories of a disaster or a near-death experience, however, may remain vivid forever. Teachers strive to develop instructional experiences that result in children's storing memories that they can use consistently at later times. If the child who is taught how to throw a ball really learns the skill, he will demonstrate it not only when it is being taught but also later and in various conditions. As discussed later, a fundamental difference exists between children's performance (visible actions) and learning (changes that take place in the brain).

Learning provides the potential for action. The child who learns to throw a ball and can accurately hit a target may not always perform well. Does this mean that the child has unlearned the skill? No, the changes in the brain that occurred during instruction are still there. It is possible that the child may not perform well because he is tired, worried, or lacks interest. One of the biggest challenges facing teachers is to construct instructional and evalua-

tion conditions that provide the best evidence of children's learning, as well as a method that results in authentic assessment, which is discussed in chapter 8.

Learning occurs only with experience or practice. Whether a child learns through trial and error or a systematic instructional program, skills are learned with practice. With experience, the changes that take place in the brain provide the learner with the capacity to begin and control actions and movements. Teachers strive to enhance children's fundamental movement skills because these skills play such an important role in learning games and sports. With practice, the child who learns to throw a ball at a target becomes increasingly more efficient and skilled in her throwing movements and more accurate in her performance.

You may remember from chapter 1 that skills differ from abilities; skills are learned and refined with practice. Teachers need to recognize the difference between the changes in children's performance that are the result of training and skill development and those that are the result of growth and maturation. As children grow, their bodies get larger, abilities emerge, and their movement control improves. The child who learns to throw a ball may later experience a growth spurt that enables her to throw a ball farther and with greater force. However, these improvements in performance may have little to do with what the child has learned about throwing. Distinguishing the effects of growth from those of learning is particularly important when evaluating children's skill development.

Learning Curve

Regardless of the skills children are taught, improvements in performance emerge in a predictable fashion. Teachers often use graphs to show students how they are progressing on class assignments. Graphs provide a visual representation of the learning process. Figure 3.1*a* shows a child's ball-throwing accuracy as measured during many practice sessions and then plotted. Researchers who have examined how various types of skills are learned note that they all progress in a similar way. Regardless of whether the person is learning

> **learning**—A process that results in relatively permanent and consistent change in behavior and is based on experience.

a cognitive skill, such as playing chess, or a motor skill, such as throwing a ball at a target, the greatest improvement in performance occurs early in training. The rate of improvement then slows as the skill is acquired (Newell & Rosenbloom, 1981). The smooth curve shown in figure 3.1b is referred to as the classic learning curve. Children may differ in how quickly and how much they learn, but the pattern of skill development remains the same.

The pattern of the learning curve is useful for educators because it not only describes how children learn with practice, but also provides a way to predict how well children will perform if they continue to practice. Educators often use the phrase *on the learning curve* to emphasize that a student is in the process of becoming more skilled. As you will see in chapter 4, keeping children on the learning curve is a powerful way to maintain motivation and mental engagement. Chapter 6 addresses how learning theory can help teachers foster new and creative ways of thinking and acting in their students.

Stages of Learning

Children's progression from being novices to achieving proficiency has fascinated parents and teachers alike. At specific ages, children show rapid changes in their skills. Parents can attest to the fast increase in their children's language in their early years. Sounds change to words, and words change to phrases. Language comes naturally and easily to children, yet they engage in huge amounts of practice during this stage of their lives. Self-talk, nursery rhymes, songs, and stories represent a large part of each day. As thousands of words and phrases are repeated daily it provides the child with the practice

needed for becoming proficient in communication. However, not all communication skills are learned as quickly as language. Consider what children undergo when learning to read. Years of instruction, practice, and hard work may be needed to become a proficient reader.

The changes in learning that take place in children as they acquire proficiency and skill have been of interest to researchers for several decades. There is a generally accepted belief that skill development requires a progression through a series of learning stages. An important early model of the stages of skill acquisition was developed by Fitts and Posner (1967) and expanded on by others (Meinel & Schnabel, 1998; Proctor, Reeve, & Weeks, 1990). Learning is hypothesized to proceed through three stages: the cognitive stage, the associative stage, and the autonomous stage. This model has considerable intuitive appeal. Virtually everyone who has learned a sport skill will attest to the physical and mental changes that take place with practice.

Cognitive Stage

Consider a child who is facing a novel task, such as learning a new game. Before beginning play, the child needs to figure out the goals of the games, how it is performed, and why it should be played. Understanding how the game is played even before making the first movement requires executive planning. Children's ability to understand what is expected when a game begins depends greatly on the availability of the necessary mental machinery that allows them to listen, see, store and recall memories, and plan actions.

Cognition involves the input of several underlying mental processes. Consider a computer, which

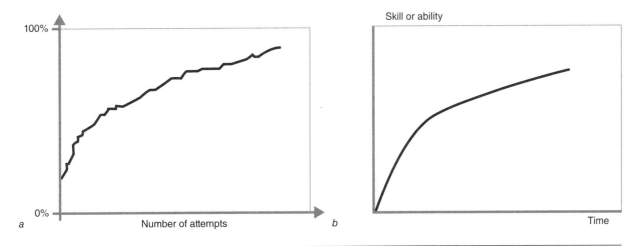

Figure 3.1 A child's ball-throwing accuracy: (a) measured over many trials; (b) the classic learning curve.

receives input from a keyboard, organizes and codes the information in a central processor, and then sends the information to storage devices. Later, information can be pulled from storage and sent to a printer, which provides output. Children are clearly not computers, but they too pull information from the world around them, can remember what they are told and what they experience, and can use those memories to plan and guide their actions. Figure 3.2 depicts one way to consider how the machinery of the mind operates. The components of cognition that are most important to learning games are attention, memory, executive functions, and movement control.

Attention is a state of focused awareness on some aspect of the environment and the ability to concentrate and maintain that focus. Attention is a gateway for incoming information. Children and adults live in a noisy environment that provides a huge amount of information, only some of which may be important at a given moment. This information arrives simultaneously from all sensory systems (i.e., eyes, ears, nose, skin, muscles). One role of attention is to analyze incoming sensory information and to determine what to allow in and what to keep out.

Memory is information about the environment that is stored for some period of time. Humans have the remarkable capacity to benefit and learn from their experiences. These experiences are catalogued by structures deep in the brain (e.g., the hippocampus, which is discussed in chapter 2) and stored in networks that are distributed throughout the brain. The total storage capacity of the brain is not known precisely, but the general consensus is that it is huge. We are also capable of storing several types of memory. Most cognitive psychologists agree that there are two general categories of memory. **Declarative memories** are memories about events, facts, and concepts; they require conscious awareness and attention to be stored and recalled. Examples of declarative memories are general facts such as the meanings of words and concepts or the name of the queen of England or the president of the United States, as well as memories unique to the child that reflect her personal experiences. **Procedural memories** are about how to do things (e.g., ride a bicycle, tie shoelaces, play a musical instrument); they can be stored and recalled without conscious effort.

Executive functions, which were introduced in chapter 1, are linked closely to consciousness and planning. Similar to the central processing unit (CPU) in a computer, the working memory executive function pulls declarative and procedural memories that are stored in the brain to solve problems. For instance, a child preparing to play a new game needs to hold instructions in mind, pull from past experiences, and formulate an action plan.

Movement control involves the selection, sequencing, and timing of the muscles contraction that guide action. Movement control is organized by **motor programs**, which are sets of commands from the brain that instruct the body to move in specified ways. They provide the child with a general idea of how to perform the actions of a new game. Some motor programs are innate and unlearned (e.g., walking and running) and underlie the develop-

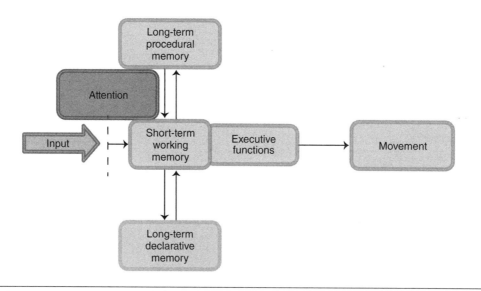

Figure 3.2   A component-process model of cognition.

ment of fundamental motor skills; learned motor programs are specific to conditions such as those in games and sports. Learned motor programs reflect the adaptive nature of experience; past learning is applied to new situations.

Understanding the components of children's cognition is important for teachers. Differences in the basic mental machinery exist among children, and they play an important role in how quickly and how much an individual child can learn.

Associative Stage

Virtually every explanation of learning since the time of the ancient Greeks to the present has explained learning by using concepts of sticking, gluing, or connecting. Contemporary psychologists focus on the connections between environmental stimuli and behavioral responses. During the associative stage of skill training, the child becomes aware of what goes with what; when certain conditions occur, he asks himself, What do I do? In answering this question, the child identifies what he sees, hears, or feels and connects those sensations to actions. These stimulus–response relationships are necessary for learning. The child learning to ride a bicycle learns that some things are more important than others.

Skill learning involves strengthening connections between environmental conditions and appropriate

---

attention—A state of focused awareness on some aspect of the environment and the ability to concentrate and maintain that focus.

memory—Information about the environment that is stored for some period of time.

declarative memories—Memories about events, facts, and concepts that require conscious awareness and attention to be stored and recalled.

procedural memories—Memories about how to do things (e.g., ride a bicycle, tie shoelaces, play a musical instrument) that can be stored and recalled without conscious effort.

motor program—A set of commands from the brain that instructs the body to move in a specified way.

explicit learning—Learning that involves conscious attention and evaluation.

implicit learning—Learning that produces habits that control movements in an almost reflexive fashion without conscious awareness.

---

behaviors. Many skills require **explicit learning**, which involves conscious attention and evaluation. For example, when a youngster learns the game of hopscotch, she needs to think about each step and how to sequence each hop based on the numbers in the boxes. Learning can also occur without conscious awareness. **Implicit learning** produces habits that control movements in an almost reflexive fashion without conscious awareness. In the hopscotch game, the child not only links her hops to the numbers in the boxes, but she also learns, without being aware of it, how to control the leg force required to move her body from one box to the next and maintain balance. Knowledge acquired in an unconscious fashion is typically stored in memory for a long time. Much implicit learning occurs when learning to ride a bicycle, for example, and it is probably one reason it comes back to us as soon as we get on a bike after not riding for a long time.

To improve, we must practice. Depending on the game or skill, the associative stage can last weeks, months, or years. During this phase, changes take place within the learner. Neural networks in the brain become progressively strengthened, and motor control programs become more refined. Along with these neurological changes, behaviors change as well. Unlike the novice, who displays slow, jerky actions, the child in the associative stage moves more efficiently and exhibits desired behaviors more readily. Improvement in skill occurs as a result of increases in the speed of mental processes, which rely on executive functions and knowledge about how to move. Note in figure 3.3 that the sizes of the boxes that reflect both the speed at which working memory works and the amount of declarative and procedural knowledge stored in memory increase with practice. As children become more skilled, they think faster and are able to draw from a larger store of knowledge.

Autonomous Stage

With practice, children's movements become increasingly more efficient and require less and less thought. The conscious mental processes that were critical for the child to connect game conditions and actions during the cognitive and associative phases come to be dominated by unconscious processes. Indeed, studies of brain activity show that early in learning, activity in cortical areas of the brain increases. However, with practice, activity in the cortex decreases and is replaced by activity in structures deep in the brain that automatically guide motor programs and actions. As skill improves, children begin to play games without even thinking

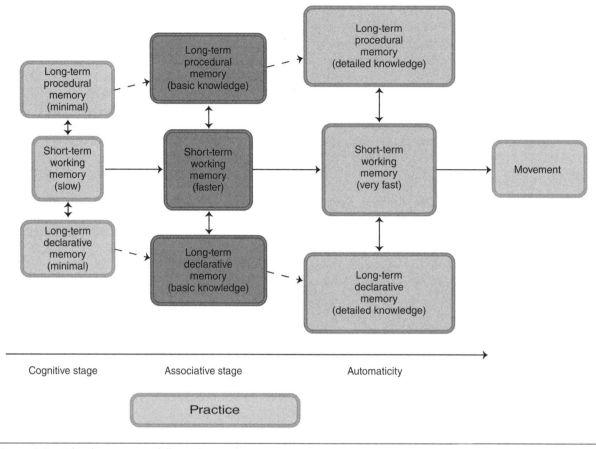

Figure 3.3   What happens as skills are learned.

about how to do it. The shift from slow, conscious mental processing to fast, unconscious processing, or **automaticity**, is a hallmark of skilled performance.

One of the benefits of automaticity is that the mental processing that was used to learn skills can now be used to employ game strategies. As described in detail in chapter 6, the release of the conscious mental processes required to guide movements provides the conditions that fuel creative thought and novel ways of thinking and acting. Also, the skill level in the autonomous stage is nearing the person's maximum. Adults who are experts are typically motivated to practice many hours each week for many years to attain and maintain their skills. Improvements in performance during the associative stage require more and more practice. Children are seldom as motivated to practice as much as adults and often reach a point at which they lose interest in the activity.

Games provide children with a natural context in which to learn and develop mental functions. Physical education scholars have emphasized the importance of children's thoughtful decision making during physical activity classes to promote critical reasoning (Kirk & MacPhail, 2002). The challenge for teachers is to construct game conditions that maximize mental engagement. Researchers who study learning have discovered basic principles that teachers can use to create game conditions that keep children on the learning curve.

What Influences the Shape of the Learning Curve?

When learning a new game, a child is faced with a movement problem: the child has a goal, but incomplete knowledge about how to act to achieve it. Solving the movement problem requires sufficient knowledge. Because the sequence of movements needed for achieving the goal of the game may not be self-evident, a child might try out many inefficient movement plans. As discussed earlier in the chapter, trial-and-error problem solving may eventually result in a solution, but improvements on the learning curve will be slow.

The shape of the learning curve reflects how fast and to what level a skill is acquired. The shape of a child's learning curve can be influenced by a number of conditions that are under teachers' control. Four of the most powerful tools available to teachers are instructions, modeling, feedback, and practice schedules. All have the potential to increase children's mental engagement and subsequent learning.

Instructions

Instructions are statements that describe how to do something. They are used to prepare children to learn. Through instructions, a teacher can direct the child's attention to what is important, describe the order of actions, and promote mental engagement. Each attempt the child makes in practice provides an opportunity for learning. The mentally engaged child who is learning to throw a ball to a target first assesses the initial conditions of the movement problem (the weight of the ball and the size and distance of the target), thinks through movements before making them, evaluates the feeling of the movements, and sees the outcome of her actions.

Teacher instructions can help the child develop a schema or general rule that he can use to solve a movement problem. With each attempt to solve a movement problem, experiences are stored as declarative and procedural memories. Teachers need to learn how to give verbal instructions as well as methods of direct instruction (these are described in detail in chapter 7). Instructions are particularly important during the cognitive and associative stages of learning and they have a marked impact on how quickly and how well skills are learned. Poor instruction that does not take into account developmental readiness, developmental differences, or information processing ability can be ineffective or even detrimental to children's learning.

Modeling

Modeling, or **observational learning**, involves learning by watching actions that are central to solving movement problems. Modeling complements verbal instructions. In much the same way that a picture is worth a thousand words, so too the actions of a teacher give a child a mental image he can use to develop a movement schema. Observing an appropriate model gives children knowledge about the consequences of actions. Effective teachers use modeling to show actions that work and actions that do not work. Children learn from seeing others' successes and failures. However, as described in chapters 6 and 7, one of the arts of teaching is knowing when (and how) to model performance and when to allow children to discover solutions to movement problems themselves.

Feedback

Feedback is information that indicates something about the consequences of movements. It is critical for learning. **Intrinsic feedback** originates from within the body during movement. Muscles, joints, skin, eyes, and ears send information to the brain that provides a sense of movement. **Extrinsic feedback** is information that cannot be obtained directly; it is provided by teachers and others who evaluate the learner's performance and movements. The learning process is influenced greatly by the dynamic interaction between extrinsic and intrinsic feedback.

As with instructions, the effectiveness of feedback depends on many conditions and how it is provided. **Scaffolding** is support given by a teacher during the learning process. The role of the teacher is to provide the support, or a scaffold, needed to progress in skill development early in training. The amount of support provided by the teacher decreases as the student acquires skill proficiency. When the teachers begin to provide less feedback, the student is forced to focus on intrinsic feedback and to think through and analyze the consequences of his actions. A child who is learning to throw a

> **automaticity**—A type of processing that is fast and unconscious.
>
> **instructions**—Statements that describe how to do something.
>
> **modeling or observational learning**—Learning by watching actions that are central to solving movement problems.
>
> **feedback**—Information that indicates something about the consequences of movements.
>
> **intrinsic feedback**—Feedback that originates from within the body during movement. Muscles, joints, skin, eyes, and ears send information to the brain that provides a sense of movement.
>
> **extrinsic feedback**—Information that cannot be obtained directly; it is provided by teachers and others who evaluate the learner's performance and movements.
>
> **scaffolding**—Support given by a teacher during the learning process.

ball at a target can be given feedback following each throw; however, this **continuous feedback** often leads to dependence on a teacher's assessment. **Intermittent feedback** is feedback given on some, but not all, learning attempts. People given the opportunity to provide their own assessments in intermittent feedback conditions learn new skills better than those who receive continuous feedback.

The type of feedback has a powerful influence on how fast and how well learning occurs. The most obvious type is **knowledge of results**, which is information about the degree to which a movement goal was met. For a child learning to throw a ball at a target, the teacher should provide not only information about how close the ball came to the target, but also **prescriptive feedback**, which is information about how to improve on the next trial (in this case, the next throw). Even more important is **knowledge of performance**, which is information about the quality of the movement. The child who is learning to throw a ball becomes more efficient as movements become coordinated. Teachers who give information about body position, stance, torso rotation, and arm positions help set the stage for effective motor control. The development of a child's efficient movement program is particularly critical during the early stages of skill learning. Part of the art of teaching is knowing when to provide feedback, how much feedback to provide, and when to let the child think for himself.

Practice Schedules

Recent research highlights the powerful effect on learning of simply rearranging practice schedules (Tomporowski, McCullick, & Horvat, 2010). It is common and appropriate during the cognitive and early associative stages to have learners repeat a movement over and over. **Constant practice** conditions are those in which a single movement is performed repeatedly. Repetition provides the central ingredients for learning a new motor program. Learning a new game requires children to sequence new movements together and establish a motor program, which defines and shapes the action. Early in learning, the child needs to pay attention to individual components of the motor program (e.g., where the feet, legs, fingers, hands, and arms go). Appropriate instruction, modeling, and extrinsic feedback help the child organize her movements. By the late associative stage, the general motor pattern is learned and the child becomes more proficient at selecting appropriate muscles, sequencing the contraction of the muscles, and timing movements.

Practice schedules may need to be rearranged so a single movement can be performed repeatedly.

During the late associative and automaticity stages, teachers can modify practice schedules in ways that promote learning. Children who practice under **varied practice** conditions in which problem-solving demands have been changed or are varied across practice trials learn more than children who continue to practice under constant practice conditions. Altering the problem-solving demands of games often improves children's ability to use their newly learned motor programs. Shifting movement plans from one condition to another requires executive functions. The child must recognize that the game conditions have changed, assess the demands of the new game, pull a movement program from memory, adjust the motor program to match the new game conditions, and then respond.

Executive functions, such as response inhibition, working memory, and mental shifting, are central to the mental processes that occur during varied practice conditions. An important benefit of varied practice conditions and the accompanying mental engagement is the opportunity to deal with unexpected changes. Thus, keeping children guessing about the changes that may occur alters how they prepare to act. When conditions change, children who have a history of experiencing change can adapt to overcome challenges in new situations. Consider the importance of generalization, as discussed in chapter 1, in the definition of learning presented earlier in this chapter. Children who cannot use knowledge in new situations have not really learned.

Attention, modeling, feedback, and practice schedules help children learn by promoting mental involvement, or engagement. Children who are mentally engaged are easy to spot. A child learning to tie her shoe may focus so much on the activity that she loses track of time, fails to hear her parents or teacher, and is in her own world. Researchers consider **mental engagement** as energized, directed, and sustained action used to meet and overcome challenges and problems. Children use their mental fuel or energy when they concentrate on mentally challenging activities such as video games, school assignments, games, and sports.

Mental Energy and Children's Learning

Genetically, children are designed to learn what is important for survival. However, because their brains are immature and their neural networks are not fully connected, they do not grasp learning problems in the same way as adults, who have fully developed neural networks (Bjorklund & Bering, 2002). Novelty attracts children's attention. Events that are no longer novel quickly lose the capacity to arouse attention. A young child may spend hours stacking blocks, knocking them down, and restacking them. But his attention to this complex game is transitory. After a while the block-building game is replaced by other, more complex and more challenging games. These behaviors reflect the concepts of disequilibrium and equilibrium discussed in chapter 1. The motivation, or drive, to achieve equilibrium explains persistence. More will be said of the motivational characteristics of games in chapter 4. However, it is important to realize that during periods of disequilibrium, changes in children's physiological states of energy and arousal occur that contribute to learning.

Children's Mental Energy

For many years, philosophers and teachers have wondered how the mind and body work together. Contemporary researchers who study cognitive energetics attempt to answer this question by studying the connections between the activities of body structures and the psychological processes of the mind. Many cognitive scientists agree that the mind does more than just process and organize information; it also has the capacity to be creative and generate new ideas. From birth to the end of life, humans face challenges that beg new and unique solutions. Children live in a chaotic world, but they bring order to chaos through the operations of their developing minds. These operations, however, require mental effort. As described earlier, children learn sequences of movements to achieve goals. Success in games, on the playing field, and in athletic competition demands that players understand the challenges they face and how to use their mental skills to overcome them.

The human mind directs voluntary, purposeful, and goal-directed behavior. Some aspects of cognition reflect "cold" reasoning—a machine-like analysis of the costs and benefits of actions. However, humans are not computers; their behaviors can be influenced by "hot" emotions and feelings. Children's psychological states reflect both cold computational processes and hot emotional processes that influence heart rate and respiration and result in feelings such as pleasure, anxiety, and fear. The balance between cold and hot cognition

continuous feedback—Feedback provided following every learning attempt.

intermittent feedback—Feedback given on some, but not all, learning attempts.

knowledge of results—Information about the degree to which a movement goal was met.

prescriptive feedback—Information about how to improve on the next trial.

knowledge of performance—Information about the quality of a movement.

constant practice—Practice in which a single movement is performed repeatedly.

varied practice—Successive practice trials in which problem-solving demands are changed (varied) across trials in no particular order.

mental engagement—Energized, directed, and sustained action used to meet and overcome challenges and problems.

can vary tremendously from moment to moment. Children's emotions greatly influence what and how they learn. Effective teachers understand the balance between the two sources of mental energy that promote children's learning.

Arousal and Learning

Teachers encounter children who are sleepy and underaroused and children who are so active that they are literally bouncing off the walls. Thus, they recognize the importance of having pupils at just the right level of arousal during classroom instruction. Considerable research conducted for over a century confirms teachers' observations about the importance of arousal to learning. Early research conducted by Yerkes and Dodson (1908) led to an important contribution to educational methods. As seen in figure 3.4, many studies have shown an inverted U-shape relation between arousal and performance: best performance occurs at moderate levels of arousal, and poor performance occurs at both ends of the arousal continuum. The **Yerkes-Dodson Law**, which describes the relation between arousal levels and performance, has maintained a prominent place in the majority of textbooks that address the effects of arousal on human performance.

Why would an increase in body activation influence what a child remembers and learns? Consider that neither children nor adults remember everything they experience. Daily routines are characterized by sameness. Repeating the same activities day in and day out makes them boring and not memorable. The human body becomes energized, however, when something unexpected or novel occurs. Children are innately attracted to new things; their attention is drawn to things they have never seen or touched before. When they encounter something new, children show widespread bodily changes—widening of the pupils, increased heart rate and respiration, and increased muscle tension. They become physically prepared to explore the new situation or object and figure it out. Children's exploration during periods of heightened arousal and increased attention and concentration set the stage for laying down memories. Indeed, research on memory storage reveals that more information is remembered when learning occurs in a state of moderate physical arousal.

Through the process of learning, children's physical and mental tension (disequilibrium) is reduced as stability (equilibrium) is attained. Learning is a naturally occurring process that helps children adapt to novel situations. The mental demands that children experience in new or restructured games lead them to engage cognitive control processes that are normal and healthy reactions to new learning situations. Further, the emotions triggered during the learning process are positive and motivate children to search out new challenging games.

Action Coupling and Children's Learning

Infants and children are biologically driven to explore and learn. Actions link movements to their consequences, and repetitive movements provide the basis for motor learning. The latter is procedural; that is, the child learns how to perform movements and goal-directed actions. As previously described in this chapter, much implicit learning occurs when learning movement actions. For example, a person may be able to ride a bicycle, but have a difficult time explaining how it is done. Action coupling automatically links the world to physical movement.

Recently, developmental psychologists have focused on the importance of physical movements to mental development. The theory of **embodied learning** states that a dynamic interaction occurs among children's body movements, the sensory experiences obtained from the movements, and the context of the movements. As a child learns to control his movements and perform actions, he begins to develop a framework to understand the world around him and how his actions provide the means to achieve goals. Learning occurs in

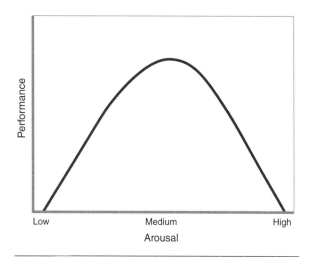

Figure 3.4 The inverted U-shape relationship between arousal and performance. Best performance occurs at moderate levels of arousal, and poor performance occurs at both ends of the arousal continuum.

real time and depends on the sensory and motor experiences obtained in the situation. Although children come to understand the environment through movement, the world limits or constrains what they learn. An unchanging, repetitive world provides few opportunities for children to learn from their movements.

Through movements and their consequences, infants and young children construct three-dimensional mental maps of the world. Infants learn where objects are and how they can control them through movements. The brightly colored mobile that dangles above an infant's crib provides an opportunity, or context, to learn how and where to move her arms or legs. The mental operations involved in remembering where objects are in space and how they can be moved are central to the mental imagery and operations necessary for solving mathematical and basic science problems (Newcombe & Frick, 2010).

Developmental Tasks and Readiness to Learn

The disequilibrium produced by a game depends on the physical and mental developmental level of the child. A game may capture a child's attention and mental engagement at one age and have little effect at another age. The game Simon Says may be an excellent game for young children, but boring for older children. Thus, how well games affect children's cognitive development depends on which games teachers select and when they present them. The importance of children's experiences during sensitive periods of development was discussed in chapter 1. Recall that there may be a limited window of opportunity in which to influence the child's developing brain.

> **Yerkes-Dodson Law**—A law that describes the relationship between arousal and performance.
>
> **embodied learning**—A theory that states that a dynamic interaction occurs among children's body movements, the sensory experiences obtained from the movements, and the context of the movements.
>
> **life span developmental tasks**—Tasks arising during certain periods of life that, if learned, contribute to happiness, success in later tasks, and societal approval.

Developmental Tasks

The mental skills that children learn and improve when they play games can help them master **life span developmental tasks**, which arise during certain periods in life. If learned, they contribute to happiness and success in later tasks. Failure to learn leads to unhappiness, societal disapproval, and difficulty with later tasks. Havighurst (1972), whose concepts of child development have influenced many generations of educators, suggested that the way a child succeeds or fails in learning a given developmental task can set the direction of his life's trajectory. Developmental tasks reflect a society's or culture's core beliefs; they reflect aspects of behavior that are considered important for group membership and physical and mental health. The developmental tasks children face are tied closely to biological maturation, social and cultural expectations, and emerging personal goals, values, and aspirations. As such, specific tasks can emerge at different points in time. Following are a few of the developmental tasks described by Havighurst that children encounter during the first two stages of development:

Developmental Tasks of Infancy and Early Childhood (birth to approximately 5 years of age)

- Learning to walk
- Learning to take solid foods
- Learning to talk
- Control/elimination of wastes
- Sex differences and sexual modesty
- Forming concepts and language to describe reality
- Getting ready to read
- Learning to distinguish right and wrong and beginning to develop a conscience

Adapted from Havighurst 1972.

Developmental Tasks of Middle Childhood (approximately 6 to 12 years of age)

- Learning physical skills necessary for ordinary games
- Building wholesome attitudes toward one's self
- Learning to get along with age-mates
- Learning an appropriate masculine or feminine social role
- Developing fundamental skills in reading, writing, and calculating

- Developing concepts for everyday living
- Developing conscience, morality, and a scale of values
- Achieving personal independence
- Developing attitudes toward social groups and institutions

Adapted from Havighurst 1972.

Havighurst emphasized that children are often primed or prepared to learn specific life skills at particular periods of development. A dynamic interaction occurs between the child and the emergence of specific developmental tasks. Children often display behaviors indicative of the **teachable moment**; that is an unplanned opportunity in which a teacher has an ideal chance to offer insight to students. As the context of classroom or game conditions change, children may be particularly receptive to learning the skills they need to meet and resolve challenges. The teachable moment is, however, transitory. Successful development often hinges on the timing of a student's readiness to learn and the teacher's readiness to impart knowledge.

Differences in Readiness to Learn

Learning depends on many conditions specific to the child. Because children do not mature and develop at the same rate, a teacher cannot rely on a child's age to determine when to introduce a particular game. Teachers need to consider the physical and cognitive demands of the game and match them to the child's physical maturation, prerequisite skills, and level of motivation, as mentioned in chapter 2 in the discussion of the optimal challenge point. Maturation does not refer only to physical abilities; it reflects changes in the cognitive domains as well. For example, a boy may have sufficient physical ability to play soccer, but lack the cognitive ability to understand complex directions or to deal with the social dynamics of a team sport. Likewise, another child may have developed the cognitive abilities to play soccer, but lack the physical characteristics needed to play the game.

Physical Development

Early childhood is a period lasting from about 18 months to about 6 years of age. The period is characterized by the emergence of **fundamental movement skills**, patterns of movements that are the basis for learning complex movements. The three categories of fundamental movement patterns are locomotor actions (walking and running), nonloco-

motor actions (bending, twisting, and balancing), and manipulative actions (knot tying, drawing). By age 6, young children's nervous systems mature and they show features of fundamental movement skills. Under the proper conditions, children's movement skills become more refined during **later childhood**, which is between 6 and 12 years of age. These improvements are partially explained by changes in body growth and stature. Sex-related changes in movement patterns become increasingly obvious after the age of 10. Boys tend to show more muscle mass and greater strength and cardiorespiratory capacity than girls do. Boys also tend to practice movements more than girls do. Evidence indicates that the quality of children's movement patterns can be improved through training.

Cognitive Development

The component-processing model introduced previously in this chapter (figure 3.2) described the interrelationship among several mental processes. Compared to adults, children process information more slowly and have less efficient memory systems. Processing speed increases with age up to young adulthood; the greatest gains occur between 6 and 15 years of age. Young children's short-term memory is less than that of older children, but increases gradually to adult levels. The greatest increases in working memory capacity are seen between 3 and 7 years. Further, young children use less refined strategies to organize and remember information than do adults. Conscious rehearsal of information increases storage in long-term memory, but children rarely use these memory-enhancing methods until about 10 years

---

teachable moment—An unplanned opportunity in which a teacher has an ideal chance to offer insight to students.

early childhood—The period of human life lasting from about 18 months to 6 years of age.

fundamental movement skills—Patterns of movements that are the basis for learning complex motor skills. The three categories of fundamental movement patterns are locomotor actions (walking and running), nonlocomotor actions (bending, twisting, and balancing), and manipulative actions (knot tying, drawing).

later childhood—The period of human life spanning between 6 and 12 years of age.

developmental disability—A pervasive disorder displayed during maturation.

of age. Thus, like fundamental movement skills, the components of young children's information processing are immature, improve with time, and are sensitive to training.

Children With Developmental Delays

Some children do not follow the developmental progression of the majority of their peers. For reasons that may be linked to genetic disorders, environmental insults, or social impoverishment, these children lag behind in domains that are critical to skill acquisition. A **developmental disability** is a pervasive disorder displayed during maturation. Some children evidence global disabilities that are reflected in virtually all measures of physical, cognitive, and emotional development. Those with severe and profound levels of intellectual disability typically evidence global disabilities. Other children evidence specific disabilities that may be detectable only under very circumscribed conditions (e.g., autism, fragile X syndrome).

A long-standing debate has taken place among researchers and educators who study developmental disabilities. Edward Zigler, a leader in the field of education, has been a central figure in what has come to be referred to as the developmental–difference debate. He and his colleagues have written extensively on the similarities and differences of two general theoretical approaches to the study of individual differences—developmental theories and difference theories (Zigler & Styfco, 2004).

Developmental theories propose that children who are free of specific genetic-based disorders, neurological disease, and environmental trauma develop and learn in fundamentally the same way. The differences among children can be best described in terms of how fast they learn a skill (rate of learning) and their terminal proficiency (level of learning). Comparisons of children's rates of learning indicate that those with global developmental disabilities learn more slowly than do children without these disabilities. However, children with developmental delays are not abnormal in the sense that they cannot learn the skill; rather, these children require additional training and practice to match the performance of children without global disabilities. Developmental theorists suggest that although some of the differences due to developmental disabilities can be explained in terms of cognitive factors, most are due to nonintellectual factors

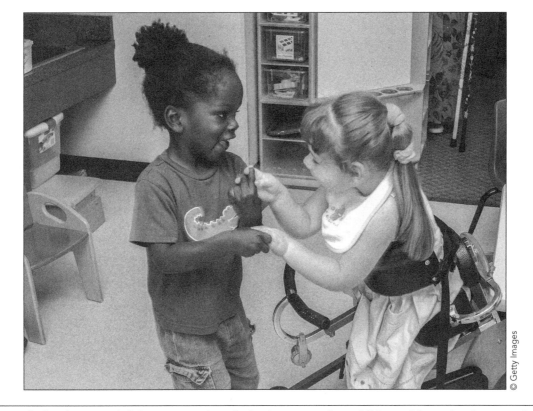

© Getty Images

Children with developmental delays can work and play just as much as children without developmental delays can; they just need more time and practice.

such as motivation, self-efficacy, confidence, and the application of appropriate teaching techniques.

Researchers have shown that children with developmental disabilities experience histories of failure and lack of success and as a result tend to be outer directed; they rely greatly on the guidance and direction of adults and less on their own abilities and skills (Zigler & Balla, 1982). Because of their low expectancies of being capable of solving problems on their own, children with developmental disabilities often display **learned helplessness**; that is, choosing to neither act nor attempt to meet the challenges that are part of skill-learning tasks because of a low expectancy of being able to solve problems on their own. When children with developmental disabilities are given the choice, they appear to behave more on the basis of their perceptions of how others behave, or how others expect them to behave, than on their own personal wishes and desires. For Zigler and other developmental theorists, fostering children's self-confidence is critical to the development of learning. As will be discussed in chapter 4, children's past experiences may have profound effects on their tendency to approach or avoid games that promote learning.

Difference theories propose that children with developmental disorders have specific defects in information processing that lead them to perform differently from children without mental disability. Children with global developmental disabilities show deficits in virtually every component of the information-processing system. Further, these differences emerge when they perform cognitive tasks in which motivational factors are expected to have minimal influence on performance. Attempts have been made to improve the components of information-processing abilities. In general, training programs have resulted in increased efficiency of information processing; however, the effects of these training programs typically are not long lasting. Thus, specific problems that exist in information-processing components can have a large effect on children's rates and levels of learning.

The issues central to the developmental–difference debate are important because they are applicable to the education of all children. Similar comparisons can be made between children with normal intellectual development and those who are considered gifted. According to the developmental position, differences between children's rates and levels of learning reflect both basic abilities and nonintellectual factors such as home environment, social support, and educational methods. Educators in the fields of special education and adapted physical education, in particular, have benefited greatly from research on differences in children's physical, cognitive, and social development. The physical activity games described in chapters 10 and 11 can be modified to address many of the differences among children.

Implications for Educators

Teachers can create environments that positively influence children's behavior, performance, and health. Unfortunately, historically, many educators have employed instructional methods that emphasize routine, repetitive exercises designed to promote physical fitness in adults. These instructional conditions, although suitable for adults who have goals of improved physical fitness (cardiorespiratory function, muscular strength, and flexibility), create conditions that most children find unappealing.

If we accept the notion that children benefit from being physically active in environments designed to meet their needs, we can easily see that knowing why and how to deliver physical activity games is essential; the old ways of doing things will not produce the outcomes we seek for children. The goal of this book is to help teachers recognize and develop instructional environments that lead children to engage in cognitive control processes that are normal and healthy reactions to new learning situations. Children's capacity to learn to control their movements is viewed as a naturally occurring process that helps them adapt to novel situations.

The games presented in this book are for children in two age ranges—3 to 6 and 7 to 11 years of age. As discussed in parts II and III, game selection and management are critical for fostering the desired level of mental engagement. The developmental changes that children go through between the ages of 3 and 11 are rapid and staggeringly complex. Some games may be well suited for younger children but less appealing for older children within a given age range. However, the game, in and of itself, is not important. What is important is that it is finely tuned to the readiness of the child. Teachers can change the context of a game; however, they cannot change a child's developmental readiness or past learning experiences.

---

learned helplessness—Choosing to neither act nor attempt to meet the challenges that are part of skill-learning tasks because of a low expectancy of being able to solve problems on one's own.

Motivating Children
to Learn by Playing

Why do children do what they do? Typically, it defies adult reasoning. A youngster may spin in circles until he gets dizzy enough to fall down. Another will walk directly through a messy mud puddle when walking around it would have been easier. Yet another will, without hesitation, bicycle off a ramp without any thought of where or how she will land. Two well-used phrases uttered by parents and teachers alike are Why in the world did you do that? and What were you thinking? This chapter addresses a topic that has been of interest to parents, teachers, and philosophers for centuries—children's motivation.

It is one thing to observe children's behaviors and quite another to develop plausible explanations for them. Indeed, early-20th-century developmental psychologists hypothesized that infants' and children's development reflects how the human species evolved. Thus, they believed that every child was innately engineered to repeat, or recapitulate, the changes that took place in their ancestors' bodies and behaviors over millions of years. Spinning, wiggling, and testing their limits were thought to mirror what the human species had gone through as a whole. Indeed, Herbert Spencer's (1820-1903) statement, "If there be an order in which the human race has mastered its various kinds of knowledge, there will arise in every child an aptitude to acquire these kinds of knowledge in the same order. . . . Education is a repetition of civilization in little," had a substantial impact on North American educators for decades. This notion that ontogeny (individual development) recapitulates phylogeny (species development) remains in some areas of education theory; however, it has largely been discredited by scientific testing.

Over the past few decades, great strides have been made in understanding how biological, cognitive, and emotional factors motivate, or drive, people to do what they do. This chapter examines how games that are both physically and mentally challenging motivate children to learn. Developmentally appropriate games, presented in the proper context, provide the mental engagement necessary for facilitating the emergence of children's executive functions. The physical and psychological benefits derived from game experiences may be far reaching, because core executive functions play important roles across multiple situations and may be critical to success not only on the playing field but also in academic and real-world situations that involve response inhibition, working memory, and mental shifting.

Motivation to Play Games

Motivation is a psychological or physiological state that energizes behavior to achieve a goal. **Needs**, which are the objects of motives, arise when a child's steady state, or **homeostasis** (the maintenance of equilibrium among body processes), is disturbed. When a child is hungry, for example, the lack of food signals to the brain to direct the child to seek something to eat. The child experiences a need state and, through goal-directed actions, reduces the need and restores a steady state. Much has been written about children's motivation to meet their physical and social needs. As discussed in chapter 1, Jean Piaget's theory of cognitive development focuses on the energizing aspects of the disequilibrium that children experience when confronted with a new problem to be solved. The world around developing children provides novel information that they have yet to understand and assimilate. Infants and children are often described as being in a constant state of unrest, which is characterized by behaviors that are repetitive and seemingly have no clear goal. A young child may hammer wooden pegs vigorously for hours at a time; then, at some point, show little interest in hammering. The child's motivation to hammer may be replaced by a motivation to drop objects to the floor and watch them bounce. The motivations for these behaviors have multiple, long-term consequences on mental development.

Importantly, the drive, or motivation, to perform movements that make the world meaningful to children is intrinsic. When the source of a child's motive to act originates from within, it is referred to as **intrinsic motivation**. Intrinsic motivators include feelings of pleasure and enjoyment. The source of

extrinsic motivation, by contrast, is external reward from the environment (such as prizes, money, and praise). A youngster who practices baseball to attain a college scholarship and then become a highly paid professional athlete is motivated by extrinsic rewards. A youngster who practices for the sheer pleasure of playing the game and the enjoyment he derives from it is motivated by intrinsic rewards.

Games and Psychological Energy

Central to understanding motivation is the notion of energy. The motivating force to achieve equilibrium is powerful. Anyone who has competed in Jeopardy, which requires recalling bits of trivia, feels compelled to stay on task until the correct answer comes to mind. Success in such games requires both attention and sustained mental effort. Some who play this kind of game report remembering and then telephoning a friend to report the answer hours after the question was asked. Once the answer has been obtained, the mental tension experienced while attempting to answer the question quickly dissipates. The mental energy we use every day to maintain our mental equilibrium is substantial. As described in the previous chapters, mental effort is drawn on as a resource when a person seeks to achieve a goal. Consider now how mental energy can serve as a source of motivation.

The notion of tension and tension release is important to understand the power of children's motives. The disequilibrium and psychological tension produced while learning games drive children toward resolution, which, in turn, releases tension and reestablishes equilibrium. Reduction of mental tension is attained only through action and

motivation—A psychological or physiological state that energizes behavior to achieve a goal.

needs—The objects of motives.

homeostasis—The maintenance of equilibrium among body processes.

intrinsic motivation—Behavior driven by internal rewards (such as pleasure and enjoyment).

extrinsic motivation—Behavior driven by external rewards from the environment (such as prizes, money, and praise).

fundamental movement skills—Movement skills that are the foundation for learning complex skills.

behavior. Games may require trying some strategies that do not work. The tension experienced during periods of disequilibrium can range from mild to intense. As such, tension plays an important role in determining the level of effort the child will allocate to play a given game or solve a particular problem. Regardless, tension release is a powerful intrinsic reward—it provides a feeling of accomplishment.

Video Games Versus Physical Activity Games

Recently, computer-based and mobile device game systems have had a huge impact on children's and adults' activity. Technological advances have made games increasingly realistic. Millions of young children are introduced to these devices. Some have been developed as teaching tools and others for recreation. Regardless, many children become mentally engrossed in video games. The degree to which these games capture children's attention attests to the motivating power of disequilibrium; great mental effort is often expended to get to the next level of the game. Indeed, some children and adults show signs of game addiction—playing video games most of the day to the exclusion of other, more important activities such as school-work and spending time with family members (Weis & Cerankosky, 2010). Game developers suggest that children can benefit mentally from playing with handheld devices. Despite the comments of computer engineers, research has yet to demonstrate any benefits of these games on children's mental development and academic performance (Gunter, Kenny, & Vick, 2008; Moreau & Conway, 2013).

Regardless of their limited benefits, games on handheld devices are very motivating for many children. As discussed later, popular video games are designed to match players' skill levels, so that players are constantly kept on the learning curve. Physical activity games can also be designed to keep children on the learning curve while providing several benefits that video games do not. First, the contexts of physical activity games are natural. Although video games strive to produce three-dimensional experiences, they are far from real-world experiences that provide developmentally appropriate action–response couplings. A youngster may be able to guide a digital bowling ball down an alley by pressing buttons on a handheld device or by moving a stylus, but these motor movements are not the real thing. Absent from video games are the sensory experiences that come from moving the

Fundamental movement and manipulative skills, such as jumping, running, throwing and catching a ball, striking objects, kicking, and agility or coordination, are the building blocks for a lifetime of movement.

body in ways that assist the development of **fundamental movement skills**, which are the foundation for learning complex skills. As discussed in previous chapters, infants and young children develop movement patterns that are refined during late childhood and adolescence to meet and overcome a variety of real-world challenges.

Another benefit of physical activity games that is absent in video games is the social interactions with parents, teachers, and other children that are critical for normal development. For tens of thousands of years, children have learned skills from their parents and families, from which they learned what constitutes normal, or appropriate, behavior. From the earliest days of a child's life, behavior is guided by a set of socially determined constraints. She learns to adapt her physical and psychological needs to the rules of the family and the social group. Recently, primary school teachers have been reporting an increasing number of children who lack social skills when they enter the educational system

(Eisenberg, Valiente, & Eggum, 2010). It is plausible that reductions in children's social play and instruction in game rules may contribute to this lack of social awareness. Indeed, some developmental psychologists have linked restrictions of motor activity and failure to learn appropriate action–response couplings to pervasive developmental delays and disorders such as autism (Stockman, 2004b). The benefits of physical activity games on children's mental health are discussed in chapter 5.

Physical activity performed in natural contexts results in energy expenditure that is developmentally appropriate and fits children's activity patterns. Computer-based games that attempt to increase children's levels of physical activity and promote physical fitness have been developed. The first generation of these exergames (*exercise* + *games*), which linked dance steps to music, was popular and provided evidence that children who played met acceptable activity intensity and duration levels. Further, some studies indicate that exergames performed in specific ways can enhance children's cognitive function (O'Leary et al., 2011). Although these studies are intriguing, evidence of long-term benefits of exergames on children's physical fitness or cognition has not been forthcoming (Papastergiou, 2009).

Games and Pleasure

Children and adults alike experience feelings and emotions during and following actions. Success feels good, and failure leads to feelings of disappointment. Disequilibrium and the changes it brings to one's steady state simultaneously influence both the body and mind. With every movement, sensations arise that produce the feelings that are the basic building blocks of emotion and mood. The step across the finish line of a footrace is like any other step of the race, but it has an immediate and widespread effect on the runner. In some conditions, it may lead to feelings of exhilaration; in others, feelings of frustration.

Researchers define **emotions** as short-term positive or negative affective reactions to objects (either real or imagined) (Wells & Matthews, 1994). **Moods** are general and pervasive negative or positive affective states that can influence thought and behavior. Unlike emotions, which are brief, moods last longer and can color how children view their world. A mood state can serve as a type of background filter that determines whether a child will choose to engage in a game, how much energy to put into the game, and how long to persist in the game. Emo-

tions and moods, which influence what children attend to and how much they involve themselves, go hand in hand with motivation. As described in later chapters, children's behaviors during games can provide teachers with insights into the games' motivational effectiveness. Research on children's emotions has revealed specific behavioral patterns that they display while preparing for and engaging in play and games. A summary of these behaviors is provided in the sidebar Children's Emotional Behaviors During Play and Games.

The emotions children show during play suggest that their actions are innately pleasurable. The feelings that arise during play fuel children's intrinsic motivation to seek out games that are challenging. Psychologists have long hypothesized that children are innately driven to attain an optimal level of arousal. More recently, researchers have been drawn to understand what is referred to as **positive psychology**, an area of study that focuses on aspects of life that are fulfilling and lead to obtaining optimal potential (Seligman & Csikszentmihalyi, 2000). Historically, psychologists have focused on the study of conditions that have a negative impact on mental health. Mainstream psychologists typically focus on the negative impacts of stress, mental illness, and disease on mental functioning. Positive psychologists focus on when things go right rather than when things go wrong. At this point, however, it is important to stress how positive experiences bring about changes in emotions and moods that can influence children's motivations to become mentally engaged and learn from the games they play.

---

emotions—Short-term positive or negative affective reactions to objects (either real or imagined).

moods—General and pervasive negative or positive affective states that can influence thought and behavior.

positive psychology—An area of study that focuses on aspects of life that are fulfilling and lead to obtaining optimal potential.

flow—A psychological state experienced when one is caught up in the moment of playing or performing a skill.

experiential motivation—Motivation derived from the feelings generated while in the act of performing.

CHILDREN'S EMOTIONAL BEHAVIORS
DURING PLAY AND GAMES

- *Situational awareness*—Emotional responses depend on a child's appraisal of the game condition. Before a child can respond to a game emotionally, he must give meaning to the game. Games that are not appraised as either positive or negative can be expected to create little emotion.

- *Arousal*—Games lead to changes in physical activity and general arousal. Increases in heart rate, respiration, and sweating are evaluated, but the emotion that is attached to these changes depends on the child's interpretation of not only the feelings, but also the game conditions. A child who falls to the ground during vigorous play may get up and get back into the game; however, the same fall may lead the child to cry and show distress if parents are nearby. Children's emotions can be influenced greatly by the context or arrangement of game conditions.

- *Facial expressions*—Basic facial expressions are innate and are similar in children across all cultures. Children express basic emotions (joy, disgust, contempt) in similar ways. Watching the facial expressions of other children, parents, and teachers provides important information about the feeling of others. Developmental psychologists are very interested in how children learn to take the perspectives of others. Being able to put oneself in another person's shoes is an important milestone of cognitive development. Also, it is an essential component of the strategic skills used in playing games.

- *Action readiness*—Children's emotional states energize and motivate them to act. However, the direction of action may be tied to the emotion. Experiences of joy and pleasure may motivate the child to continue in play or games; on the other hand, experiences of sadness and despair may set the stage for withdrawal, lethargy, and lack of movement. Positive emotions that are linked to success in physical activity games generate mental engagement.

Adapted from Parkinson 1995.

When absorbed in play, children use their developing mental skills to find ways to take virtually any object or situation and turn it into a play activity. They can use their minds to take simple objects, words, or situations and turn them into sources of pleasure. **Flow** is a psychological state experienced when one is caught up in the moment of playing or performing a skill (Csikszentmihalyi, 2000). **Experiential motivation** provides the basis for the flow experience; it is motivation derived from the feeling generated while in the act of performing. The flow experience is not related to extrinsic external rewards, but rather, to intrinsically generated emotions (Csikszentmihalyi, 1978).

Achieving a state of flow requires a balance between what the child is asked to do in a game and the child's physical and mental skills. In Csikszentmihalyi's general model shown in figure 4.1, the emotions generated by a game are determined by three conditions: the child's current skill or ability level, the behavioral demands

placed on the child, and the child's perceptions of his ability to meet game challenges. Boredom occurs when game conditions are not challenging. A worried state can occur when game demands are greater than the child's skill level. This state may evolve into an anxiety state as environmental demands overwhelm the child. A flow state is experienced only when a match exists between the environmental demands and the person's skill level, which is referred to as the optimal challenge point from the perspective of learning theorists in chapter 2.

Conditions that produce flow states in children are believed to be optimal for creative thinking (Csikszentmihalyi & Bennett, 1971). A child's creative thinking occurs only when the conditions are right, however. The child must possess the mental abilities and skills required to address a novel problem, have the opportunity to think through and solve the problem on her own, and persist until the problem is solved (Collins & Amabile, 1999).

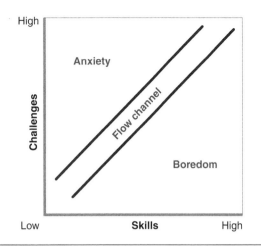

Figure 4.1 Flow model of motivation.

Children's Self-Efficacy

Initiation and persistence are behaviors that have received considerable study by developmental psychologists. Albert Bandura developed an influential theory of self-efficacy that focuses on how peoples' beliefs influence their motivation and persistence (Bandura, 1997). Unlike a sense of confidence, which reflects a global belief about one's ability to deal with problems, self-efficacy beliefs are tied closely to specific tasks. **Self-efficacy**, which is the belief that one can perform adequately in a given situation, plays the central role in determining children's willingness to engage in games, the level of intensity of their behavior, and the persistence of their behavior. Children's motivation is linked to what they have learned about themselves and to their perceptions of their abilities. A child may have a high sense of self-efficacy when playing the goalie position on the soccer field, but a low sense of self-efficacy when solving mathematics problems in the classroom.

At any moment, a child's self-efficacy and level of motivation are the products of several factors. As seen in figure 4.2, four clusters of experiences are integrated and result in self-efficacy.

Performance accomplishment reflects the child's personal history of success and failure. When introduced to new games, children are faced with a decision to play or not to play. Their motivation to play the game is based on their memories of past experiences. Added to the decision are their perceptions of the demands of the games and of their skill levels. Further coloring the decision is the perception of the **locus of control**, which is the belief about whether the outcomes of their actions are due to internal or external factors. For instance,

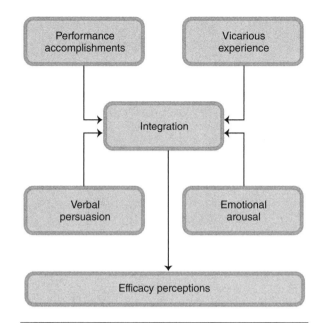

Figure 4.2 Self-efficacy model.

are they playing a game because it was decided by others (parents, peers, or teachers) or because they want to?

Vicarious experiences are obtained from seeing the success or failures of others in a game. Children do not necessarily have to play a game themselves to develop a perception of its difficulty; often, they watch others who serve as models. Modeling is a form of learning in which people perceive how to act by observing others. As noted in chapter 3, modeling is a powerful instructional method for physical education teachers; it is often used to show children how to move. The use of modeling to affect children's self-efficacy is not a simple process, however. First, the model needs to be relevant to the child. A youngster's older brother or older friend may be a better model than an adult teacher. Second, a clear connection needs to be made between the model's actions and specific outcomes or consequences. For example, a youngster may be motivated to play a game after seeing his older brother receiving praise and being rewarded for his performance in the game.

Verbal encouragement provided by teachers, parents, and friends is typical during game play. A youngster's motivation to increase effort and to persist can be influenced greatly by the exhortations and encouragement of others. The effectiveness of such input may depend on how much a youngster values the comments, as well as the significance of the person providing them. Parents and coaches may say the same words, but the child may be influenced more by a coach or a role model than by her parents. Also, children soon learn to tell the difference between motivational speeches that are authentic and believable and those that are generic and have little meaning.

Emotional arousal reflects how a child interprets changes in sensations that occur during and following periods of physical activity. With game play and increases in physical activity, the child's body responds with increased muscle tension, breathing rate, and sweating. Young children, who have limited game experiences, may interpret these sensory events as negative feelings (pain, fear, anxiety) or positive feelings (pleasure, fun, joy). Teachers, through their feedback during the initial stages of learning, can help children understand and appreciate the physical arousal that is central to game play.

Integration processes determine the child's momentary perceptions of self-efficacy. A child's beliefs that she can perform well in a given situation is based on a weighting of factors. Developmental readiness, information-processing capabilities, memory, and attentional capacity all contribute to differences in how children integrate their experiences. These topics were discussed in previous chapters.

The moment a child makes the decision to become involved in a game or sport, she has established **outcome expectations**, which are the results she anticipates will happen. Self-efficacy precedes the initiation of behavior, and outcome expectations follow behaviors. Children's outcome expectations play an important role in determining whether they develop positive, adaptive views of their abilities and skills, or negative, maladaptive views.

---

self-efficacy—The belief that one can perform adequately in a given situation.

locus of control—The belief about whether the outcomes of one's actions are due to internal or external factors.

outcome expectations—The results that someone anticipates will happen.

stress—A pattern of behavior in response to events that disturb equilibrium and tax the ability to cope.

eustress—A state in which people are confident that they have the skills and resources necessary for meeting and overcoming potentially stressful situations.

Challenge and Children's Development

Children and adults alike confront challenges every day of their lives. Each day, children are challenged to perform well in school, in social situations, or in games or sports. Young children are expected to learn to play games and get along with others; older children are expected to attend school and learn basic academic skills. Parents invest a tremendous amount of time and effort in teaching their children how to behave, teachers give their students the opportunity to benefit from education, and coaches provide instruction in how to play games and sports. How well children learn from these experiences may well determine their success in adulthood and how they feel about themselves throughout their lives.

Stress of Learning

The term *stress* is perhaps one of the most overused words in modern society. Indeed, it has been used by many people to describe their everyday lives. **Stress** is a pattern of behavior in response to events that disturb equilibrium and tax the ability to cope. Historically, psychologists have tended to define *stress* the way a builder or engineer would, as something that exerts great pressure to the point of causing collapse. Stress typically is viewed negatively and thought of as the great evil of the modern world. Some, however, point out that stress can have positive consequences as well. A pioneer in the study of stress, Hans Selye (1907-1982), noted that although stress has a threat component and can cause harm, it also has a challenge component that can facilitate growth. Selye coined the term *eustress* to describe a state in which people are confident that they have the skills and resources necessary for meeting and overcoming potentially stressful situations (Selye, 1974).

Several researchers have proposed that controlled levels of physical or mental stress promote a type of hardiness that leads to improved physical and mental health and an increased capacity to deal with the rigors of life (Dienstbier, 1989; Kobasa, 1979). Children's histories of success and failure determine how they face and overcome challenges on the playground, in academic classes, or at home. One key to quality physical activity games lies in teachers' abilities to create conditions that challenge children. Game performance is accompanied by emotion and self-appraisal. The appraisal process is critical to the developing child's self-efficacy.

A child's perceptions and responses can range between "This is too much for me" and "I can take this on." Children's beliefs in their ability to cope with challenging situations result in positive feelings of control and reinforce expectations of future success.

Successful experiences have both short-term and long-term physiological and psychological benefits. As shown in figure 4.3, a child who seeks challenges and believes that she has the capacity to succeed and has positive outcome expectancies is likely to reinforce an adaptive "toughening" arousal pattern, which sets the stage to meet and overcome new challenges (Dienstbier, 1989). The positive physical and psychological changes associated with mastering challenges lead the child to seek the very tasks that toughen her. **Toughening manipulations** place learners in challenging situations that evoke strong physiological responses. Alternatively, a child who lacks self-efficacy when faced with a potentially stressful situation will develop a stress pattern and accompanying levels of fearfulness, anxiety, sadness, and distress.

Transfer of Learning

It was once said that the success of the British military in the 19th century was founded on schoolyard playing fields. Many believed that children who grew to be competent young military men learned the value of teamwork, leadership, and command through competitive sport. That is, the strategies used in game and sport settings were thought to be used later in military settings. Educational psychologists have long been interested in **transfer**, which is the degree to which learning in one setting is used in another setting. Indeed, modern education is based on the belief that students who are introduced to

core information gain knowledge that they can use after they graduate in their occupations. Likewise, physical educators assume that the games they design for children result in learning that transfers to sports and activities in other life domains.

Recently, there has been an interest in the cognitive skills children develop through play and game experience and whether they transfer to other academic areas and improve academic achievement (Diamond & Lee, 2011). Early research on **metacognition**, which is children's awareness of what they know and how they can use it (Bransford, Brown, & Cocking, 1999), and current research on executive functions highlight several characteristics that promote transfer (Diamond & Lee, 2011):

- *The necessity of initial learning.* Teaching must promote understanding rather than memorization. The more the child organizes and restructures the learning experience, the greater the transfer.
- *The importance of abstract knowledge.* Teaching for transfer requires teaching general solutions and strategies that can be used in different situations.
- *Learning is an active and dynamic process.* Children's transfer of knowledge can be improved with teacher guidance and prompts.
- *Learning builds on prior learning.* Teachers can facilitate transfer through the logical organization of instructional activities that are conceptually linked.

Contemporary researchers view executive functions as mental skills that can be developed and refined with practice (Diamond & Lee, 2011). The fact that executive functions can be honed via play and games reveals the important influence

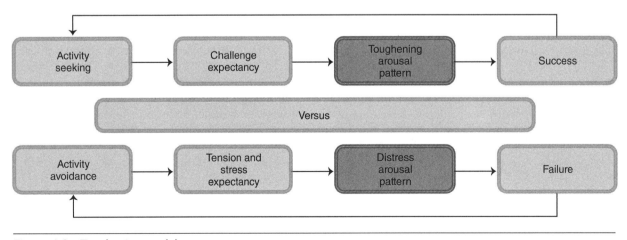

Figure 4.3   Toughening model.

physical educators have on children's development. Because of children's natural motivation to play, games provide vehicles for arranging learning conditions that can alter the trajectory of their mental development. Through the attentive arrangement of instructional conditions and the careful use of feedback, teachers can guide the emergence of children's core executive functions. The mental skills that children use to control their actions have been linked to applied intelligence (Sternberg, 2005). Real-world intelligence requires the capacity to restructure problems to maximize problem-solving strategies.

Creating a Motivational Climate for Learning and Enjoyment

A general theory of learning introduced in chapter 3 proposed that learning involves a progression through three stages: cognitive, associative, and autonomous. The stage model of learning can help teachers understand how motives influence learning. As discussed earlier, children's motivation

toughening manipulations—Placing learners in challenging situations that evoke strong physiological responses.

transfer—The degree to which learning in one setting is used in another setting.

meta-cognition—Children's awareness of what they know and how they can use it.

goal setting—The process of targeting outcomes.

outcome goals—Goals that focus on comparing performances—who is best, second best, and so on.

performance goals—Goals used to judge one's own progress (e.g., a personal best).

process goals—Goals that focus on the quality of movement patterns (e.g., keeping a good body position when kicking a ball).

extraverted—A description of people who tend to be outgoing, impulsive, and active because their general brain arousal is relatively low and as a result they seek stimulation.

introverted—A description of people who tend to have relatively high levels of general brain arousal and avoid situations that are stimulating.

depends on many factors, and it plays a particularly important role in every stage of learning.

Motivation in the Cognitive Stage

In the cognitive stage, the child is put into a situation that requires an initial appraisal: What is the significance of this game and how important is it to me? Her appraisal process dictates the quantity and quality of the effort she will expend to play the game. The next questions are Do I have the ability to learn this game? and How much effort should I put into this problem? Teachers play a critical role in helping children answer these questions in ways that maintain their motives. Through verbal instructions, teachers can describe the major theme of the game, the actions that are required, and why the child should be able to succeed. **Goal setting**, which is the process of targeting outcomes, is critical during this stage. Teachers can, with input from the child, identify short-term, intermediate, and long-term goals. During the initial stage of instruction, short-term goals that are easily achieved can be powerful motivators. Children can have several types of goals. **Outcome goals** focus on comparing performances—who is best, second best, and so on. **Performance goals** are goals used to judge one's own progress (e.g., a personal best). **Process goals** focus on the quality of movement patterns (e.g., keeping a good body position when kicking a ball). All three goal types can motivate children. Teachers play an important role by helping children focus on goals that are important at a given time. For example, process goals may be particularly useful during the cognitive stage when children are challenged to understand game rules and plan their actions.

Getting children to take the first step in game play is not as simple as it seems. Although children are intrinsically motivated to move and explore their worlds, they exhibit considerable personality differences. An influential personality theorist, Hans Eysenck (1916-1997), proposed a prominent theory of personality that describes people in terms of their arousal and activity. On one end of a continuum, **extraverted** children tend to be outgoing, impulsive, and active. Because of genetics, general brain arousal in these children is relatively low and as a result they are natural sensation seekers. At the other end of the continuum, **introverted** children have relatively high levels of general brain arousal and avoid situations that are stimulating (Eysenck, 1967; Eysenck, Nias, & Cox, 1982). Children can also differ because of social and cultural forces. Messages given early in life concerning appropriate behaviors for boys and girls can influence a child's willingness and motivation to participate in vigorous physical activity. Preparing physical activity games for children who differ in personality and social backgrounds can challenge teachers. However, as described in part III of this book, teachers can alter game conditions to accommodate children's differences.

Once a child chooses to participate in physical activity games, the teacher can use guidance and feedback to facilitate the learning process. **Guidance** is any procedure (e.g., physical, verbal, visual) that directs learners as they perform a task. For instance, a teacher is guiding when physically moving a child's limb and body to appropriate positions, using gestures to aid movements, or describing the steps involved in complex actions. Physical guidance is particularly useful for young children because it provides support and reinforces the social connection between the child and teacher. Guidance helps the child focus on aspects of moving that are important for achieving short-term goals. Children who are not provided feedback can learn through

trial and error, but such learning is slow and may result in frustration, which can decrease motivation.

A **task analysis** involves identifying the key components of a game and then breaking the game down into a series of movements that are central to learning the game. The advantage of a task analysis is that it makes clear how a game can be made more or less complex. Teaching separate parts of the game also helps maintain children's motivation because learning is more manageable.

Planning game interventions and being prepared to teach games differently to meet children's individual differences is critical to drawing children into games. The skill of teaching involves matching children's abilities, skills, and personalities to the physical and mental challenges of the game. Direct observation of their students' behavior provides teachers with evidence of how well they are motivating them.

Numerous books on motor skill learning have introduced readers to task analysis and how to apply it. However, the descriptions of task analysis methods differ markedly. These differences are linked to the histories of two academic specializations: applied behavioral psychology research and individual differences research.

Task Analysis From the Applied Behavioral Psychology Approach

Starting in the 1960s, the focus of applied behavioral psychology was on the application of learning

Providing some guidance as children learn new movements or games can help them reach their goals.

guidance—Any procedure that directs learners as they perform a task.

task analysis—Identifying the key components of a game and then breaking the game down into a series of movements that are central to learning the game.

forward chaining—Applying behavioral principles to learning to strengthen the connections between the steps of a complex skill.

behavior shaping—A general term often used to describe how the application of reinforcement principles alters or modifies a learner's actions.

time out (from reinforcement)—A method used to change the frequency of behaviors by the contingent withdrawal of the opportunity to obtain rewards or reinforcers.

psychometrics—A field of study that uses standardized tests to measure and classify abilities.

principles advocated by a pioneer in psychology, B.F. Skinner (1904-1990), and others (Kazdin, 1994). The principles of contingent reward were central to the application of behavior modification methods. In the view of applied behavioral analysis researchers interested in motor skill learning (Rushall & Siedentop, 1972), a complex skill could be learned by first breaking it down into its components and then arranging them in a logical sequence.

The task analysis shown in figure 4.4 describes the steps involved in teaching a child to throw. In this example, the instructional method of **forward chaining** (applying behavioral principles to learning to strengthen the connections between the steps of a complex skill) is used to teach the skill of ball throwing. The instructional context is arranged so that a reward follows the performance of the first step in the task analysis. Then a reward follows the execution of both the first and second steps. The process of rewarding behaviors continues until all the steps of the task analysis are performed. The contingent use of rewards, or reinforcers, strengthens the connections between the steps of the skill.

Behavior shaping is a general term often used to describe how the application of reinforcement principles alters or modifies a learner's actions. The methods used by applied behavioral psychologists were incorporated and remain in many areas of education, special education, business, and training. Indeed, few American children

have not been told "If you do that again, you'll be sent to time out." **Time out** is the application of a principle of learning to modify the frequency of a child's behaviors. As intended by B.F. Skinner, the behavior modification method of "time out from reinforcement" means that the consequence of an undesirable behavior is a period of time during which the child does not have the opportunity to obtain a reward or reinforcer.

Task Analysis From the Individual Differences Approach

The second task analysis method is linked historically to **psychometrics**, a field of study that uses standardized tests to measure and classify abilities. Intelligence tests, first developed in the early 20th century, were designed to both measure abilities and predict how well the person could learn specific types of knowledge. Today, standardized tests such as the Scholastic Achievement Test (SAT) and the Graduate Record Examination (GRE) are used in the United States to identify the abilities of those entering higher education. Psychometric testing has been used extensively in business, industry, and the military.

The focus of psychometric research is to assess differences in abilities and determine whether a given task fits the learner. For example, each year researchers in military training facilities use physical and mental tests to assess the basic abilities of

Task Analysis Using Forward Chaining

Description of task: Overhand throwing movement for children 6 years and older

The child stands sideways to the target with feet shoulder-width apart and holding a ball in the dominant hand. The child points the nonthrowing arm toward the target and brings the throwing arm back with the ball in hand. At this point the child is now making a T with the arms. The child then transfers the weight from the back leg to the front by stepping through with the back leg and bringing the throwing hand forward. Keeping the ball in hand, the child extends the throwing arm in unison with the forward step and completes the movement by allowing the throwing arm to continue until the arm touches the opposite hip. Initially, the steps are performed slowly, following each cue. This is part-task training because ball release, trajectory, and accuracy are not addressed.

Movement sequence	Cues
1. Stand sideways to target, feet shoulder-width apart, ball in hand.	Ready position
2. Point with nonthrowing hand; bring ball hand back and up.	Make a T
3. Transfer weight; initiate arm extension.	Step, rotate, and extend
4. Follow through touching opposite hip with throwing arm.	Hip

(continued)

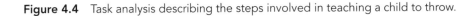

Figure 4.4 Task analysis describing the steps involved in teaching a child to throw.

Task Analysis and Behavior Modification Evaluation Sheet

Objective: To complete a ball-throwing movement in the proper sequence without any verbal cues

Scoring

I = Initiates segment following cue. (If not, provide feedback and guidance.)

P = Performs segment satisfactorily. (If not, provide feedback and guidance.)

Y/N = Completes all movements in proper sequence. (If not, provide feedback and guidance.)

Name:	Trial 1	Trial 2	Trial 3	Trial 4	Trial 5	Trial 6
1. Ready position						
2. Make a T						
3. Forward stride						
4. Follow through						
5. Entire sequence						

Notes: _____

Steps Involved in Throwing Movements

Step 1: Ready position   **Step 2:** Make a T   **Step 3:** Forward stride   **Step 4:** Follow through

Figure 4.4   *(continued)*

thousands of recruits. Based on the pattern of test scores, men and women are assigned to training programs designed to develop specific areas of expertise and skill (Fleishman & Quaintance, 1984). The task analyses seen in the majority of textbooks on skill learning reflect the individual differences approach (Magill & Anderson, 2014; Schmidt & Wrisberg, 2008). For example, figure 4.5 shows a task analysis that links basic motor abilities as measured by psychometrics tests to select movement skills; it can be used to channel learners into optimal instructional conditions (Schmidt & Wrisberg, 2008).

Both the applied behavioral psychology and the individual differences approaches to task analysis have their place in teaching physical activity games to children. Indeed, in chapter 3 the topic of individual differences in basic abilities was introduced in terms of the speed and level of proficiency skills that can be acquired. In later chapters you will see the merits of the applied behavioral psychology task

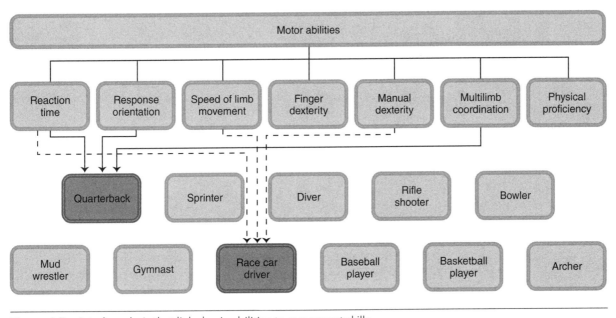

Figure 4.5 A task analysis that links basic abilities to movement skills.

Adapted, by permission, from R.A. Schmidt and C.A. Wrisberg, 2008, *Motor learning and performance*, 4th ed. (Champaign, IL: Human Kinetics), 179.

analysis approach for assessing interventions (chapter 8) and developing games (chapters 10 and 11).

Motivation in the Associative Stage

In the associative stage of learning, practice conditions lead to such questions as Is learning this game worth the amount of effort that is required of me? and What benefits will I gain from this practice? The answers to such self-generated questions may determine to a great extent a child's effort and willingness to persist. Children who begin to learn new games are novices and, by definition, not skilled and not efficient in their movement, and they make errors. A concept important for both teachers and children to understand is that errors are not bad! Indeed, an **error**, which is the difference between an expected outcome and the actual outcome, can actually improve learning. Each action provides an opportunity for youngsters to think about the movements they planned to make and the movements they actually made. Teachers who encourage children to reflect on their movements and the reasons for the outcomes of their actions provide opportunities for mental engagement.

error—The difference between an expected outcome and the actual outcome.

Practice is critical for learning; however, it is the type of practice that is important. Practice that keeps children mentally engaged is superior to mindless, repetitive physical actions. Simply going through the motions during games is not enough; children must be continually mentally engaged and view the challenges at hand as demanding but capable of being overcome. Teachers can increase children's mental engagement and motivation by appropriately applying practice structures and varying game conditions so that they involve executive functioning.

Unexpectedly changing the rules of games during the cognitive stage of learning would not be good for learning because children are just beginning to understand how to organize their actions—which limbs to move, in what order, and at what time. However, once basic motor movement programs are established during the cognitive and early associative stages, introducing unexpected rule changes increases mental engagement. In the game Simon Says, with each variation in the game, the child who is in the middle to late associative stage must notice the change, stop what he is doing, change his action pattern, and reengage in action. The themes of stop, think, and switch are embedded in games in part III of this book. Instructions that prepare children to adapt to upcoming game changes can increase their attention and motivation.

The appropriate use of feedback can also increase children's levels of motivation. It is important to recognize, however, that the motivational properties of feedback depend greatly on how and when it is delivered. Although a teacher may believe that giving a lot of feedback is always a good idea, researchers have found that feedback can improve learning, have no effect on learning, or actually slow learning. For example, during the cognitive and early associative stages of learning, the development of movement programs can be facilitated by generous feedback from teachers. However, as children refine their movement patterns during the mid-to-late associative stage, their learning improves when feedback is provided less often and they must think for themselves. The skilled teacher recognizes when it is time to gradually remove the scaffolding that feedback provides during the crucial early stages of learning. The overuse of feedback leads to an overdependence on teachers' assistance.

The amount and type of teacher feedback also determines its effectiveness. Children's actions during game play can be quite complex, and excessive feedback can overwhelm their memory systems. Likewise, feedback is only helpful when the child understands it. Using words and concepts that do not match the child's level of language and mental development represents poor feedback. Highly detailed descriptions may be well suited for adults, but may baffle young children. The old saying "Practice makes perfect" is only partially true. Perhaps better is the phrase "Practice with appropriate feedback makes perfect." Teachers guide children through the stages of learning. As they improve, they should be encouraged to be more independent and to think creatively.

Motivation in the Autonomous Stage

Children experience rapid improvements in game-play performance during the cognitive and associative stages; however, with continued practice, performance gains become less evident. Even though the movement patterns involved in game play become increasingly more automatic, children begin to see the games as less challenging and ask questions such as Can I get any better at this game? Children may continue to improve their skills, but without adequate challenge, they may experience boredom. Although teachers cannot make flow happen, they can modify game conditions to facilitate mental engagement.

One of the characteristics of performance during the autonomous stage of learning is that children direct less conscious attention to the control of their movements. Structures deep in the brain begin to take over the control of movements that were previously controlled by networks in the cortex. During the cognitive and associative stages of learning, networks in the frontal lobes are involved in the selection of movement sequences. During the autonomous stage of automaticity, these networks can be used to create strategies and solve complex problems in creative ways and to update or change action plans.

Teachers can take advantage of the changes that take place during learning to maintain children's motivations to continue game play. Children can be involved in establishing long-term goals that involve individual and group game play. Teachers can structure a series of interrelated games that are increasingly more complex and also require children to work with each other to achieve goals. Through thoughtful planning, teachers can have older children serve as models for younger children and emphasize the importance of leadership and teamwork in achieving short-term and long-term goals. Developmental psychologists have proposed a **theory of mind**, which explains how young children learn to take the perspectives of others (Sabbagh et al., 2006). Many of the challenges children face in school are linked to social skills, and appropriate behaviors and executive functions play an important role in social development.

Strategic problem solving is an acquired skill that people need throughout their lives. Further, being skilled in high-level cognitive processes takes considerable practice and time. Researchers who study expertise and people who are highly skilled in games such as chess and sports such as tennis suggest that at least 10 years of deliberate practice is required to rise to high levels of proficiency (Ericsson, 1996). **Deliberate practice** is performed with

---

theory of mind—A theory that explains how young children learn to take the perspectives of others.

deliberate practice—Practice that is performed with the primary goal of improving skill and expertise. It is characterized by much mental effort and low levels of inherent enjoyment.

deliberate play—Games and sports that are intrinsically motivating, provide immediate gratification, and maximize enjoyment.

autotelic personality—The personality type of a person who is internally driven and exhibits a sense of purpose and curiosity.

Deliberate play depends on intrinsic motivations, such as tons of fun!

the primary goal of improving skill and expertise. It is characterized by much mental effort and low levels of inherent enjoyment. Deliberate practice is considered the work necessary for becoming highly skilled. Few novices consider the hours spent repeating musical scales on a piano to be fun. The requirements of deliberate practice probably explain why so many learners burn out and why there are so few true experts in the world.

The physical activity games described in this book are not designed to make children experts in sport; they are designed to be fun! As discussed in chapter 6, games can be arranged to promote **deliberate play**, which is used to describe games and sports that are intrinsically motivating, provide immediate gratification, and maximize enjoyment (Cote, Baker, & Abernethy, 2007). Regardless of the type of practice, however, children get better at problem solving when they experience variations in the problems they encounter. Depending on the skills being learned, the autonomous stage of learning may be very long, and teachers' roles will need to change. Indeed, teachers of children in this stage may consider their role as that of a mentor—one who observes and is there to consult and give guidance when needed.

As some children become proficient in their movements and skilled in high-order problem solving,

they become increasingly intrinsically motivated to learn. Indeed, after learning the basics, some develop a "rage to master" and spend all of their available time in practice (Winner, 1996). Playing a musical instrument, for example, requires a minimal level of skill before even the simplest musical pieces can be played. When the conditions are right, however, the novice musician may feel a sense of exhilaration, or flow, when she first masters a musical piece. With improvements in her skills, however, simple pieces begin to lose their ability to challenge, and the musician's mental state shifts to one of boredom. Retaining the flow experience requires a more challenging musical score or a more demanding variation of the piece. People who find their own actions rewarding are described as having **autotelic personalities**; they are internally driven and exhibit a sense of purpose and curiosity (Csikszentmihalyi, 1990).

Implications for Educators

Children are motivated to play games by both intrinsic pleasure and external rewards. Teachers who understand the sources of children's motives appreciate how instructional methods can bring about fundamental changes in children's brains and behavior.

Taking Advantage of Children's Intrinsic Motivation

Observations of children's game-playing behaviors reveal the pleasures they derived from meeting and overcoming challenge. However, pleasure wanes as games become less challenging. Games that challenge children promote more mental involvement, motivation, and long-term effects on executive functions than games in which conditions are predictable and unchanging. Maintaining mental engagement requires keeping children on the learning curve. Not only do games in which goals and demands are frequently changing promote intrinsic motivation, but they also promote better learning.

Children's self-efficacy in the arena of game and sport play can be modified through instructional methods. Teachers who instruct young children should be aware of the important role they play in establishing their students' personal perceptions of their capabilities. A supportive instructor can arrange conditions that promote feelings of self-efficacy; likewise, failure to provide such conditions may have negative consequences that can profoundly color children's views of their ability to meet and overcome challenges that emerge during the first two decades of life.

Teaching Styles

Two approaches are often used to teach children new skills. One builds on the notion of toughening manipulations that place learners in challenging situations that evoke strong physiological responses. Advocates of this approach believe that children who learn to perform in moderately stressful situations develop the physical and mental resources required to act adaptively, and in doing so acquire a sense of competence and self-efficacy. The other approach, self-selection, advocates allowing children to make choices about the activities they pursue. Advocates of self-selection believe that forcing children to participate in activities that they find undesirable can lead to negative psychological and behavioral consequences. These two approaches may, however, be conceptualized as representing two sides of a coin. Effective teachers recognize the value of each approach but also are aware that each has its strengths and weakness.

One of the greatest difficulties of teaching is knowing when to control the learning environment and students' behaviors and when to allow students to take charge and choose their own paths. An important factor to consider when attempting to determine the right mix of control and freedom is the youngster's perceptions of the skill to be learned and whether the learning situation elicits positive or negative emotions. Learning situations that are perceived as challenging are accompanied by positive emotions and the desire to approach and participate. Learning situations that are perceived as threatening are accompanied by negative affect and the desire to withdraw and avoid participation. Observing children's approach or avoidance behaviors reveals a great deal about them. Although a child's perception of a learning situation may be caused by any factor or a combination of factors, ultimately, these perceptions are translated into approach or avoidance behaviors.

Common to both views of teaching is the notion that positive training depends on a match between the demands of training and the child's skill level. Children approach and engage in games when they have the knowledge they need to keep up with the demands of the task. A child with insufficient knowledge or experience will perform poorly and begin to withdraw from the game. Moreover, an ineffective instructional environment is created when a teacher provides directions or feedback that are too complex and overwhelm the child's processing capabilities.

When children are placed in learning environments in which they can explore and solve problems, they have fun. A coach or teacher can make skill development enjoyable by capitalizing on children's innate motivation to seek challenging tasks. There are several ways teachers can provide structure to game and play activities so that children acquire essential skills without becoming bored. Gross-motor physical activities such as dance, tumbling, and yoga permit children to experience the pleasures of movement and controlling their bodies. Fine-motor activities such as crafts, painting, model building, and pottery let children experience the pleasure of creating objects or images. Mental activities such as singing, shouting, and reciting poems provide the opportunity to learn how to make use of and enjoy knowledge. Learning how to play with words, to make puns and analogies, can make the educational process challenging and fun. Children who are given the opportunity to experience and learn from their own actions evidence a lifelong motivation for creativity (Csikszentmihalyi, 1990). Children who learn that they can derive pleasure through their own actions are seldom bored or sedentary. They constantly manipulate and search out activities that present challenges. As adolescents and adults, their drive to play and experience the pleasures of new challenges continues.

Part II

Translating Research to Practice

Translating evidence obtained from scientific research into good teaching practices is a complex undertaking. The long-term rewards of good teaching methods are worth the effort, however. Methods that promote movement in the very young are crucial because the level of physical activity in childhood predicts activity levels later in life. Part II addresses how to translate scientific evidence about movement into new practical means to promote children's cognitive development.

The chapters in part I described why physical activity is good not only for children's physical health and fitness but also for their mental development. The key to maximizing both physical health and mental functioning is to keep children active and moving and to keep them on the learning curve. Movement-based learning is a powerful way to challenge a child's developing brain. However,

promoting cognitive development through movement is more than just an issue of prescribing the correct dose of physical activity.

As emphasized in the Society of Health and Physical Educators (SHAPE) guidelines, quality physical education requires opportunities to learn, meaningful content, and appropriate instruction. The chapters in part II reflect these standards by showing how to use information about children's mental development, physical activity, and learning to improve teaching effectiveness. Theory-based principles of teaching are presented that show how, when, and why to vary specific components of movement games. We also describe how to verify the effectiveness of games through the use of appropriate assessment and evaluation. Part II concludes with a chapter that explains how to integrate physical activity into children's everyday lives.

Capitalizing on Physical Activity to Benefit Children's Physical and Mental Health

Scientists and philosophers alike regularly use analogies to describe how events in nature operate. The analogy of the flowing stream is often used to describe children's development. Like a stream, the direction and speed of the flow may change from moment to moment. A large boulder may slow down the stream and force it to take a different path. Likewise, small rocks can create turbulence that determines whether the water flows smoothly or churns violently. As a child develops, his progress, like that of a flowing stream, can be affected by a multitude of experiences. You might consider physical activity as one of many rocks that influence children's stream of development. Although not life-changing, the physical activities infants and children engage in can subtly affect how they develop and influence their behaviors throughout their lives.

Previous chapters addressed child development and the ways physical activity affects physical and cognitive functions. This chapter expands the discussion to address how movements experienced early in life can set the trajectory for health behaviors across the life span. Of particular interest are the benefits of movement activities for children with developmental disorders and those who develop sedentary behaviors.

63

How Physical Movements Create Mental Maps

As we move, our bodies are constantly sensing the world around us. Sensory experiences provide a view, or perception, of how we are moving as the world around us moves. During movement, our actions and our perceptions become linked. Consider how we can walk in the middle of a crowded corridor and seldom bump into others moving past us or ahead of us. Our eyes and other sensory systems provide our brains with information concerning the position of our bodies and limbs and the movements of others moving past us and out in front of us. The brain converts that information into signals that guide our walking patterns, gaits, and movements. All of this complex processing and movement control is going on without much, if any, conscious awareness.

Athletes show the uncanny ability to make game movements faster than the mind can make decisions. The highly practiced movements of elite athletes reflect the fusion of perception and action; as game conditions change, so do the athlete's movements, without deliberate thought, in milliseconds.

How Infants Learn What Goes Where

The brain of the developing infant is creating connections between changes in the world and what she perceives both during and following physical movement. The contraction and lengthening of every skeletal muscle send information to areas of the brain that build and refine neural networks that serve as the building blocks of skilled movement. These emerging networks also receive input from the eyes and ears concerning the location of objects in the infant's world. The integration of information from skeletal muscles and visual and auditory structures allows the infant to learn from her actions—how her movements lead to sensory experiences. An infant who reaches out and touches a mobile dangling over her in a crib learns to connect controlled body movements to changes in her world. Learning to control the world through her own psychomotor skills is a very powerful psychological event.

Self-initiated actions are critical for learning. It has been known for decades that brain development is strongly linked to movement experiences. More recently, Ester Thelen (1941-2004) and her colleagues conducted a large body of systematic research with infants that demonstrates the critical role of body movement in cognitive development (Thelen, 2004). Movements that couple changes in sensation and perception provide the basis for embodied learning.

Similar to the theory of children's cognitive development proposed by Jean Piaget, whose ideas were introduced in chapter 1, Thelen linked the movements of infants to intrinsic rewards and pleasure. As infants gain control of muscles and establish sufficient strength to move their bodies, they begin to use their actions to make things happen in their world. They also use their movements to find solutions to new problems. For example, the infant who is placed on her abdomen can alter her perception of the world tremendously by organizing the skeletal muscles needed to turn to her back. Often to the delight of parents, the reactions of the infant when she performs her first few flips are clear. The infant invariably shows all the facial expressions of surprise and enjoyment. When placed back on her abdomen, the infant quickly learns to flip to her back. Although this action may appear simple, consider the involvement and control of muscle groups needed to initiate and control such a movement. Also remember that these actions are occurring prior to the emergence of the executive functions involved in planning and problem solving.

The importance of embodied learning was introduced in chapter 3, which outlined various types of learning. Most people think of learning as the ability to remember information—reading, writing, and arithmetic—academic learning. There are other types of learning, however. Learning that is grounded in action provides information concerning the body's movement in space. The child who picks up a toy learns about distance and depth, and the action provides the basis for guiding his arms and hands to objects. The capacity to understand the relationship between the body and objects in space is believed to underlie mental imagery, the ability to create mental representations and alter them. This ability to see things in the mind is critical to understanding mathematical computations and the arrangement of molecules, as well as for having an eye for drawing and creating art (Woodlee & Schallert, 2006). It is often said that artists are born

movement effectiveness—The ability to achieve a particular goal.

movement efficiency—The degree of effort required to achieve a particular goal.

with certain abilities that others do not possess. It is plausible that early experiences, together with genetics, provide the budding artist or scientist with unique abilities.

Movements are the central agent for the stages of cognitive development described by Jean Piaget. Similarly, to Thelen, "the foundations of complex human thought and behavior have their origins in action and are always embedded in a history of acting" (Thelen, 2004, p. 49). The physical movements of infants may appear simple, limited, and random; however, even the earliest actions provide knowledge on which more complex behavior is organized. Long before the emergence of executive functions, infants are already learning about the world in ways that can have lifelong consequences.

Although physical movement is important for infants' learning, it is not a prerequisite. For example, historically, in Asian and traditional Native American communities, infants were swaddled and placed in cribs that restricted movement. Researchers who examine cultural rearing methods have found that these infants' movement skills may lag behind those of children reared in less restrictive conditions; however, differences in movement pro-ficiency disappear rapidly during early childhood. Further, infants who have movement disorders, such as spina bifida or cerebral palsy, can evidence typical mental development. However, even though physical movement may not be a requirement for mental development, it is plausible that crawling, walking, hopping, and skipping may enhance and enrich the quality of a child's mental experiences and the way the brain develops.

Self-generated movements may work like an enzyme: they may not directly cause the emergence of a specific mental skill, but they can promote mental and behavioral efficiency by accelerating and amplifying the effects of experiences on the development of the brain and its functions. Psychologists consider **movement effectiveness** to mean the ability to achieve a particular goal. **Movement efficiency**, on the other hand, refers to the degree of effort required to achieve that goal. Therefore, although two children may be able to reach the same goal, one may be able to reach the goal with less effort and more rapidly than the other because of the efficient use of mental skills. Children who gain knowledge through physical movements and experiences become efficient in their thinking and problem solving.

Movement helps infants and young children learn about the world.

Pervasive Developmental Delays

Over the past decade, there has been a substantial increase in the number of children worldwide showing signs of **autistic spectrum disorder**, a neurodevelopmental disorder that impairs social skills, delays language development, results in repetitive behaviors and restricted interests, and impedes academic and social involvement (Stockman, 2004a). Proponents of embodied learning suggest that the cause of many developmental delays and autism (pervasive developmental delay disorder) lies in problems in movement control. Thelen explained the importance of being able to control movements when she wrote: "Children without a sensitive sense of their own movements and body positions cannot monitor them and will lack any sort of predictive control. If body sense is poor, sequencing behavior is difficult and social interactions are unpredictable, then normal skills are very difficult to acquire. Each of these difficulties can lead to frustration, emotional withdrawal, or aggressive and inappropriate behavior. Even small distortions in basic processes can cascade over development and lead to multiple, overlapping problems" (Thelen, 2004, pp. 70-71).

Many explanations for the increase in the diagnosis of autism have been proposed. In all likelihood multiple factors underlie the disorder. Nevertheless, linking the disorder to movement merits consideration. The ability to move plays a major role in developing attachment between young children and their parents. As children move toward their parents, they provide social signals that parents respond to with physical contact and comfort—the basic components of lasting bonding. With attachment with parents come feelings of safety, comfort, and security. Parents serve as a safe harbor from which children can explore their world. Supported by feelings of security, they systematically increase the distances they travel to explore the new world. Young children's independent movements are not random, but rather, goal directed. Some goals are achieved and others are blocked, resulting in frustration and other emotions. With the resolution of frustration and support from parents, children develop a sense of accomplishment and self-confidence.

Why Self-Initiation of Movement Is Important

For many decades, movement-based interventions have been developed to treat developmental disorders. The **patterning therapy** programs developed by Doman (2005), for example, were based on the notion that ontogeny recapitulates phylogeny, described at the beginning of chapter 4. Doman's theory was that passively guiding children's limbs through patterns that reflected evolutionary-linked motor movements would benefit cognitive growth. A critical difference between these early movement intervention programs and those of embodied action learning described earlier lies in the source of infants' and children's movements. Patterning involves the passive movement of children's limbs: several practitioners work together to move a child's arms, legs, and head in sequences of movements that simulate basic crawling and reaching actions. The central assumptions of patterning therapy, however, have not been supported by research (Sparrow & Zigler, 1978).

Embodied learning occurs when infants and children initiate their own movements. The importance of self-initiated movement in learning was highlighted in chapter 3. Recent advances in the study of skill acquisition highlight the importance of feed-forward processes in learning. When actions are initiated and signaled from the frontal part of the brain, instructions for movements are sent not only down the spinal cord and to the muscles, but also to other brain structures that await predicted incoming feedback information.

Perhaps you have noticed that you cannot tickle yourself. When you think about moving your finger to a sensitive area, your brain expects input from that area even before your touch. When someone else touches your side, even when you see it coming,

autistic spectrum disorder—A neurodevelopmental disorder that impairs social skills, delays language development, results in repetitive behaviors and restricted interests, and impedes academic and social involvement.

patterning therapy—A form of therapy that uses the passive movement of body limbs in sequences to simulate basic reflexes.

habits—Learned behavior patterns that are engrained and enduring.

sedentary behavior—Behavior that results in an energy expenditure equal to that of sleeping, sitting, lying down, or watching television.

metabolic equivalent units (METs)—A unit of measurement of physical energy cost that is computed as the ratio of metabolic rate to a reference metabolic rate.

the brain is unprepared and you sense being tickled. Although tickling may seem an odd example, it illustrates the importance of the feed-forward system; it provides the brain with the capacity to predict upcoming movements that are critical for learning and their sensory and perceptual consequences. Without mental involvement, learning is hindered.

Watching infants learn to plan, execute, and control their movements reveals how physical activity, mental effort, and cognitive development are intertwined. As infants move, they learn about their environments and how tasks are solved. Advancing into childhood, histories of movements are accumulated and continue to provide the basis for understanding the nature of the environment. Clearly, the impact of physical activity interventions can go far beyond motor skill development and sports. Physical activity interventions that are appropriately designed can have far-reaching effects across the life span. When infants and children acquire physical and mental skills, the movement patterns are stored as memories that can be retrieved, modified, and applied at later times. Children with a dearth of movement experiences are at a disadvantage when exposed to new games and sports.

Childhood Inactivity and Sedentary Behavior

Infants and young children are physically active throughout each day; crawling, walking, pulling themselves up, and playing all require physical effort. However, activity levels drop off around age 6 in the United States (Faigenbaum et al., 2011; Tudor-Locke, Johnson, & Katzmarzyk, 2010); boys and girls show similar reductions. Some of these changes can be linked to sex-related changes and body changes, and others are related to social and cultural factors. Some researchers suggest that many children exhibit an exercise deficit disorder that leads to long-term negative consequences on physical and social habits (Faigenbaum, Stracciolini, & Myer, 2011). **Habits** are learned behavior patterns that are engrained and enduring. Without specific interventions that promote motor skill development and movement confidence, children miss the opportunity to develop health-promoting habits. Faigenbaum and colleagues pointed to the importance of developmentally appropriate motor skill instruction over general physical fitness programs designed by adults for adults. They also emphasized the importance of providing teachers with sufficient knowledge to develop and implement physical activity programs that develop fundamental motor skills, enhance coordination, and encourage self-confidence.

Children who fail to acquire the basic skills of hopping, throwing, jumping, and kicking tend to doubt their abilities when asked to participate in games. Furthermore, these are fundamental movements that make up more complex motor skills. For example, to skip, a child must know how to hop. By middle school, children recognize their skill levels; those who lack skills choose sedentary, solitary activities over games and sports that promote socialization and physical activity habits. School coaches typically recruit students to play sports based on physical characteristics and skills. Seldom do children who are not selected for sports receive additional skill training. Proponents of the exercise deficit disorder model suggest that teachers and medical providers be trained to identify children who lack basic motor skills and draw those children into programs that are fun and develop those skills.

Inactivity Versus Sedentary Behavior

Physical activity is defined in chapter 2 as bodily movement produced by skeletal muscle contraction that requires energy expenditure. Physical activity lies on a continuum from minimal to maximal. Physical inactivity implies the absence of activity (Marshall & Welk, 2008). Exercise scientists define **sedentary behaviors** as those that result in an energy expenditure equal to that of sleeping, sitting, lying down, or watching television. Technically, the energy cost would be 1.0 to 1.5 **metabolic equivalent units (METs)**, which is a unit of measurement of physical energy cost that is computed as the ratio of metabolic rate to a reference metabolic rate. Although the terms *sedentariness* and *inactivity* have been used extensively and interchangeably in the public health domain, clear definitions of the terms are lacking (Pate, O'Neill, & Lobelo, 2008). The vast majority of research conducted by exercise scientists has focused on the health benefits of moderate-to-vigorous physical activity (MVPA). Many researchers have considered physical activity levels of less than moderate intensity to be sedentary behaviors.

The lack of a clear description of low-intensity physical activity has led some researchers to stress the importance of understanding these behaviors, particularly in children. Indeed, many behaviors that are desirable are considered sedentary; for example, socializing and spending quality time with family. Health experts have considered other sedentary behaviors, however, as undesirable. Social media and television time are often viewed as unhealthy behaviors. As discussed previously, children's activity patterns differ from those of adults; children display more bursts in physical activity throughout the day. The problem for researchers and health professionals has been to separate low levels of physical activity that are appropriate and healthy from those that are unhealthy. The American Academy of Pediatrics recommends limiting children's total daily entertainment media time to two hours; discourages television viewing for children younger than 2 years old; and encourages more interactive activities that promote talking, playing, singing, and reading.

Television time has been linked to childhood obesity since the 1980s; by the 1990s, it was believed to cause increased weight. Similarly, media time and video play have been linked to increases in children's sedentary behaviors, decreases in health-promoting physical activity, and increases in overweight and obesity. Despite the general appeal of blaming children's increased weight issues on television and media time, a strong link between these activities and weight gain has not been shown. It is clear that many factors play a role in changes in children's physical fitness and weight status.

Worldwide Trends in Children's Physical Fitness and Motor Coordination

Have children's levels of physical fitness declined over the past few decades? Experts differ in their answers to this question. The complexity of measuring children's physical fitness and tracking changes over long periods of time has resulted in differing opinions. Some assert that evidence of global declines in physical fitness is clear. A landmark study examined aerobic fitness data obtained from 1958 to 2003 on almost 2.5 million children and adolescents living in 27 countries and five geographical regions (Tomkinson & Olds, 2007). The pattern of aerobic performance was clear for both boys and girls and across all geographical regions: from 1958 through the 1960s, children's and adolescents' physical fitness improved. However, beginning in the 1970s, fitness levels began to decline rapidly. These **secular trends**, which are alterations in the average pattern of growth or development in a population over several generations, have been explained in many ways. One view is that children

who are less active fail to adequately condition or physically train their bodies, and as a consequence show lower levels of fitness. Others have proposed social, cultural, and psychological explanations for changes in children's physical fitness levels. The environmental changes that have taken place around the globe over the past three decades are staggering. Migration to large cities, the increasing use of automobiles, and laborsaving devices all have been considered as explanations.

Other researchers have suggested that children's physical fitness capacity has not changed much (Olds, Ridley, & Tomkinson, 2007). What has changed, however, are factors that reduce their performance on tests of physical fitness. This is especially true when aerobic fitness is measured using running tests. Consider the worldwide increase in children's body weight. Fatness can compromise measures of aerobic fitness; excess body weight hinders the ability to attain the levels of fitness performance of which children are capable.

Understanding why children's levels of physical fitness have changed is important. At first glance it might seem that the reasons are clear. If physical fitness declines are due to fat increases, programs that emphasize dietary control would be desirable. However, if declines are due to low physical activity levels, then programs that emphasize vigorous physical activity are important.

Another possible reason for poorer performance on physical fitness tests that has received much less attention is motor coordination. European studies show decreases in the ability to perform coordinated movements over generations, which are exhibited as early as preschool age (Roth et al., 2010). These decreases seem not to impair movement performances that rely on speed and power, but those that rely on motor coordination. This might be due to the

secular trends—Alterations in the average pattern of growth or development in a population over several generations.

body mass index (BMI)—A mathematical method used to describe the relation between body weight and stature.

obesogenic—Promoting excessive weight gain.

metabolic syndrome—A combination of health measures such as body fat, blood pressure, and cholesterol that are combined and used to predict the onset of cardiovascular disease and type 2 diabetes.

decreased quality of physical activity experiences that children have in contemporary societies. Australian studies have convincingly shown that children who master skilled movement and feel competent in moving enjoy moving and remain active later in life (Barnett et al., 2008; Barnett et al., 2009). However, physical fitness in childhood is not a strong predictor of physical activity levels and fitness in adolescence. These studies seem to suggest that to have more active adolescents and adults, we should focus on the quality of physical activity experiences early in life, so that children experience feelings of enjoyment and mastery from physical activity.

Worldwide Trends in Childhood Obesity and Health

A few decades ago, overweight children were an exception; today, over a third of American children are classified as overweight or obese. **Body mass index (BMI)**, a mathematical method used to describe the relation between body weight and stature, is an accepted metric of body weight. Childhood obesity is defined as a BMI at or above the 95th percentile according to the U.S. Centers for Disease and Control BMI for age growth charts (Ogden et al., 2010). Since 1980, rates of obesity in children ages 2 through 5 doubled; they quadrupled for children ages 6 through 11 (Bleich, Ku, & Wang,

2011). Figure 5.1 shows the incidence of childhood overweight and obesity in the United States; some believe the country is experiencing an obesity epidemic. The term **obesogenic** means "promoting excessive weight gain."

Concern about weight gain in children has increased as a result of data showing the likelihood that overweight children will grow to be overweight adults. The costs of being overweight are high for both individuals and society. There has been considerable interest in recent years in the **metabolic syndrome**, which is a combination of health measures. In adults, measures such as body fat, blood pressure, and cholesterol are combined and used to predict the onset of cardiovascular disease and type 2 diabetes. Recently, measures of the metabolic syndrome and associated risk factors have been extended to children. Numerous studies have found that children who are physically active have reduced metabolic syndrome scores compared to less physically active children. Indeed, a dose–response relation appears to exist, in that greater doses of physical activity are associated with higher levels of cardiovascular and metabolic health.

Health-related behaviors developed during childhood show great promise for decreasing the likelihood or severity of diseases in adulthood and later life. Physical activity may exert much of its influence on cardiovascular and metabolic health by enhancing fitness and reducing fatness, which

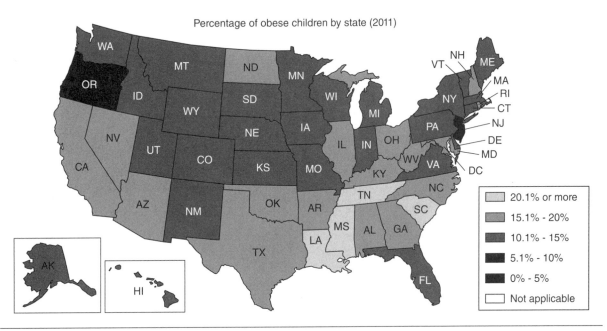

Figure 5.1 Percentage of obesity in children in the United States.

Adapted from National Conference of State Legislatures, 2014, *Childhood Overweight and Obesity Trends*. Available: http://www.ncsl.org/research/health/childhood-obesity-trends-state-rates.aspx.

in turn influences the underlying processes leading to cardiovascular disease and type 2 diabetes. The evidence is clear that physical activity intervention can decrease the body fat of children who are overweight or obese (Gutin, 2011). However, it has not been established that exercise interventions help lean children avoid weight gain. Assessing the impact of exercise interventions on children's and adolescents' weight gain is difficult, considering the developmental and sex-related changes that occur during this period. Indeed, the benefits of planned exercise may be quite modest, and it may take years of routine physical activity to see its effects on the metabolic risk profile.

Understanding the conditions that affect physical activity behaviors and diet is critical for appreciating the obesity epidemic affecting children's health worldwide. Much has been written over the past decade in an attempt to identify the causes of the phenomenon. Despite many studies, specific factors that drive children's weight gains have not been identified. A detailed overview of the causes of children's increase in body weight is beyond the scope of this book. However, the academic community agrees that reductions in children's sedentary behaviors and increases in physical activity contribute to healthy bodies and minds. Presently in the United States, national and regional organizations, both in the public and the private sectors, are becoming increasingly involved in programs designed to persuade children to be more physically active. Virtually all promote programs that emphasize fun activities.

Overweight, Cognitive Function, and Academic Performance

Several researchers have measured the relation between obesity and cognitive function. A summary of those studies reports that, across the life span, executive functions, intelligence, and processing capabilities are negatively related to body weight or BMI (Smith, Hay, Campbell, & Trollor, 2011). Further, the clearest findings were obtained from childhood research; several studies linked overweight to lower levels of executive function. Although the link between adiposity and cognitive function is understudied, several explanations have been offered. Overweight is linked to inflammation, increased triglyceride levels, disruptions in insulin production, and impaired hippocampal function— all of which have been implicated in brain health.

Several large studies have reported that as weight increases, children are more likely to have aca-

demic difficulties and behavioral problems (Datar, Sturm, & Magnabosco, 2004; Davis & Cooper, 2011). Again, many social and psychological factors may contribute to the relation (Krukowski et al., 2009). Nevertheless, sufficient data link being overweight with negative academic consequences.

Overweight and Physical Activity

Children who are overweight or obese engage in less routine physical activity than nonoverweight children. Overweight children typically view physical activity negatively and seek sedentary activities. The combination of a lack of physical activity, increased sedentary behavior, and unhealthy eating contribute greatly to the childhood obesity epidemic.

Few games that children play are solitary, and children are more active when playing with a friend and peers than when alone. Overweight children, however, are often alone. Negative experiences and rejection by other children on the playground can have long-lasting negative effects on children's motivation to be physically active, as well as on feelings of belonging, self-esteem, and mood. Researchers have noted that the pain that children feel when they are ostracized is similar to physical pain. Breaking the vicious cycle of a child's failed attempt to participate in games and increased isolation and withdrawal from physical activity is difficult (Salvy, Bowker, Germeroth, & Barkley, 2012).

Positive peer support is critical for motivating overweight children to move and be active. Recent research has found that overweight children are particularly sensitive to social messages sent by other children and teachers. Overweight children who perceive criticism when engaging in games or sports show increased signs of depression, feelings of loneliness, and reductions in enjoyment. On the other hand, experiences of cooperation and respect, as well as positive interactions, increase children's motivation to engage in physical activity.

Children's and Adolescents' Mental Health

The World Health Organization (WHO) defines mental health for children and adolescents as the ability "to achieve and maintain optimal psychological and social functioning and well-being." Healthy children and adolescents have a sense of identity and self-worth, sound family and peer relationships, an ability to be productive and to learn, and a capacity to tackle developmental challenges and use cultural resources to maximize growth.

Moreover, mental health is crucial for active social and economic participation (World Health Organization, 2005).

Worldwide, approximately 20 percent of children and adolescents exhibit mental health problems. Risk factors for these problems are genetic, social, and cultural. Specific types of disorders are linked to developmental periods. During infancy and early childhood, **attachment disorders**, which are characterized by difficulty bonding with parents and poor socialization behaviors, as well as pervasive developmental disorders and childhood autism, can be detected. **Hyperkinetic disorder**, which is an enduring disposition to behave in a restless, inattentive, distracted, and disorganized fashion,

and **conduct disorder**, evidenced by excessive defiant or impulsive behavior, are typically diagnosed between 4 and 6 years of age. Symptoms of anxiety disorder and mood disorders increase in some children after the age of 6. These age ranges, of course, can be influenced by a wide variety of factors. Of importance, however, is that early diagnosis and treatment have the best chance of producing mental health gains in children. Given that conduct, anxiety, and mood disorders can set the stage for cycles of negative mental health behaviors that extend into adolescence and adulthood, early interventions are of particular importance.

Childhood mood disorders are the most common problems that occur in children and adolescence. They include all types of depression and are sometimes referred to as affective disorders. **Depression** in young children is characterized by pretending to be sick, refusing to go to school, clinging to a parent, or worrying that a parent may die. Older children may sulk, get into trouble at school, be negative, act grouchy, or feel misunderstood. It is difficult to identify depression in children because of the massive changes that children go through. Detection often requires an evaluation by someone who specializes in treatment of children.

There are several types of **childhood anxiety**, which is characterized by a state of worry, apprehension, or tension that often occurs in the absence of real or obvious danger. **Generalized anxiety disorder** (GAD) is characterized by worrying excessively about grades, family issues, friendships, and performance in school and sports. **Obsessive-compulsive disorder** (OCD) is characterized by unwanted thoughts and feeling the need to perform rituals and routines that ease anxiety. **Separation anxiety disorder** typically occurs between 18 months and 3 years of age. Behaviors include not wanting to go to school or social activities and not wanting to be separated from someone.

Does Physical Activity Help Children With Mental Health Problems?

Practitioners and researchers who use routine exercise as treatments for adults with mental health problems have found that it can reduce symptoms of anxiety and depression. In some cases, the benefits of exercise for adults with depression are as large as those obtained with drug treatments (Buckworth, Dishman, O'Connor, & Tomporowski, 2013, chapter 11). Much less is known about exercise and physical activity interventions for children. However,

---

attachment disorders—Disorders characterized by difficulty bonding with parents and poor socialization behaviors.

hyperkinetic disorder—An enduring disposition to behave in a restless, inattentive, distracted, and disorganized fashion.

conduct disorder—Excessive defiant or impulsive behavior.

childhood mood disorders—Disorders that include all types of depression and are sometimes referred to as affective disorders.

depression—A disorder characterized in young children by pretending to be sick, refusing to go to school, clinging to a parent, or worrying that a parent may die. Older children may sulk, get into trouble at school, be negative, act grouchy, or feel misunderstood.

childhood anxiety—A state of worry, apprehension, or tension that often occurs in the absence of real or obvious danger.

generalized anxiety disorder (GAD)—A disorder characterized by worrying excessively about grades, family issues, friendships, and performance in school and sports.

obsessive-compulsive disorder (OCD)—A disorder characterized by unwanted thoughts and feeling the need to perform rituals and routines that ease anxiety.

separation anxiety disorder—A disorder characterized by not wanting to go to school or social activities and not wanting to be separated from someone. It typically occurs between 18 months and 3 years of age.

the few studies conducted suggest that routine physical activity can favorably affect many mental health problems. The U.S. Department of Health Services' Physical Activity Guidelines Advisory Committee Report (Physical Activity Guidelines Advisory Committee, 2008) summarized the results of available research.

Physical activity programs have been shown to reduce symptoms in children who are depressed. For example, Annesi (2006) found that a 12-week physical activity program decreased depression and significantly improved mood in children 9 to 12 years of age. Furthermore, physically active children were less likely to report symptoms of depression (Motl, Birnbaum, Tykubik, & Dishman, 2004). Many children's symptoms of anxiety were also reduced as a result of being physically active (Strong et al., 2005).

Does Physical Activity Help Children Who Do Not Have Mental Health Problems?

Thankfully, most children enjoy suitable mental health. For them, it is important to consider factors that can contribute to promoting, maintaining,

and maximizing their potential. Traditionally, the focus of psychologists has been to identify and treat mental illness. Over the past two decades, a branch of psychology has emerged that focuses on the positive qualities of human experiences. As described in chapter 4, the goal of positive psychology is to make normal life more fulfilling and to help people live life to the fullest.

Flow theory, which was introduced in chapter 4, emphasizes the positive feelings experienced when coping well with challenging conditions. When skills are lacking to meet a challenge, feelings of worry and anxiety occur. When challenge is minimal and skill levels are high, feelings of boredom and monotony may occur. Adults often report feelings of pleasure when they are totally mentally engaged in performing challenging activities. Actions occur as if on automatic pilot, and feeling of complete control and assuredness ensue. Regardless of the task, pleasurable states occur most often when people face challenging situations that match their skill levels.

It is plausible that physical activity games that match challenge and skill levels provide feelings of pleasure similar to the experience of flow. Such a match also ensures that children reap the greatest

© Digital Vision

Physical activity can help to turn that frown upside down. Don't wave off a sulky kid as just being grumpy; it could be depression or anxiety. Get them moving and playing, and watch their moods improve.

benefits from learning-through-play experiences, as discussed in chapter 2 where the optimal challenge point was introduced. The primary emphasis of previous chapters was how to apply teaching principles that help children reach and maintain consistently high levels of mental engagement. The physical activity games described in chapters 10 and 11 are designed to enhance children's pleasure and positive experiences.

Children face many real-world developmental challenges. Those who lack the needed skills may experience anxiety, worry, and feelings of stress that lower their motivation to continue. For children, the very process of learning a new game can be stressful. As discussed in chapter 3, during the early stages of learning, children experience a sense of disequilibrium and tension—stress. As they learn the game, tension is reduced and they feel a renewed sense of stability. Social scientists suggest that the process of meeting and overcoming stress plays a role in social development and mental health.

An important characteristic of good stress management skills is that children believe they can achieve their goals using their own physical and mental resources. Faced with learning a new game, a child must assess the game and decide whether she has the abilities to meet the challenge. Her estimation of the game may lead her to decide, This is too much for me—I'm going to fail. On the other hand, her estimation of the game may lead her to decide, I can take this on—I'm going to be successful. This appraisal process is critical to the development of stress management. The mental engagement that occurs during challenging games alters children's belief in their ability to overcome stressful conditions more than does engaging in mindless physical activities. Going through the motions of physical training programs is not enough; children must view the task at hand as one that, although demanding, can be overcome by employing their skills and abilities. The belief that they can cope with challenging situations results in positive feelings of control over the environment and leads to expectations of future success.

Childhood self-esteem refers to how much children value themselves, which often guides their behavior. A sense of self-worth in childhood has been linked to satisfaction in adulthood. A child's early experiences in games and sports can have a

---

childhood self-esteem—How much children value themselves.

---

big influence on self-esteem. Most children under the age of 10 develop self-esteem from feedback from parents and self-appraisals of their own performance. In later childhood, peer appraisal plays an increasingly important role. Throughout childhood, the feedback provided by teachers and coaches can set the trajectory of children's views of who they are. Historically, games and sport have been seen as ways to help develop the self. Success and failure are both important outcomes because they provide realistic information about children's capabilities and what they can expect. Physical competence is a component of self-esteem. Games and sports give children the opportunity to develop beliefs concerning their strength and endurance. As such, they can have a substantial impact on children's views of themselves. Because children lack a complex sense of who they are, of their selves, early experiences can profoundly influence their psychological makeup.

Recently, concern has been voiced about how body weight may influence children's body image and self-esteem. Overweight children are aware of the media images and stereotypes associated with obesity, and these messages can contribute to low levels of self-esteem. Concerns about body image are also expressed in normal-weight elementary children. Girls commonly feel the need to be thinner; and boys, to be bigger, taller, and more muscular (Gibbs et al., 2008). Dissatisfaction with body image is linked to eating problems, eating disorders, and depression.

Childhood self-efficacy is reflected in the belief in the ability to succeed in specific situations. As discussed in chapter 4, children's sense of self-efficacy can play a major role in how they approach goals, tasks, and challenges. Bandura proposed that feelings of self-efficacy provide the basis for developing positive health behaviors and health maintenance across the life span (Bandura, 1997). Children who learn that they have the power to control their destiny approach new challenges with the expectation of success. A sense of self-efficacy can influence both body and mind as well as health and disease.

Learning a new skill is both challenging and stress producing. Learning to cope with the stress of learning new skills is thought to result in a buildup of a physiological reserve that can shield against the negative consequences of stress. Children who believe that they can deal with challenges grow into young adults who can adapt to the stress of everyday life. How people respond to life stress is determined greatly by their perceptions of their coping capabilities.

Implications for Educators

The impact teachers have on children may not be immediately apparent. Children accumulate knowledge over years of interacting with others. The games and their consequences experienced in preschool, kindergarten, or elementary school have the potential to provide memories that can be recalled later in life. In adolescence or young adulthood, people can recall memories of early experiences that they can reevaluate and appraise quite differently from when they first experienced them. Experiences gained though play and games in childhood can lead to optimal physical and mental health in later life.

For generations, parents and teachers have recognized that children's early experiences set a course for the remainder of their lives. Much has been said about the benefits of influencing children while they are young and impressionable. The notion of simply keeping kids active has merit, given that, left to their own devices, children do explore and learn. However, teachers' knowledge of the progression of children's physical, mental, and social growth can help them create instructional settings that promote optimal development and help children make good personal health decisions.

Teachers are uniquely positioned to create environments that foster general self-efficacy, as well as positive efficacy beliefs when confronted with challenging tasks. Recall that a child's efficacy beliefs are the result of a past history of success or failure, observing the consequences of other people's actions, feedback and guidance, and an interpretation of feelings. Physical activity games conducted in the proper manner can set the stage for children to develop skills and realistic perceptions of their capacities.

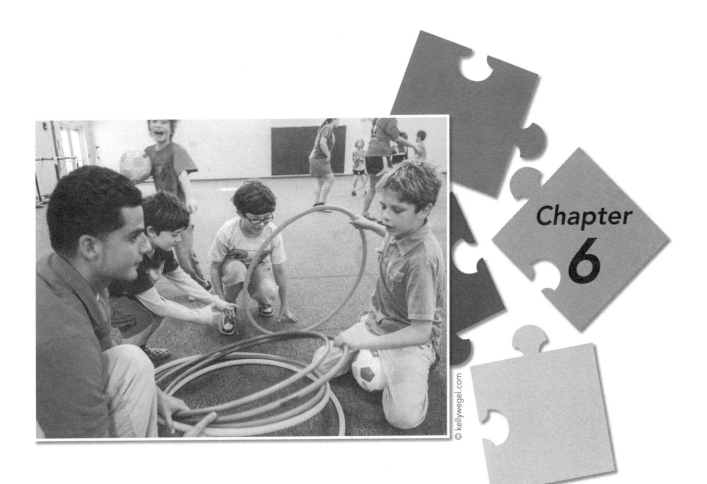

© kellywegel.com

Engaging Children in Playful Learning

Recognizing that someone is mentally engaged in a task is not too difficult. The child twirling objects on a string attached to the front of his stroller, the young girl arranging her dolls around a table and taking the lead in an animated pretend tea party, and the college student typing on his handheld media device while walking down the hallway all exhibit similar characteristics. For a brief period, virtually all of their attention is focused on the task at hand. They block out everything else to concentrate on the problem.

When presented in specific ways and at the right time, tasks can capture people's attention. As long as the conditions remain, attention is focused. When the challenge of a game is set just right, or optimally, it captures players' attention and fosters mental engagement. Recent studies of mental effort and engagement build on theories of learning that

have been accepted in the fields of psychology and education for many decades. Consider Jean Piaget's theory of cognitive development, introduced in chapter 1. He asserted the importance of mental balance and how a sense of equilibrium and a sense of disequilibrium motivate children to learn. Consider also the three-stage model of learning described in chapter 3. Children experience shifts in attention and mental involvement across the cognitive, associative, and autonomous stages. For the past five decades, these theories of learning have provided a general road map for teachers.

This chapter introduces recent advances in learning theory and teaching methods that have been shown to enhance physical and mental development. This information can increase the precision of the teaching road map and lead to better learning.

Children's Mental Engagement

Children are genetically programmed to be drawn to new experiences. Early developmentalists described childhood as the skill-hungry years, highlighting their natural drive to explore and enjoy the progressive development of movement skills. Today, some educators propose that children should participate in a wide range of activities involving deliberate play, which focuses on enjoyment, rather than participate in a single sport involving deliberate practice, which focuses on training and skill improvement. The variety of activities children experience in deliberate play is important for satisfying their skill hunger and maintaining their motivation and interest. Early learning experiences are considered important for ensuring lifelong participation in physical activity (Kirk, 2005).

Optimal Challenge Point

The importance of providing challenges tailored to children's developmental status was addressed in chapters 2 and 4. An optimal challenge is like a coin with two sides: one is emotional-energetic, and the other is psychomotor-cognitive. Motivation helps the child maintain an optimal level of emotional arousal to remain on task during game play. Games that are enjoyable and playful ensure the necessary emotional energy. However, to reach and maintain an optimal challenge point for learning, the complexity of the tasks composing a game must be fine-tuned to the gradually increasing skill level of the child. If children have become skilled at playing tag, reducing the playing field or the number of safe spots will challenge them physically and cognitively. Although children are primed to learn, optimal learning requires specific environmental conditions. The context sets the stage for learning. Without a movement problem that attracts and channels children's attention, learning will not occur. The greatest challenge teachers face is creating the optimal context to keep each child on the learning curve. Effective teachers know how to change instructions to maintain an optimal challenge point.

Recently, researchers have begun to examine more closely the optimal challenge point, which is defined as an unstable point of balance between the degree of task complexity and the child's skill level in a given learning environment (Guadagnoli & Lee, 2004). Finding and maintaining a child's optimal challenge point is crucial for promoting the development of executive functions. In fact, researchers have found that executive functions must be continually challenged to improve performance. Children who perform the same activities, but do not experience challenge, evidence no gain in executive functioning (Diamond & Lee, 2011). To maximize cognitive challenge, movement games should be neither too simple nor too difficult.

Variability of Practice

Researchers who have examined the optimal challenge point highlight the importance of variability of practice. This chapter focuses on this very important issue. What can be varied, or changed, when teaching movement games, to reach an optimal level of cognitive engagement for learning? Consider a game that involves throwing and catching. A girl needs to deal with two primary challenges: learning the movement skill and then applying it to changing game conditions. When learning a movement game, children must first master the motor skills involved. Teachers commonly begin by teaching one game-relevant skill in a constant fashion. For instance, they teach children throwing a ball with the same arm at the same speed toward a target located the same distance away. However, performing a given skill in a constant environment is only the first step in the long process of learning to play the game.

When a child's throwing performance has become stable, the teacher can introduce variability into children's practice. For instance, children may be requested to perform the same skill (e.g., an overhead throw) over and over, but changing each attempt in some way, such as the force or speed of the throw or the throwing arm. The child may also throw overhead while stepping backward, forward, or sideways, thus changing the throwing distance and direction. She may also alternate throwing balls of different sizes and weights, or throw the ball alternately with the right and left arm. Variability of practice progressively increases cognitive engagement and improves learning.

Promoting Variability Across the Learning Curve

As discussed in chapters 3 and 4, learning begins with a cognitive stage, continues through an associative stage, and is concluded when the person

> **contextual interference**—A phenomenon in which a practice schedule results in less efficient performance but produces better long-term learning.

reaches the autonomous stage. Theories of motor learning describe learning as a progression toward movement automaticity, or movements that require progressively less mental engagement (figure 6.1a). Thus, automaticity is the end point of the motor learning process. At that point, the educator who wants to maintain a child's mental effort must introduce changes that generate new cognitive challenges and keep the child at an optimal challenge point. Games can be altered in two ways: (1) by arranging conditions so that the child needs to use newly introduced or different skills (e.g., throwing a ball with a scoop instead of his hand) or (2) by changing the game so that the child needs to adapt a skill to new conditions (e.g., throwing a ball at multiple targets that vary in size).

According to Eastern European movement researchers (Meinel & Schnabel, 1999), when children learn and refine movement skills, they pass through the first two stages of learning: the raw stage and the refined coordination stage (figure 6.1b). Similar to the cognitive and associate stages of learning depicted in figure 6.1a, the raw and refined coordination stages involve an initially high level of mental engagement that progressively decreases. However, at the end of the learning curve, these researchers identified a stage they called the variable availability stage, in which children learn to adapt their refined movement skills to changing situations. This is a stage of renewed mental engagement in which such executive functions as response inhibition, working memory, and mental shifting are particularly challenged. The emphasis of this last stage has important practical implications regarding cognitive flexibility and adaptability. To understand the central role of variable adaptability in the movement games provided in this book, and in their ability to promote executive function development, let's look at three principles of instruction used to introduce changes and generate new cognitive challenges.

Three Principles of Mental Engagement

The classic stage theories of child developmental and learning and advances in neuropsychology can be pulled together and summarized in three principles of mental engagement: contextual interference, mental control, and discovery. Each principle can be used by teachers to promote children's physical activity and advance their mental development.

Contextual Interference

When the context, or conditions, of a game change and require a child to make unpredictable sequences of actions, **contextual interference** is created, which, in turn, enhances mental engagement. The importance of contextual interference to children's learning comes from a counterintuitive observation. One might think that children learn better when they are more proficient during practice, but this is not so. It is true that children who practice skills in repeated sequences perform them better than do children who practice them in nonrepeating, random sequences. However, random

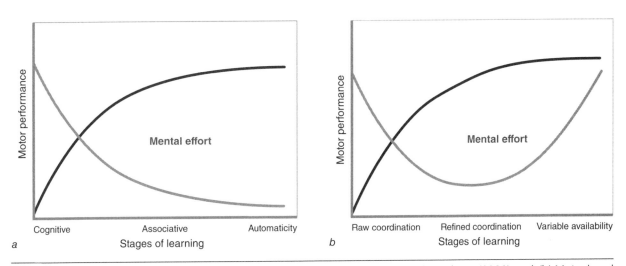

Figure 6.1 Two views of mental effort during motor learning. *(a)* Schmidt and Wrisberg (2008) and *(b)* Meinel and Schnabel (1998).

(a) Adapted from Schmidt and Wrisberg 2008.

(b) Based on Meinel and Schnabel 1998.

practice leads to better and more stable learning in the long term.

Why does this contextual interference effect occur? Two factors explain why learning is better under nonrepeating, random game conditions. First, when children alternate between action plans, they elaborate and think deeply about the features of the game. This mental effort results in their memorizing the requirements of various movement plans. Children who develop meaningful or distinctive memories can draw on them when confronted with changing game demands. Second, contextual interference leads to better learning because mental effort is required to reconstruct and plan prior to action. Children often forget when they move from one game to another. When they return to the original game, they must reconstruct and then execute a new action plan. Under contextual interference conditions, children must perform multiple mental operations to be successful. Games that apply the principle of contextual interference challenge children's executive functions (Tomporowski, McCullick, & Horvat, 2010).

Mental Control

Executive function reflects a number of interrelated mental processes. Previous chapters described the executive functions of response inhibition (stopping), working memory (updating), and mental shifting (switching). These functions provide the basis for the principle of mental control, and each of them can be drawn on during physical activity games.

Stopping Games

Movement games that challenge response inhibition are particularly useful for younger children. These games focus on the first building blocks of executive function development. To stimulate response inhibition, movement games involve having children stop and go at unpredictable time intervals. Children given alternating signals to go and to stop must react by overriding prior actions. These are called **stopping** games.

Traditional games played by children worldwide apply the principle of stopping. In chapter 10, for example, The Statues Game includes several alterations that require response inhibition. You will see how to apply the principle of stopping in both **simple** and **complex response inhibition** games. In simple inhibition games, children must delay well-learned habits; for example, choose a larger delayed reward instead of a smaller immediate reward. In

other words, children must behave opposite to the saying "A bird in the hand is worth two in the bush." In complex inhibition games, children may be asked to hold a rule in mind, respond according to this rule, and inhibit a habitual response. For example, in a typical inhibition task for preschool children, the "grass-snow" task, the child must point to a white object when hearing "Grass" and to a green object when hearing "Snow."

Updating Games

As discussed in previous chapters, working memory involves the capacity to hold and manipulate information in the mind. Games can be created that differ in their memory demands. In a **simple working memory** game, children are required merely to hold information in mind over a delayed period. A typical example is holding one rule in mind prior to the start of a game and then using the rule during the game. **Complex working memory** games require children to avoid repeating previ-

---

stopping—A description of tasks in which an external stimulus signals the person to interrupt an already initiated motor response.

simple response inhibition—The ability to withhold or delay an automatic, habitual response (e.g., trading a smaller, but immediate reward for a larger, but delayed reward).

complex response inhibition—The ability to hold a rule in mind, respond according to this rule, and inhibit another response (e.g., point to white when the teacher says "Grass" and to green when the teacher says "Snow").

simple working memory—The capacity to hold information in mind over a delayed period.

updating—Changing and manipulating information that is no longer relevant as new information becomes relevant to an ongoing task.

complex working memory—The capacity to hold information in mind and to manipulate it.

switching—Stopping what one is doing and acting in a totally different way.

response shifting—When a change in task conditions requires players to stop one movement and perform a different one.

attention shifting—When a change in the task requires disengaging attention from one cue and refocusing on a different cue.

ously used solutions by updating information held in memory. Complex working memory is defined as the capacity to hold information in mind and then to update it as new information is acquired. To follow this rule, children need to monitor the information held in working memory and remember the solutions they have already used so they can avoid repeating them. Recall that children's memory capacities are smaller than adults', so the information load in games needs to match their capacities. Also remember that because children's working memory capacity increases with age, teachers should alter games to ensure that they continue to meet children's optimal challenge point.

Switching Games

In physical activity and sport training, children are often required to respond quickly to signals, such as the voice of the teacher or the movements of other children. In most cases, they must make the same response each time a signal is presented. For example, a teacher repeatedly gives go and stop signals, and children must perform the same action in response to each. A child waiting to receive the baton in a relay race, upon seeing an approaching teammate, responds with only one correct motor response. This promotes automatic responding, and mental effort progressively decreases. However, a child cannot develop automaticity when the associations between signals and movements are unpredictable. As you will see in later chapters, some games alternate the use of voice and visual signals for stopping and going.

Teachers can also deter the development of automaticity and maintain mental engagement by associating the required response with more than one stimulus. In several tag games described in chapters 10 and 11, children do not have fixed tagger and taggie roles; rather, each child must try to tag certain children, but avoid being tagged by others. Therefore, a child seeing another child approaching cannot always make the same response, as in the case of a relay race; he must either try to tag or avoid the approaching child according to changing rules and unique situations.

In **switching** games, children must stop what they are doing and act in a totally different way. This rule can be applied by using **response shifting**, in which a change in task conditions requires players to stop one movement and perform a different one, or by using **attention shifting**, in which a change in the task requires disengaging attention from one cue and refocusing on a different cue. In response shifting games, children may be asked to

Using switching games can help hone mental skills.

learn two actions in response to two colors (e.g., hopping when a red flag is shown, and skipping when a green flag is shown), and then to reverse their actions (hopping for a green flag, and skipping for a red one). With attention shifting, the type of stimulus cues is changed. For example, a teacher may ask children to hop around or over red hoops or sticks, but to skip in the presence of green hoops or sticks, and then to shift their attention to a new stimulus cue and disregard color altogether (e.g., hopping around hoops and skipping over sticks regardless of color).

Discovery

For many decades, our understanding of movement learning has been dominated by the idea that our brain functions like a computer and stores motor programs that enhance our skills. The concepts of contextual interference and mental control described earlier belong to this theoretical approach to learning. In recent years, advances in **ecological psychology**, which focuses on the interdependence of the individual and the environment, have sharpened our understanding of how people learn to move. Much like the perspective of Jean Piaget described in chapter 1, the ecological point of view is that children are constantly acting and reacting to the world, which helps them solve movement problems. The ecological model has led teachers to emphasize games that promote **exploration**, which is focused investigation, and **divergent discovery**, which encourages multiple solutions to a problem. Central to these games is the fact that a broad range of actions are possible, rather than only one correct solution (Corbetta & Vereijken, 1999).

As you will see in chapters 10 and 11, games that use the principle of discovery allow children to discover and use multiple solutions to a movement problem. Discovery games are typically **open-ended games** in which the starting point, the rules, and the goal are explained, but not how to perform the game. Open-ended games are particularly useful when the children in a group differ in their levels of physical and mental development and their basic abilities. Cognitive engagement generated by applying the principle of discovery learning leads to **dexterity**, which is the ability to find a solution for any situation; that is, to solve an emerging movement problem with available physical and mental resources. Tailoring physical activity games to promote this ability is important because, as explained in chapter 5, physical activity games can have a substantial impact on children's views of themselves. Open-ended movement games and divergent discovery tasks can generate high levels of mental effort and promote the development of specific executive functions and creativity.

Repetition Without Repetition

What does **repetition without repetition** mean? At first blush, it seems to be a contradiction, but it isn't. It means coming up with more than one action plan; the person solves the problem in many ways to find a solution that is best for her and the game situation. For example, in a hurdling task, a child must try to go over the obstacles several times (repetition), but is encouraged to use a novel way to do it each time (repetition without repetition). Searching for as many solutions as possible requires her to inhibit highly learned automatic responses in favor of unusual and novel ones and to continually update the information in her working memory

to avoid repeating formerly chosen solutions. The principle of repetition without repetition fosters the development of executive functions and creativity.

Promoting Movement Creativity

The games in chapters 10 and 11 promote children's creativity, which was defined in chapter 2 as the ability to produce work that is novel and useful. Novelty and usefulness are the key features of a creative product, which is the result of a child's creative ability and creative processes. Considering that the aim of this book is to show how physical activity games can be tailored to aid the development of those cognitive functions that broadly transfer across the life span, creativity games cannot be neglected. In fact, creativity is one of the most intriguing of all human abilities, an extraordinary feature that explains facets of giftedness in various domains and considered a key to success in many professions.

---

ecological psychology—A theoretical approach to psychology that focuses on the interdependence of the individual and the environment.

exploration—Focused investigation through which children gain familiarity with new objects or environments; may lead to play.

divergent discovery—A teaching style that employs open-ended tasks and encourages learners to discover multiple responses to each problem.

open-ended games—Games in which the starting point, the rules, and goals are explained, but not how to perform the game.

dexterity—the ability to find a solution for a problem using available physical and mental resources.

repetition without repetition—A learning approach in which people do not repeat the same solution to a practiced motor task; rather, they solve the problem many times in various ways to identify the best solution(s).

direct instruction method—A method of teaching in which the instructor prescribes how students will accomplish a goal.

exploration and discovery method—A method of teaching in which students are given the opportunity to choose the method that best suits them to accomplish a goal.

In physical activity games that promote creativity, children must go over (or under) obstacles and find as many solutions as possible. Solving the movement problem requires the activation of executive functions. A child who generates a creative idea (e.g., hopping over obstacles while turning and clapping her hands) must think about and plan her movements. The ability to inhibit habitual responses seems to be necessary for producing unique and creative movement solutions (Scibinetti, Tocci, & Pesce, 2011). For this reason, we present both games that specifically challenge inhibitory function, and games more broadly tailored to promote creativity.

Both early play and age-appropriate forms of enriched sport games can promote the development of creativity in children (Memmert, 2011). The games in chapters 10 and 11 challenge creativity by means of both play activities that foster the discovery of divergent solutions without time pressure and team games that require finding individual and cooperative solutions under time pressure. The games for younger children (chapter 10) apply the principle of creativity in more stable situations. The unpredictable, but slowly occurring changes in the play environment give children time to come up with many ways to solve the problem according to the rules. Discovery games for older children (chapter 11) allow them to find new, possibly unexpected, and original ways to achieve goals mostly under time pressure (e.g., put a ball in a can while keeping the other team from doing so, under the limited time demands central to all invasion games).

Teaching for Engagement

Children's mental development follows a clear sequence. Age-related differences in mental processing play an important role in determining the effectiveness of physical activity games. Games that involve discovery learning are especially good for young children; older children are particularly responsive to games that have prescribed outcomes. Age is an important factor in eliciting and maintaining mental engagement. For example, inhibitory abilities that are essential for ignoring environmental distractions and suppressing inappropriate responses come online in infancy and early childhood and can be therefore effectively challenged by means of stopping games at preschool age. Also, preschool and early elementary school (up to 7 years old) is an age of flourishing creativity, whereas later, both biological and environmental factors lead to a reduction in creative potential. Therefore, divergent

discovery and creativity games are particularly appropriate at preschool and kindergarten age. The more complex executive functions of mental shifting and working memory, which involve abilities such as the ability to plan actions, develop and can be challenged by appropriate physical activity games in the elementary school years.

Selecting the Teaching Approach

Imagine that you want to teach young children to become skilled in moving over obstacles, such as hurdles. You can accomplish this in one of two ways: through the **direct instruction method**, in which you prescribe how your students will accomplish the goal, or through the **exploration and discovery method**, in which your students are given the opportunity to choose the method that best suits them. In both cases, variability of practice challenges children's cognition. If you choose the first method, you may decide to teach the skills you consider most effective in going over a hurdle. When the children master the hurdling movements, you can introduce variability by changing hurdle height and distance

Children should be allowed to explore and learn how to solve problems.

or by asking them to alternate running between hurdles with hopping between hurdles. This progression from constant to variable aids both motor learning and executive function development.

Using the exploration and discovery method, children explore the many ways they can find to go over the hurdles. This type of teaching is central to the games designed for children 3 to 6 years of age (chapter 10). These are open-ended games in which you define the starting point (children stay in front of the hurdles), the goal (they must go over the hurdles), and the rule (they must go over the hurdles several times, but can use a novel way to do it each time). To facilitate, and not hinder, the discovery process, you alter the task requirements and the environmental conditions and do not demonstrate possible solutions. If, for example, you use relatively high hurdles, you can expect that most children will attempt only stepping solutions. If you add some low hurdles or use other small objects as obstacles, you can expect children to explore solutions involving other movement skills, such as jumping or hopping over the obstacles in various ways. Recall that the focus of physical activity games is not to teach specific sport skills, but rather, to teach movement skills.

Let's compare the teaching methods used in the hurdling example. In the first case, you used direct instruction (Metzler, 2011), and in the second case, you used exploration and discovery (Bjerke & Vereijken, 2007). This is an important issue that we address in later chapters, because different tactics for introducing variability in movement games challenge children's executive functions in different ways.

Keeping Children Engaged

Teaching is part science and part art. The science of teaching is primarily reflected in the direct instruction method (described in more detail in chapter 7) and primarily applies to teaching games to elementary school–age children (chapter 11). Using this method, teachers organize their lessons to ensure that their students learn specific concepts and actions. The art of teaching that guides children to discover concepts and actions on their own is reflected in the use of methods also described in chapter 7, but primarily applied to teaching games to preschool- and kindergarten-age children (chapter 10). We should not forget, however, that artists can exploit their artistic potential by acquiring specific technical skills. This same premise also holds in the case of the art of teaching. Both meth-

ods of teaching are essential to the development of children's higher-order thinking. A child's capacity to use executive functions to plan and solve problems hinges on teachers' providing both direction (prescription) and freedom (discovery) and can shift between these two ends of the teaching style spectrum.

Previously in this chapter, we spoke about a key challenge teachers face when delivering games to promote children's cognitive development—how to find and maintain the appropriate balance between repetition and change. This issue can be addressed in terms of **stability**, in which games are played until children reach and maintain movement precision, and **flexibility**, in which children are required to adjust movements in response to changes in the game (Bjerke & Vereijken, 2007). Repetition leads to stability and to a reduction of mental effort; change leads to flexibility and to an enhanced involvement of executive functions. To maintain children's cognitively optimal challenge point, teachers must provide game experiences that generate destabilization by changing rules or modifying the game environment after children have reached a given level of stability.

Implications for Educators

Focusing solely on either physical activity or cognitive stimulation to develop children's executive functions will not reap the same benefits as combining quality physical activity and mentally engaging activities. Variability of practice promotes mental engagement and fosters the development of executive functions along with motor skill learning. As we have seen, multidisciplinary advances give teachers ways to apply basic principles of learning, cognitive development, and movement training to reap benefits in the biological, cognitive, and social-affective domains.

We have embedded cognitive training in the physically and socially engaging games described in chapters 10 and 11. In fact, integrated into the games are specific cognitive demands that engage

stability—Movement precision that is achieved during game play.
flexibility—Adjustments of movements as game conditions change.

all core executive functions: response inhibition, working memory, and mental shifting. To ensure that our games challenge these executive functions in an age-appropriate way, we base them on cognitive developmental research at preschool, kindergarten, and elementary school levels (Garon, Bryson, & Smith, 2008; Huizinga, Dolan, & Van der Molen, 2006). The three principles of instruction (i.e., contextual interference, mental control, and discovery) are stressed.

The way games are taught influences their effectiveness in promoting cognitive development. This chapter presented two instructional methods to generate engagement—direct instruction and exploration and discovery—and emphasized that they are not mutually exclusive, but complementary. The challenge for educators who want to use physical activity games to promote children's cognitive development is threefold. They must (1) choose games that involve both motor and cognitive processes, (2) match games to the cognitive and motor developmental level for each child, and (3) make the games either easier or more complex to reach and maintain each child's optimal challenge point. To achieve maximal benefits from instruction, teachers must deliver games that balance repetition and change in ways that promote mental engagement.

Teaching Physical Activity Games for Cognitive Engagement

Cultural anthropologists study the progress of human cultures and societies. Their research has revealed that about 12,000 years ago, humans transitioned from living in nomadic clans as hunter-gatherers to living in established centers of agriculture and commerce. With the rise of complex cultures in various areas of the world came the need for such specialists as farmers, traders, builders, artists, and warriors. In all emerging cultures, there were people who specialized in teaching and gathering knowledge.

Teachers have traditionally been held in high regard and for good reason! For a culture to be stable, specialized knowledge must be passed from one generation to the next. The successful farmer, for instance, knows when, where, and how to plant and harvest crops. Should that specialized agricultural knowledge fail to be passed on to the

next generation of farmers, mistakes will be made, crops will fail, and the community will suffer. For thousands of years, teachers have played a critical role in the storage of knowledge and the instruction of specialized skills. Indeed, those who teach in modern universities can lay claim to being part of the longest-standing legal profession in human history. Access to education has been a trademark of democratic societies, and educational institutions play important roles in communities and governments.

Teaching has been considered a noble profession because teachers help society immensely but are paid little for their efforts. Further, the esteem given to teachers often depends on their areas of specialization. Consider the well-worn adage that was extended by the movie director Woody Allen, when he said, "Those who can, do; those who can't, teach; and those who can't teach, teach physical education." This implies that teaching is a job that requires experience but little specialized skill and that teaching physical education requires neither. This chapter highlights why both of these beliefs are misguided and examines the importance of the teacher in physical activity games. Well-prepared teachers have the knowledge and skills to deliver physical activity experiences that are developmentally appropriate, challenging, and therefore motivating. Quality teaching, as we have said, is part science and part art.

Who Are Physical Activity Teachers?

Physical activity teachers are people who intentionally teach children how to be efficient movers. They come in many forms and are found in many settings. What they have in common are skills and knowledge that can be used to deliver movement-based games in ways that mold the way children think and solve problems.

School-Based Personnel

The success in promoting physical activity in school settings depends on the joint efforts of several specialists. Physical education specialists have been part of school curriculums for more than a half century (Kirk, 2005). Recently, school policy makers in the United States have stressed the need for all teachers, paraprofessionals, and parent volunteers to take on the role of physical activity coaches during class time, recess, and break time. Increasingly, classroom teachers are asked to become physical activity coaches because of the limited time children are formally taught by physical education specialists in preschools, kindergartens, and elementary schools.

Physical Education Specialists

Perhaps the most able and qualified physical activity teachers are those employed in schools as physical education specialists. In almost every state in the United States, physical education specialists are required to be certified to teach the subject (National Association for Sport and Physical Education and American Heart Association, 2012). Similar academic training is required in many other countries. However, being certified is not the same as being qualified. Qualified physical education specialists are teachers who, like their classroom counterparts,

have been trained in physical education teacher education (PETE) programs and demonstrate that they have the knowledge, skills, and disposition to be teachers (National Association for Sport and Physical Education, 2007).

Physical education specialists have the best opportunity to influence children during the school day. They are in an optimal position to deliver quality physical activity experiences, and a majority of schools in the United States and Europe have such teachers. Today's physical education teachers have a broad mission that extends beyond teaching a host of physical activities; they are often called on to teach nutrition, drug awareness, personal hygiene, and other wellness classes to promote healthy lifestyles (Schempp, 2003). As a result of these expanded teaching duties, time allocated to physical activity coaching has been reduced in many schools worldwide.

Recess Coaches

As school time devoted to physical education has decreased, some have suggested that children be given opportunities to be physically active during recess or break times (Beighle, Morgan, Le Masurier, & Pangrazi, 2006). Unfortunately, traditional recess focuses on children's social skills rather than physical activity (Nettlefold et al., 2011; Pellegrini & Bohn, 2005). Moderate-to-vigorous physical activity can occur during recess, but is not central to its purpose.

Nontraditional recess programs have emerged recently that emphasize the role of recess coaches (Hu, 2010). The recess coach is charged with ensuring that recess is organized to help children develop and maintain conflict resolution skills while maximizing physical activity time (Burnette, 2011). Although the effectiveness of recess coaches in promoting children's physical activity has yet to be determined, the approach is praiseworthy and indicates that schools are beginning to see the need for people (e.g., paraprofessionals, parent volunteers) who can provide physical activity instruction.

Classroom Teachers

Classroom teachers are also in key positions to deliver quality physical activity experiences. In some schools, classroom teachers are charged with teaching physical education to their students in addition to math, reading, science, and social studies as part of their daily responsibilities (Graber & Woods, 2013; Hastie & Martin, 2006). In other schools, classroom teachers are encouraged and sometimes tasked with integrating physical activity into other classroom subjects. Preparing classroom teachers to provide quality physical activity opportunities is challenging. However, with proper training and support, nonspecialist physical education teachers (classroom teachers) can provide quality physical activity experiences (Faucette, Nugent, Sallis, & McKenzie, 2002).

Before- and After-School Programs

Physical activity is increasingly provided in before- and after-school programs. Traditionally, adults in these programs serve as supervisors rather than teachers. Nevertheless, out-of-school proctors can be valuable teachers of physical activity. Programs in many locations offer excellent opportunities for children to be physically active. Places such as the Boys and Girls Clubs, Young Men's Christian Associations (YMCAs), and Young Women's Christian Organizations (YWCOs), day care centers, and other community-based programs provide environments that encourage children to be physically active.

In most instances, these program proctors are not certified (licensed) teachers, and they are even less likely to be trained physical education teachers. Typically, little more than a personal background check and a high school diploma are required to be a proctor. Although those working in Boys and Girls Clubs, YMCAs, YWCOs, and community-based programs may be required to have a measure of postsecondary education (especially if in a managerial position), specific training is not required to teach. Regardless, before- and after-school proctors are uniquely positioned to deliver quality physical activity experiences for children—especially with the right preparation and support. For example, the BOKS program is a well-designed before-school physical activity intervention designed for parents and teachers to promote children's academic achievement (www.bokskids.org).

Youth Sport Coaches

Certainly, youth sport is as popular as ever. However, the limited frequency and duration of sport practice and the minimal time spent in moderate-to-vigorous activity restricts children's physical fitness and health gains. In addition, not all children have the opportunity to participate in youth sport. The financial and time commitments (e.g., equipment, multiple practice times, and sport-specific costs) exclude a sizable number of children.

As with after-school proctors, the qualifications needed for coaching youth sport are minimal. Usu-

ally, this is due to a large number of children participating and few adults who volunteer to coach. When youth sport teams need a coach, often a well-meaning parent fills the role. These days, most youth sport organizations offer coach education programs; however, they are typically more focused on first aid, safety, minimally developing skills, and teaching good sporting behaviors than on promoting physical activity. Some youth sport coach certification programs are delivered online and include a brief test at the conclusion (see www.recreation.slco.org/centralcity/youthSports/Coaches_Certificatio.html). Rarely are youth sport coaches required to display a body of knowledge or set of teaching skills for the sports they are coaching. Those who want to acquire that knowledge and those skills are often left to their own devices.

Skills Needed by Physical Activity Teachers

The good news is that many people can contribute to teaching children how to be physically active. The weak link, however, is the lack of sufficient training and preparation for those people. Teaching is a skill set that can be learned (Rink, 2010; Siedentop & Tannehill, 2000). The notion that people are born to teach is as flawed as the notion that anyone can teach. To that end, we identify and discuss the pedagogical (teaching) skills needed for teaching physical activity games that affect children's cognitive development.

Planning and Structuring the Learning Environment

Before conducting a physical activity program for children, teachers much establish their intent. Physical activity games do not just happen. Specific elements must be considered and planned prior to teaching if the games are to have any impact on mental development.

Planning Physical Activity Games

Consider the saying "Failing to plan is planning to fail." Rarely are goals achieved without having a plan. For example, if you want to drive from the East Coast of the United States to Yellowstone National Park in Wyoming, you would need a plan for getting there. Your arrival would depend on a number of elements that you must consider and evaluate. Selecting your route, choosing a vehicle, and gathering resources would be important. Then you need to answer some questions: Do you want the trip to be scenic, or do you want to arrive as quickly as possible? Are you traveling by car or bike? Answers to these questions would affect your plan. To plan well, a goal needs to be identified and the steps needed to achieve the goal need to be determined. This holds true for teaching physical activity games to children.

Before planning physical activity game sessions for children, teachers must decide what they want the children to experience. Based on evidence provided in previous chapters, the games should be mentally engaging, foster skill learning, and elicit moderate-to-vigorous levels of physical activity. The next step is to choose games to teach. This decision depends on such factors as (1) the children's previous experiences, (2) the children's developmental levels, (3) the available space, (4) the available equipment, and (5) the number of children in the class. Perhaps the greatest challenge is to accommodate differences among children's physical and mental developmental levels. In a typical third-grade physical education class, most of the children are 8 or 9 years old; thus, they share a number of physical, emotional, and cognitive developmental characteristics. However, even children who are nearly the same age differ in their backgrounds, skill levels, and knowledge. In before- and after-school programs, children may find themselves in multiage or multigrade groups; in such cases, the spread among the children's physical, cognitive, and emotional developmental levels is quite wide.

Once the games have been chosen, teachers must consider how to deliver them and modify them, and how to make changes should the games and children fail to match (which can happen to even the most experienced physical activity teachers). During a 45-minute activity period, each activity must have a purpose, and the teacher must have a step-by-step protocol for demonstrating and explaining the game. Also required are clues to look for that indicate when the game should be stopped and reexplained, when questions should be answered, or when the game should be modified.

Planning the Physical Environment

For dynamic games, the physical environment and instructional space is of utmost importance. Thinking about, planning for, and preparing the game environment is important for two reasons. First, the content (games planned) and the space are linked. Children will be moving about (sometimes quickly) and concentrating on evading, chasing, holding objects, and carrying out strategies. For this reason planning game-play space is critical. The space available often dictates whether a particular game can be played. Nothing is worse than showing up to teach a game and realizing five minutes before the children arrive that the plan will not work because the physical environment is either insufficient or unsafe. Even worse is realizing this after the children are engaged in play. The second reason the game environment is important is that it affects children's enjoyment. We know that children remain motivated when they are enjoying the game.

Part of planning also includes ensuring that the play area is free of rocks, glass, sticks, and other objects commonly found on outside play areas. Because children will be moving, it is likely that a child will fall in even the safest physical activity class. Even falls on a carpeted gymnasium floor can be painful, but falls on pavement or grass fields are even more so.

A key factor that determines the quality of the games described in chapters 10 and 11 is the level of physical activity. A well-structured class includes demonstrations, explanations, and questioning time. Noninstructional time is also part of a well-planned and well-implemented lesson. For example, the time required to go from one game to another requires a regrouping of teams or partners and the addition or deletion of equipment. These transitions are unavoidable, but the key is to ensure that they are done as efficiently as possible. We provide three recommendations for planning and organizing the physical environment for games.

The teacher should first count the number of pieces of equipment needed for playing all the games (and versions of those games) planned for the day. Second, the teacher should set out all equipment so that it is ready to be retrieved safely at the right time. This means having the equipment properly grouped and spaced so no traffic jams occur when children are retrieving their equipment. If possible, the teacher should have the first activity set up before the children arrive so they can begin the game as soon as the demonstration and explanation are over. The third recommendation is to have the children retrieve and replace equipment. They can also help with transitions that require altering the physical environment; this increases the time available for games. However, keep in mind that children must be taught the procedure so that it becomes routine. Explaining to them that more time will be left to play the games when they can complete the transition tasks quickly is one way to motivate them to help.

Another mini-strategy is to provide a motivational objective that makes the transition tasks

Preparing for physical activity games means structuring the time with children so that there is time to help them understand the game, as well as having the physical environment set up and ready for play.

more gamelike. For example, the teacher might say, "When I say go, I would like you all to put your polo sticks down and quickly and safely get a Nerf ball from the far wall. I will give you 18 seconds to do this; let's try to beat that time. Ready, set, go!" The teacher then follows those directions with an audible countdown and offers praise after the students have completed the task. Even if it takes them 20 seconds, it's not necessarily a failure because it resulted in a quick transition. Without a protocol, such a transition could take nearly 45 seconds. With five transitions during a 45-minute class, a savings of 25 seconds per transition adds just over two full minutes that can be dedicated to physical and cognitive engagement.

Managing the Educational Environment

Often the layperson observing an educational environment determines its value (effectiveness) on the basis of whether the class runs smoothly and there is little off-task behavior. Undoubtedly, managing a class is a condition for learning. Without proper management, children can become bored and demotivated to be physically active. However, it is essen-

tial to remember that a well-managed educational environment (e.g., gymnasium, classroom, outside play area) is a prerequisite to quality teaching—not the sole indicator of it.

No matter how developmentally appropriate the physical activity games are or how well they engage children, their effects will be weakened if the teacher cannot manage the pupils and the environment. A well-managed class is one that allows children to be both physically and mentally engaged. To maximize engaged time, physical activity teachers must (1) establish behavioral expectations and consequences, (2) institute and use a clear set of signals, (3) visibly display enthusiasm, (4) reinforce appropriate behavior, and (5) create an inviting climate.

Establishing Behavior Expectations and Consequences

Just as in the classroom or any other learning environment, behavior expectations and consequences for not meeting them must be set, taught, and reinforced in physical activity sessions. Without these, less time is spent playing and learning the games. Furthermore, children are less likely to be motivated to participate when they feel unsafe, and this runs counter to our objectives.

Four simple guidelines help physical activity teachers create safe learning environments. (1) Behavior expectations (rules) should be few. Most children cannot remember more than four rules. (2) The expectations need to be stated in short, simple, clear language to reach children of various ages and language skill levels. (3) The expectations should be stated positively. Traditionally, we think of rules as don'ts rather than dos. Stating them as expectations (e.g., do be respectful) makes it very clear what behaviors are anticipated and lends a more positive meaning to the concept of rules. (4) The language must be general to cover a number of possibilities. For example, an appropriate expectation might be: Be safe. This expectation is brief, clear, and positively stated. At the same time, being safe covers a lot of ground, such as keeping shoelaces tied, not chewing gum or eating candy, and following the rules of the game. Teachers should be careful, however, not to confuse *general* with *vague*. The rule is clear, make no mistake, but *safe* could mean different things in different contexts, and those contexts must be discussed with children.

Setting expectations is not enough; teachers must teach them to their students. Behavior expectations must be introduced, discussed, and, if possible, posted. Reviewing the rules at the start of each session should not take much time if they are few, brief, and positively stated. This will ensure that the children know what is expected of them.

Setting and teaching expectations will not guarantee that rules will not be broken; it only decreases the likelihood. Children should be held accountable for meeting expectations, and when they do not, they should face consequences. As with expectations, consequences should be communicated (via drawings, written statements, or verbal statements) in brief but clear language that is easily understood by all children and (in the case of drawings and written statements) posted throughout the learning space. The consequences also should represent a fair but hierarchical and systematic procedure that implies that one slip-up does not result in a major consequence or dismissal from the program, but that continual failure to meet the behavior expectations will not be tolerated.

One note about the term *consequence* is that it connotes a negative experience. However, it is helpful to teach children that positive behavior results in positive consequences. Although reward systems are used by many, the simplest reward is uninterrupted physical activity playing time. That is, "the usual" is a positive consequence for meeting behavior expectations.

Instituting Signals

The whistle is traditionally associated with physical education teachers and coaches. Even though it has a shrill sound that strikes fear in the hearts of many who have unpleasant memories of their school physical education or sport experiences, it serves a purpose. As we have mentioned, the physical activity learning environment is different from that of the typical classroom because of the dynamic nature of the content. Physical activity games, especially the ones presented in this text, encourage children to make noise, move quickly from place to place, and have fun while becoming better game players. When children have fun, they laugh, and it can get loud. Furthermore, when they are moving with a purpose, their attention is focused on playing the game and the combination of noise level and their focus necessitates something other than a verbal command to grab their attention. Thus, they need to learn clear signals that represent commands such as "Start" and "Stop." Yes, whistles work because the sound is noticeable, and they are easy to use. Other options are horns, drums, clapping sequences, and flashing lights.

Some advocate turning on and off music as a signal. The advantage of this is twofold: music can easily be controlled via a remote device from many places in the gym, and children enjoy moving to music. However, there is an important disadvantage. The music must be loud enough so that children notice when it is turned off. Yet, most of the games in this book require children to communicate with one another, and loud music renders that quite difficult. Therefore, we advise that music signals be used sparingly. We present some examples in which music can be used in the second and third games sections of chapter 10.

Displaying Enthusiasm

Some people claim that dogs can smell fear in humans. Whether it is true remains a debate for animal scientists and dog lovers. Although there is no evidence to indicate that children can "smell" enthusiasm in a teacher, it would be hard to argue that children do not sense enthusiasm in their teachers. When a teacher is enthusiastic, children are more likely to mirror that enthusiasm, and vice versa.

Enthusiasm is often thought of as a personality trait that is hard to define but easy to identify. A person's behavior indicates enthusiasm to others, and that behavior is undoubtedly influenced by age. Children are likely to attend to tangible clues in teachers, such as smiling, knowing names, laughing (when appropriate), and reassuring them about how great it is to be doing those activities. Although careful, thoughtful planning and having a well-run classroom are without question hallmarks of an enthusiastic teacher, enthusiasm needs to be both genuine and easily perceived. Teachers should identify daily behaviors that children can see and make them conclude that they are enthusiastic about what they are teaching. Their enthusiasm must be explicitly clear; children often miss subtle clues.

Reinforcing Appropriate Behavior

"Stop that. Maria, don't bother LeBron." "You're not supposed to be talking, Ellis. Shh." "Class, please be quiet . . . Shh!" At one time or another, you have probably heard teachers use similar expressions, and we would be willing to bet that all teachers have used these phrases at one time or another. They are typical responses to pupils' off-task behavior. However, continually commenting on inappropriate behaviors is just a reactive tactic. Most classes consist of an overwhelming majority of children exhibiting appropriate behavior (both social and skill). Unfortunately, it is easier to remember the child who always got in trouble and not that he or she was just 1 among 25.

Using a proactive approach of reinforcing appropriate behavior is a good way to accomplish two important managerial tasks. Publicly pointing out pupils' appropriate behaviors reminds all of them of correct and incorrect actions. Spotlighting good behavior (especially of those who do not always exhibit it) is a motivational tactic. Not surprisingly, teachers who recognize appropriate behaviors foster a positive classroom climate.

Creating an Inviting Climate

Successful physical activity games classes encourage children to be physically and mentally engaged. This atmosphere is developed over a period of time and cannot be established in one lesson. Teachers must intentionally plan and act and hold the children accountable for exhibiting the behaviors

Part of managing a classroom involves modeling enthusiasm about games and encouraging good behavior and a positive environment.

that contribute to such an environment. Chapter 4 addressed the importance of creating an appropriate motivational climate to promote learning and ensure enjoyment. In this section we discuss how to create a positive climate.

Unlike classroom performance, the performance of game content is quite public. When a child takes a spelling test, only three people, at most, are informed about her performance: the child, her teacher, and possibly a parent. A child could go an entire school year without any of her classmates having any idea about her spelling ability. However, in physical education and when teaching physical activity games, children are interacting with both the content (skills and strategies for using them) and one another. Their abilities are exposed to others, which could deter some from wanting to be physically active. To many children, especially those less skilled or knowledgeable, this outward display is a demotivating factor and can be a source of fear. For others, it is an opportunity to show their competence. Both groups of children are best served by a class atmosphere that is welcoming and emotionally safe. Children should be encouraged to try and fail without fear of chastisement or bullying. All students should have opportunities to display their skills and knowledge. Perhaps more important, classmates should not be permitted to make fun of others' abilities. Teacher silence is tacit approval of such behavior. Although they will not always hear or see it all, teachers must remain alert for such negative behavior and shut it down immediately.

Selecting an Approach to Teaching

There are numerous approaches to teaching physical activity, and most are supported by considerable research (Mosston & Ashworth, 1986). Regardless of the method used to teach physical activity, it must be developmentally appropriate and align well with the intended outcomes. This chapter introduces two instructional methods that provide the flexibility and options teachers need when working with children who differ in age and ability. The exploration and discovery method (Bjerke & Vereijken, 2007), introduced in chapter 6, maximizes physical activity in preschool- and kindergarten-age children. This method helps children between the ages of 3 and 6 years move smoothly from spontaneous play to structured game activities. The direct instruction method of teaching (Metzler, 2011) maximizes physical activity time in children between the ages

of 7 and 11 who have completed the transition from spontaneous play to deliberate play and practice.

Teaching physical activity games well depends on the ability to tie the appropriate teaching method to the children's characteristics (e.g., age, experience, individual differences), the games (e.g., tag games, ball games, improvisation activities), and the goals of the games (e.g., motor skill learning, executive function development). Good teaching reflects the ability to competently shift between different but complementary teaching methods. With the direct instruction method, the teacher describes the path that leads to a goal; with the exploration and discovery method, children create their own paths. A common feature of the games presented in chapters 10 and 11 is problem solving. Challenges posed by means of both exploration/discovery and direct instruction give each child an opportunity to explore and overcome the challenge in his or her own unique way.

Exploration and Discovery Method

As introduced in chapter 6, direct instruction and exploration and discovery are two sides of the same coin—both are valid methods of teaching children. The games in chapters 10 and 11 maximize the use of both methods. The processes of physical and mental development are complex; as a result, they require teachers to use learning approaches that best fit each child at a specific point in time. The following sections describe how to modulate and properly constrain or release children's freedom to help them discover solutions on their own and develop creativity.

Teacher as Facilitator and the Discovery-Promoting Climate

Problem solving and mental effort are key concepts in games and many sports. Success is often determined by a child's ability to find many ways to reach a goal. Games that offer many options increase mental engagement and meaningful reflection, which are fundamental ingredients of **core-based motor teaching-learning** (Eloranta & Jakkola, 2007). It offers numerous problem-solving situations that engage children in meaningful reflection and lead them to focus on practice and process rather than on a final outcome, and is central to our approach for teaching games. The teacher who uses the discovery model acts as a facilitator who primes and supports children's discovery and creativity. The games presented in chapter 10 for preschool- and kindergarten-age children especially focus on promoting creativity in action and movement, encouraging children to seek their own solutions without the pressure of time. The games for elementary school–aged children presented in chapter 11 promote the discovery of solutions to game problems generated by opponents in a changing environment under time pressure.

Promoting creativity in movement and action is challenging because there is not a single correct response. The teacher's job is to create an environment that supports children's exploration and creative processes through movement and action using appropriate self-generated strategies, tasks, and cues. Observations of effective instructional methods by Tocci and Scibinetti (2003, 2007) led them to highlight key ways that teachers can help children think and act creatively. Their model highlights key points to promoting movement creativity, which should be integrated when put into practice:

- *Type and progression of game activities*—To promote creativity, teachers need to use semistructured, open-ended games in which only the starting conditions and the goal are indicated. They should not explain how to reach the goal. Giving children a goal constrains their creative process and focuses their efforts on a specific theme. By not instructing them in how to reach the goal, the teacher gives them the opportunity to follow many action paths. When they become more skilled, they can move from open-ended activities with goals defined by the teachers to activities that are open at both the beginning and the end; that is, they must also search for and define the goal.

Creativity-promoting game activities must be adapted to children's ages. The games for preschool- and kindergarten-age children in chapter 10 have features of symbolic, or pretend, play, which dominates at that age. We propose fable and **sociodramatic play**, which is social pretend play, common from around 3 years of age, in which children take on the roles of others (e.g., parents, siblings, teachers) in make-believe situations characterized by imaginary scenes. Real-life situations can be the starting point for a child to pretend play—for example, pretending that a ball is something else and using it in unusual ways. Initially, the teacher may limit children's range of solutions, and as they learn to play, the teacher can vary game demands and provide more possibilities. Young children start the learning process with very few actions; however, as they explore the boundaries of the game, they come to see many new ways of moving and acting.

- *Teaching strategies*—As facilitators, teachers can use the following teaching strategies to help children develop their creative processes:

  ° *Checklists*—Using a checklist consists of choosing a list of action words or descriptive words that are applicable to the game activity. For example, children can be instructed to move from one area to another in various ways based on an action word (e.g., crawling, hopping) and a descriptive word (e.g., tired, excited).

  ° *Forced relationships*—Using forced relationships entails connecting make-believe conditions. For example, children can be asked to move in the playing area while pretending they are on the sea and must reach an island.

  ° *Analogies*—Analogies involve generating unusual associations as children pretend to be objects or other people, to act out an emotion, or to move in a space different from the playing area. For example, they can be asked to move like a ball, a stretched elastic band, a log, or an old person; to show anger; or to act as they would at home or on the way to school.

  ° *Attribute listing*—Attribute listing entails focusing on a specific object or body part. For example, children can be asked to move around faster or slower, make large or small movements, or touch the floor only with a specified number and type of body part (e.g., moving on all fours, or only on their knees).

These teaching strategies can be combined in many ways. For example, the attribute list and checklist strategies can be combined by asking the children to move slowly on their knees (an attribute of their bodies) while pretending they are tired (a descriptive word).

---

core-based motor teaching-learning—A model of movement-based teaching and learning that offers numerous problem-solving situations that engage children in meaningful reflection and lead them to focus on practice and process rather than on a final outcome.

sociodramatic play—Social pretend play, common from around 3 years of age, in which children take on the roles of others (e.g., parents, siblings, teachers) in make-believe situations characterized by imaginary scenes.

- *Creativity-promoting environment*—Organize a creativity-promoting environment by doing the following:
  - ° *Objects*—Using a variety of objects from sports as well as everyday life. Promoting the search for different ways to use objects helps children overcome habits that hinder their thinking about alternative, less usual uses of objects.
  - ° *Music*—Using music to generate an emotionally loaded experience of improvisation.
  - ° *Perception*—Exploiting visual, acoustic, and tactile perceptions to develop children's ongoing creative process.
  - ° *Space*—Using space in a way that limits or frees children's actions (e.g., varying the boundaries of or the degree of light in the playing area).
- *Creativity-promoting climate*—Foster a creativity-promoting environment by doing the following:
  - ° *Cooperative learning*—**Cooperative learning**, an educational approach based on structuring positive interdependence among learners who work collectively toward a common goal. Cooperation enhances both the quantity and the quality (originality) of actions and allows groups of children to work together to reach the goal of the activity, capitalizing on the differences in skill levels. The search for cooperative solutions may turn into an exploration of new actions that can be used in ways that would not be possible for an individual child. The search for individual solutions, even though more difficult, promotes autonomy, self-confidence, and risk taking.
  - ° *Variation of time constraints*—To generate novel insights and evaluate their appropriateness, children need time. Setting time limits generates pressure that limits the emergence of insight that results in the execution of a creative movement action.
  - ° *Teacher's role*—Defining the teacher's role as a facilitator of the creative process. To facilitate the creative process, teachers must be attentive to the children's needs and their individual learning potential, encourage them to remain on task, help them enjoy effort and learning (**task orientation**), and use teaching methods that promote autonomous learning and evaluation, integration, and cooperation.

  - ° *Feedback*—Feedback that promotes creativity differs from error feedback, which is usually given to get children to precisely model specific movements and sport skills. Rather than giving information about the only correct movement performance, teachers can guide children toward the discovery of new ideas, directions, and alternatives.
  - ° *Suspension of judgment*—Last but not least, suspending judgment about the quality of a child's performance. Suspending judgment is one of the most powerful ways to promote the creative process. A child must feel free to explore a variety of solutions and clearly perceive that the teacher considers all attempts equally correct and valuable as long as they are linked to the game activity.

Text provided by N. Tocci and P. Scibinetti

Direct Instruction Method

The direct instruction method is a systematic way of approaching physical activity instruction that is characterized by six key elements. This method is considered one of the easiest ways to teach and is perhaps the most widely used method for teaching physical activity. It includes (1) a review of previously learned material, (2) a presentation of new content and skills, (3) initial pupil practice, (4) feedback and corrections, (5) independent pupil practice, and (6) periodic reviews during class time. The use of these elements is underpinned by a set of general teaching skills that, when combined, allow for the delivery of games that promote mental engagement.

The direct instruction method addresses two major misconceptions regarding teaching. The first is that good management is good teaching. Although management is an essential element in teaching, it is insufficient by itself. The second misconception is that physically active children are learning. Consider the saying "Never mistake activity for achievement." To learn from their actions,

---

cooperative learning—An educational approach based on structuring positive interdependence among learners who work collectively toward a common goal.

task orientation—A motivational disposition that leads people to focus on mastery through effort and persistence, doing their best, progressing over time, solving problems, and learning.

children must do more than simply be physically active. They must be mentally engaged in the control of their movements. "Move with a purpose" is a phase teachers commonly use to help their students understand when and why one action is better than another. What the teacher does during the delivery of the game is critical.

Beyond good planning and management skills, a set of basic teaching skills is important for knowing when to extend the tasks, providing appropriate and valid feedback, and noticing when children are bored or frustrated because the game is too easy or too difficult. The direct instruction method identifies essential pedagogical skills for teaching physical activity games.

Demonstration and Explanation

Demonstration and explanation are like peanut butter and jelly: they are better together than alone. To communicate clearly with children, physical activity teachers must provide a show and tell. At the same time, they must be clear and succinct while not sacrificing game time. As games are altered and become more complex, explanations and demonstrations usually take longer. Thus, teachers must find effective yet efficient ways of communicating game information to children.

To comprehend the structure and rules of the game, children need a visual display of the game and any important skills involved. Ideally, teachers should take part in demonstrations, but they do not have to be the sole source. Using children to demonstrate how to play games provides models children can relate to. Also, the teacher can explain what is supposed to happen while children demonstrate.

Quality demonstrations show the game in segments that are then put together to show the full version of the game. For example, a demonstration of a game that requires an offensive team and a defensive team is probably best shown initially with only one participant from each side. This isolates and clearly identifies the two roles the children will eventually play. Perhaps after demonstrating with one-person teams once or twice and answering questions and checking for understanding, the teacher can add more players to show how the game looks with more players in the area.

Demonstrations need not always be live. Other sources of information can be used, such as videos and pictures. Relying solely on videos and still pictures is not advised, however. An effective demonstration is accompanied by clear explanations of how and why certain actions occur. Further, teachers have to make certain that their language is clear and their vocabulary is developmentally appropriate when explaining a game. A limited number of points should be communicated at one time. Even though games may have many rules and restrictions, a well-delivered explanation would summarize them as brief points. The teacher should begin by explaining only the most important rules before moving on to others. An overlooked aspect of verbal explanations is the use of a consistent vocabulary. Referencing terms used in previously played activities is a good way to increase children's familiarity with a new game and perhaps help them learn other game-specific terms more quickly.

Observation and Analysis

Eliciting the maximum benefits of physical activity games requires that the teacher follow, or see, what is happening in the game. Seeing in this context is not merely watching; seeing children play involves witnessing how well they are playing, whereas watching is simply making sure they are safe and on task. Of course, observing for safety and on-task behavior is important and, in fact, the first thing to do when the children are engaged in a game. After determining (and monitoring) safety and on-task behavior, teachers can then make observations and provide guidance regarding children's game play. Teachers who concentrate on seeing children playing a game are in a better position to make appropriate alterations to the game and to determine whether the children are ready to move to a more complex version of the game, as well as to decide what questions and feedback to provide to enhance their learning.

Feedback and Questioning

The rate at which a skill is learned and the quality of the skill depend on feedback about performance. Although the outcome of a game can provide some feedback, this information alone is insufficient for optimal learning. Feedback that describes the quality of the child's movements is critical to comprehending the game. Teachers are in a position to provide extra feedback that children can use to improve their understanding of game challenges and how they can be overcome. A nice bonus is that when teachers provide feedback, they indicate that they care about the children and their improvement.

There are two ways to use information to enhance children's learning. One way is to provide specific feedback directly to the child about skill performance and tactical decisions. An example of this would be, Fiona, that was an excellent use of the head fake to evade the chaser. Even if Fiona knew she did it well, the teacher's affirmation is reinforcing and makes it more likely that Fiona will use that skill in future play. Providing this type of information is only possible if the teacher is seeing Fiona play the game and exactly what she is doing well, rather than just watching her. Another way to enhance learning is through questioning. The teacher can purposely form questions that require students to think about them, contrast them with their current knowledge or performance, and then use the answers to inform themselves. If the questions are asked and answered in front of the class, other children can use the exchange to compare, contrast, and alter how they play the game. An example of how this may look is illustrated here:

> Mr. Moak notices that Fiona is having difficulty evading a tagger because she is not using a head fake or another type of feint. After seeing this happen a couple of times, he sees it again exhibited by two other children. Mr. Moak stops the game and says to Jose, a child he saw using multiple types of feints who was rarely tagged, "Jose, I noticed that you got tagged only once. Tell me and the class some of the things you did to stay away from the taggers on the other team." Jose replies, "I used fakes to escape." Although that was the answer Mr. Moak was looking for, it was not enough information to help the others. He probes deeper and asks Jose, "OK, why did you use a fake?" But, before Jose can answer, Brenda, who is also participating in the group discussion, raises her hand and Mr. Moak calls on her. "Because he wanted them to think he was going in one direction, but then he went in another," says Brenda. With these two questions, Mr. Moak knows he has nearly collected all the information he wanted children to hear. To make sure he lets Jose know that his answer was also acceptable (and not stymie possible further responses) he follows up Jose's original reply with one more probe informed by an incident that he saw during the game. He says, "Good idea, Jose, but what type of fake did you use when you were being chased by Kevin? Please show it to us."

In this instance, Mr. Moak could have presented the information directly to Fiona and the others, and he could have had Jose immediately show the class how to do a head fake. However, the questioning process not only informed the rest of the class but also allowed Mr. Moak to thoroughly check

for Jose's understanding of both the skill (the head fake) and the tactics of the game (when to use the head fake).

The decision to use either direct feedback or questioning to inform children about performance depends on the context and the teacher. As part of the art of teaching, a physical activity teacher must know the children in the class and determine whether they have sufficient awareness to answer questions or whether being told directly would be more appropriate. Although questions can be mentally stimulating, providing information directly may be necessary before such questions can be useful.

Ensuring Adherence to the Model

By now you probably understand that for games to help children learn, teaching matters. Physical activity alone cannot be counted on to foster children's mental development. Both the delivery and the deliverer of the physical activity games are important. Without a conscious and intentional delivery, the prospect of mental engagement is decreased and children who are less able or knowledgeable are more likely to be excluded.

The teacher's job is to present the game clearly and quickly, let children play it, determine what should or could be changed in the game, and then present the game's new form while asking questions to promote students' thinking. Perhaps the easiest way to check on program fidelity is through a major-element checklist. An example of a checklist is presented in figure 7.1. Checklists have a long history of use in public school teacher performance evaluations and are easy to use (van der Mars, 1989). A checklist provides information about the presence or absence of a behavior, not the quality or duration of that behavior. Regardless, tracking how faithful they are to the instructional method they are using not only helps teachers teach the games correctly but also enhances their ability to teach within the method.

Enhancing the Effectiveness of Teaching Methods

Teaching is a social science in which the effectiveness of pedagogical skills is not a yes-or-no determination. Three factors shape the effectiveness of teaching physical activity games: (1) recognizing the need for alteration, (2) having sufficient content knowledge, and (3) appreciating children's sense of fairness and dominance.

Direct Instruction Model Teacher Fidelity Behavior Checklist

Name: _____ Date: _____

Benchmark	Criteria met?	Comments (e.g., what went well, what didn't go so well, changes you made during the lesson, what you need to do to improve)
The game was broken down into a series of small learning tasks leading to larger learning goals.	☐ Yes ☐ No ☐ Partially	
The previous experience content was reviewed.	☐ Yes ☐ No ☐ Partially	
A clear and effective presentation of the game was given.	☐ Yes ☐ No ☐ Partially	
A brisk pace was used through content progression.	☐ Yes ☐ No ☐ Partially	
Much positive and corrective feedback was used.	☐ Yes ☐ No ☐ Partially	
Learning tasks had a mastery criterion.	☐ Yes ☐ No ☐ Partially	
Regular reviews of the game were made.	☐ Yes ☐ No ☐ Partially	
Learners had high rates of engagement during the game.	☐ Yes ☐ No ☐ Partially	
Initial practice of the game was led by the teacher.	☐ Yes ☐ No ☐ Partially	
Later practice tasks allowed students to play independently.	☐ Yes ☐ No ☐ Partially	
Students mastered the game.	☐ Yes ☐ No ☐ Partially	

Figure 7.1   The direct instruction model.

Recognizing the Need for Alteration

Central to physical activity games that promote cognitive development is the teacher's ability to recognize when a game needs to be altered. A good teacher knows when to make an alteration in the activity to provide the right amount of challenge. Recall from chapter 6 the central issue of balancing repetition and change to help children acquire and properly alternate stability and flexibility in their movement behaviors. Changing the game is critical and depends on several factors. Teachers must be able to recognize when the game is starting to become stale and children are no longer challenged physically or mentally, or both. A game might also need tinkering to make it safer or more inclusive. Without the ability to modify a game, a teacher risks demotivating children who are then turned off to playing games in general. Once this occurs, games devolve into supervised recreation rather than play for learning.

Learning the cues that signal when to alter a physical activity game is complex. A good starting point is to pay close attention to factors that indicate boredom, frustration, and staleness. One indicator is simply inactivity. When children are either bored or frustrated, they often stop participating. If a child is standing still or moving with obviously minimal effort, she is likely either bored because the game is not challenging enough or frustrated because the game is too complicated. By no means is this an absolute, but when a physical activity teacher notices one child minimizing her effort, that should be a clue that something might be amiss. If a teacher notices more than one child doing this, it should be a red flag that an alteration might be due. Conversely, a child might be acting with vigorous effort but inefficiently. This is also a clear indicator that the child is not sufficiently challenged or perhaps overly challenged by the game or does not comprehend how to play it. Both behavioral inactivity and inefficiency are undesirable and serve as cues for the need to alter game conditions.

One caution should be noted, however. Teachers can best determine whether inactivity is due to the level of challenge if they know their children. It may be that a child is acting in this manner because something is emotionally or physically bothersome. For example, if this occurs toward the end of a vigorous class, inactivity might be an indicator of fatigue. Regardless, the teacher should notice and respond to this child's behavior in some way.

Having Sufficient Content Knowledge

Undoubtedly, content knowledge is imperative for good teaching. As noted previously, many adults are in positions to teach physical activity games but lack a depth and breadth of physical activity content knowledge. This book provides the content knowledge needed for teaching physical activity games. The games provided in chapters 10 and 11 link research and application. We are aware that increasing content knowledge is more than simply replicating activities from a book or website. A teacher must be able to break down physical activity games and understand the skills and tactics needed for playing them, as well as which games are predicated on the mastery of others. To this aim, we provide alterations of each basic game and information on the physical, cognitive, emotional, and social demands of those alterations.

Most of the games described in this book require the use of locomotor, nonlocomotor, and manipulative skills that are relatively straightforward. However, the tactics and strategies needed for instructing these games require careful thought and consideration. Teachers who invest time in learning the direct instruction method and the exploration and discovery method can profoundly influence their students. Good teaching is more than just rolling out the ball and letting children have play time.

Appreciating Children's Sense of Fairness and Dominance

Children have a keen but not necessarily refined sense of injustice, and when they sense they are not being treated fairly, the results can be devastating. At best, children will properly express their dissatisfaction with the situation. At worst, they will verbally or physically express their outrage. A child who experiences injustice in game environments at a young age may develop a negative attitude toward being physically active.

Although a child's sense of injustice might be acute, it may differ from that of other children and certainly that of adults. An adult who loses a game because of a questionable officiating call may understand that even officials make mistakes, but a young child is likely to interpret the bad call as an intentional and personal attack. Thus, teachers must be aware of how the games are being played and whether any children are constantly finding themselves on the losing side or are rarely able to fully participate because older, stronger, or more skilled children are dominating.

It is important not to confuse this point with the notion that every child must win. For any game to be worthy of participation, it must be fair. Losing hurts much less when a child believes that the teams were fairly built, the rules were clear and adhered to by all participants, and the officials were judging the game as objectively as possible. Unfortunately, in many before- and after-school environments, as mentioned earlier, children of various ages and developmental levels are often placed together. This can lead to teams in which 7-year-olds are playing against 10- and 11-year-olds who are stronger, faster, and more experienced. Heterogeneous classes are not always ideal and often have the potential for games to appear (and sometimes actually be) unfair.

Considerations for Implementing Physical Activity Game Programs

A well-developed physical activity game program requires that administrators and teachers be aware of some pre- and corequisites beyond the games and pedagogical approach used. Three main criteria are important for novice teachers or youth sport coaches to learn before teaching physical activity games: **(1) know how to allocate time to teaching the games in such a way that they are not presented as recreation, (2) emphasize the importance of being physically active, and (3) watch themselves or another teacher model the process.**

The real world of before- and after-school programs and youth sport programs is full of obstacles that can hinder the training of physical activity teachers. These obstacles are difficult to overcome even with maximal motivation and commitment. However, it can happen with the proper technology and a teacher educator (individual or group) who understands the teacher's workplace and can navigate within it. Three obstacles are particularly common in many environments. The first is the lack of time for deep discussions about teaching, given the need to care for children. The second obstacle is grouping children of widely varying ages and skill levels (e.g., physical, cognitive, and emotional maturity; skill level; game-play experience). The third obstacle is a lack of resources. Minimal equipment or space (or both) can lessen the quality of physical activity programs. All of these obstacles working together make learning how to teach, and teaching, physical activity an undertaking that is conducted in an ever-changing environment.

Finally, teacher training is crucial. Ideally, novice physical activity teachers should be trained by experienced teacher educators who can model the instructional method and then act as mentors as they acquire the necessary skills. This process should occur over a period of weeks, during which the novice teacher gradually takes full responsibility for game delivery. Unfortunately, many environments make teacher training difficult. In out-of-school programs, for instance, teachers are likely to be people with other part-time jobs or responsibilities that conflict with teacher training. We look forward to the increased use of social media and online training to reach inexperienced physical activity teachers. Through the use of individual instructional supervision techniques, communication through e-mail, and digital video, novice physical activity teachers can be prepared to implement quality physical activity games.

Integration With SHAPE America Guidelines

The Society of Health and Physical Educators (SHAPE America, 2014) was formerly known as the American Alliance for Health, Physical Education, Recreation and Dance (AAHPERD) and includes the suborganization formerly known as the National Association for Sport and Physical Education (NASPE). SHAPE America is the leading organization for the development of standards and guidelines for sport and physical education in the United States. Its membership consists of sport and physical education professionals who work in a variety of environments, as well as those training to become professionals. Among other goals, SHAPE America exists to (1) define, promote, and recognize best practice and professional excellence in physical education, sport, and physical activity; (2) support and disseminate research contributing to the advancement of knowledge and evidence-based practice in physical education, sport, and physical activity; and (3) facilitate the establishment of public policy that supports physical education, sport, and physical activity.

Toward that end, SHAPE America and its members established the National Standards & Grade-Level Outcomes for K-12 Physical Education, which outline what K-12 children "should know, and be able to do as a result of instruction in physical education" (2014, p. 3). The standards describe a physically literate person as someone who has "the

knowledge, skills, and confidence to enjoy a lifetime of healthful physical activity" (p. 11). SHAPE America's "Physical Education Position Statement" (2011) provides an overview on the "whole child initiative," which is based on the assumption that physical education is critical to educating the whole child. Our physical activity games are in line with this fundamental statement, because they promote children's development in a variety of domains.

Although you may not be a physical education teacher, if you are using the physical activity games in this text, you are teaching content that can contribute to children's development into physically educated people. Therefore, at the beginning of chapters 10 and 11, we provide a table that illustrates how the games in each chapter align with the SHAPE America guidelines, and specifically how the games align with the child expectations and sample performance outcomes for the two age groups targeted (ages 3 to 6 and 7 to 11).

Developing the Physically Engaged and Literate Child

Broadly, SHAPE America's position is that children "should engage in daily physical activity that promotes movement skillfulness and foundations of health-related fitness" (NASPE, 2009, p. 4). The National Guidelines for Physical Activity, both for younger and older children, recommend the FITT model, which addresses (1) frequency, or how often children should engage in physical activity; (2) intensity, or how difficult or strenuous the activity should be for each child; (3) time, or the duration of the physical activity bout; and (4) type, or the

nature of the activity. Educators must use games that ensure both a sufficient quantity and an adequate quality of physical activity experiences. This is recommended in the guidelines for preschoolers (table 7.1) and for children ages 5 through 12 (table 7.2).

Our games are in line with guideline 3 for preschoolers, which recommends promoting the development of competence in fundamental motor skills that will serve as the building blocks for future motor skillfulness. Guidelines 1 and 2 recommend that young children accumulate at least 60 minutes of structured physical activity and engage in at least 60 minutes of unstructured physical activity each day. Although this might seem to go beyond the scope and possibilities of our games, we have designed games for preschoolers and kindergartners that have the potential to affect the movement habits of young children. Consider that the games, centered on deliberate play, embed features of spontaneous play into structured activities and mainly require only a safe, open space and low-cost, often self-made, equipment. When playing our games in the context of structured physical activity, children may import elements of spontaneous play, contributing their own story lines. Conversely, they may easily export these experiences to unstructured physical activity contexts. Thus, our games should facilitate the flow between spontaneous and deliberate play in unstructured environments and deliberate practice in structured environments.

Although the SHAPE America national standards were developed for physical education teachers involved in educating K-12 students, we are convinced that they can be pursued with

Table 7.1   National Guidelines for Physical Activity for Preschoolers

Guideline	
PRESCHOOLERS SHOULD . . .	
1	. . . Accumulate at least 60 minutes of structured physical activity each day.
2	. . . Engage in at least 60 minutes—and up to several hours—of unstructured physical activity each day, and should not be sedentary for more than 60 minutes at a time, except when sleeping.
3	. . . Be encouraged to develop competence in fundamental motor skills that will serve as the building blocks for future motor skillfulness and physical activity.
4	. . . Have access to indoor and outdoor areas that meet or exceed recommended safety standards for performing large-muscle activities.
CAREGIVERS AND PARENTS IN CHARGE OF PRESCHOOLERS' HEALTH AND WELL-BEING ARE RESPONSIBLE . . .	
5	. . . For understanding the importance of physical activity and for promoting movement skills by providing opportunities for structured and unstructured physical activity.

Based on National Association for Sport and Physical Education, 2009, *Active start: A statement of physical activity guidelines for children from birth to age 5* (Reston, VA: NASPE).

Table 7.2 National Standards for Physical Education

Standard	The physically literate individual . . .
1	. . . Demonstrates competency in a variety of motor skills and movement patterns.
2	. . . Applies knowledge of concepts, principles, strategies, and tactics related to movement and performance.
3	. . . Demonstrates the knowledge and skills to achieve and maintain a health-enhancing level of physical activity and fitness.
4	. . . Exhibits responsible personal and social behavior that respects self and others.
5	. . . Recognizes the value of physical activity for health, enjoyment, challenge, self-expression, and/or social interaction.

Based on Society of Health and Physical Educators, 2014, *National standards & grade-level outcomes for K-12 physical education* (Champaign, IL: Human Kinetics).

preschoolers and, not only by physical education teachers in schools, but also by caregivers and health care professionals working in recreational settings. We further believe that anyone who is using the physical activity games in this text is teaching age-appropriate content that can contribute to children's development into physically literate people.

Implications for Educators

This chapter should have made one point crystal clear: teachers matter! Although adults supervise children in many environments both in-, after-, and out-of-school, supervisory roles should not be confused with those of physical activity teachers. Physical activity teachers recognize their need for a distinct set of skills that allow them to both manage and instruct with an enthusiastic disposition. Children are more likely to experience quality physical activity experiences that combine fun, vigorous movement, and learning when a teacher is leading them. Physical activity environments without attentive teachers leave the possibility to chance. Well-informed teachers surely recognize that gambling with a child's development is too important to be left to chance.

Planning is fundamental to good teaching. Preparation means truly understanding the children one will be guiding. Games for children should reflect not only the usual physical and behavioral indicators (age, size, and activity level), but also their psychological characteristics. Because each child has a unique set of abilities, enduring characteristics, and past experiences, teachers should choose games that are not only developmentally appropriate but also of value to each child. The way a game is played is not written in stone. Indeed, as emphasized in part III, games should be constantly modified and altered to meet the needs of individual children as well as the needs of the entire group.

How to Assess Children at Play

Most adults have firm ideas about how children should be educated. Public education plays an important role in society, and we have all been influenced by it. Debates arise and discussions ensue concerning the best way to teach. Over the decades, teacher education programs in universities and colleges have introduced many teaching methods to aspiring teachers. Some have been found to work well; and others, less so. However, what determines the success of a teaching method? The answer to this question is simple: a successful method is one that transforms the way children think and act. Unfortunately, this is not easy to determine. Indeed, consider the flowing stream analogy introduced at the beginning of chapter

5. The impact that a teacher has on a child may not be seen immediately, but much later on.

Verifying the effectiveness of a teaching method requires an assessment. To assess the impact of games on children's thinking and behavior, teachers must use systematic observations from many sources. First, however, they need a clear understanding of the rationale for and components of a good assessment before determining what should be assessed, how it should be assessed, and from whom assessment data should be collected. The rationale for assessment reflects the core building blocks of the scientific method—measurement reliability, objectivity, and validity.

What Is Assessment and Why Do It?

Assessment is the gathering of data to document student learning and teacher effectiveness. When students or teachers hear the words *assessment*, *evaluation*, or *test*, their eyes often glaze over. Few seem to enjoy the process. However, a proper assessment is not difficult to conduct, and it has been shown to help children learn and help teachers improve. Quality assessments provide confirmation of game improvement, a fine-grain determination of what works and what does not work, evidence of the effectiveness of physical activity games in making children competent movers, and a way to promote teacher excellence. Regardless of the focus, assessment is imperative; it must be done continuously, pragmatically (i.e., without causing undue stress or additional labor), and with validity (i.e., truthfully).

Fundamentals of Good Assessment

The Society of Health and Physical Educators (SHAPE America) has articulated four components of a quality physical education program. One is student and program assessment, and SHAPE America stipulates that it

- be an ongoing, vital part of the program;
- include formative and summative measurements of student progress;
- be aligned with state and national standards and the written curriculum;
- assess program elements that support quality physical education; and
- include a periodic evaluation of total program effectiveness by stakeholders (NASPE, 2003; 2009).

Although the SHAPE America criteria for quality program assessment are specific to physical education programs, most of them hold true for student assessment in physical activity game programs. Aside from the fact that physical education and physical activity games share content similarities, they also both help children learn. To illustrate how these criteria for quality assessment can be realized, it might be helpful to refer to five simple features that distinguish good assessment (Graham, Holt/Hale, & Parker, 2013).

First, assessment and instruction should be inseparable; that is, assessment should be a part of the entire learning process. When assessments are performed well, children do not view them as tests, but as part of the program.

Second, assessment should be a form of feedback about how well children are progressing toward a target. For example, a paper returned to a student by a teacher with only a mark of 85 percent on it provides no information about what was good about the performance and what needs to be corrected or improved. Assessment should be focused on helping students acquire knowledge and skills.

Third, assessment must be continuous; it should not be performed only at watershed moments during the year (i.e., before and at the conclusion of a program). Assessment is best when it occurs all the time and thus is intertwined with the entire learning experience.

Fourth, assessment is best when measures are obtained in the proper context. Imagine a scenario in which a coach implements a plan to improve a player's basketball free throws. After a few weeks, the player shows big improvements when tested during practice, sinking 17 out of 20 free throws (85 percent). However, during games, the player's performance plummets. The coach may be dumbfounded given the results of the assessment. In this case, performance during practice did not transfer to game conditions. Likewise, assessment measures recorded during practice may not reflect those recorded during game conditions. During games, other factors may affect performance (e.g., tired legs, crowd distractions, game pressure). This scenario illustrates how conducting skills tests in isolation or out of context provides misleading information that can hinder the learning process.

The fifth characteristic of good assessment is communication. People being assessed must be

---

assessment—The gathering of data to document student learning and teacher effectiveness.

reliability—An indicator of how well an assessment would produce the same data if it were given twice or more times in a relatively short period of time to the same person or people.

objectivity—A condition that results when two people conduct separate assessments on the same person and see the same results.

validity—The determination of whether an assessment truly measures what it is intended to measure.

Teachers should assess skills while students are actually playing a game, not in practice situations.

informed about the assessment criteria before data collection begins. For instance, children who know that they are being assessed and what the assessment expectations are provide the clearest evidence of learning. More important, they are not left wondering what they are supposed to be doing during practice and can more intentionally practice the skill that will be evaluated and, therefore, learn it more thoroughly.

Reliability, Objectivity, and Validity

Measurement is fundamental to scientific inquiry, and it drives the quality of teachers' assessment and implementation plans. The core characteristics of scientific inquiry are reliability, objectivity, and validity. Without them, "little faith can be put in the measurement [assessment] and little use made of it" (Baumgartner, Jackson, Mahar, & Rowe, 2007, p. 96). The three characteristics are intertwined in a well-designed assessment plan; you cannot have one without the others.

- **Reliability** is an indicator of how well an assessment would produce the same data if it were given twice or more times in a relatively

short period of time to the same person or people. A simple example would be the written test to obtain a driver's license. If you took the test on a Monday morning, went home and did not study or learn more about the rules for properly driving a car, and then took the test again on Tuesday morning, your scores on both those tests should be very close if not identical. This would indicate that the test is reliable.

- **Objectivity** results when two people conduct separate assessments on the same person and see the same results. Using our driver's license example, two officials from the licensing office should be able to assess your performance on the test according to established criteria and reach the same conclusion. That is, both assessors should agree on your score. This would indicate that the test is objective.

- **Validity** is the determination of whether the assessment truly measures what it is intended to measure. For example, when you pass your driving test it reveals that you are a safe driver whenever you get behind the wheel of a vehicle. There are several types of validity (Baumgartner, Jackson, Mahar, & Rowe, 2007), but for the purposes of this chapter, we focus only on the general characteristics.

To compare the characteristics of reliability, objectivity, and validity, consider again the driver's license test example. Imagine that the test included questions about world history. Chances are good that you would score low (unless you are a historian). If you took the same test the next day without preparing for questions about history, you would again score low. We could say that the test has good reliability. Further, if the two licensing officials looked at your test performance, both would agree that you failed. We could say the test has a high degree of objectivity. The major issue, however, is that the test is supposed to measure how well you know the rules regarding how to drive safely and legally, not what you know about history. Thus, this test is not a truthful, or valid, measure of the knowledge it was intended to assess.

Managing the Process

Now that you know the importance of assessment quality, and that assessment should be linked to learning and be a continuous process, the next step is learning how to conduct a good assessment. Many believe that quality assessment is a laborious process that can detract from teaching. This is not the case. Strategies are available that can help teachers evaluate their students' behaviors in a practical way without sacrificing the quality of the intervention. Because this is particularly true when assessments are integrated into the learning process, teachers should select assessments that they can complete while they are teaching; for example, via checklists or exit slips, which are covered in more detail later in this chapter.

Teachers can also use video and media technology to assist in the assessment process. A video camera set up in a corner and out of the way with the lens set for wide-angle recording provides records of both teachers' and children's actions and interactions. Digital voice recorders are affordable and small enough to fit in a shirt pocket. Keeping a voice recorder on during a physical activity game is an easy way to record what both teachers and students say. This can be a treasure trove of assessment data.

Volunteers can also help manage the assessment process by being trained to assess both children's and teachers' behaviors. One thing to remember is that reliability, objectivity, and validity are not necessarily stronger when the assessment is complex. Simple assessments can provide quality data, too.

Selecting Appropriate Indicators of Program Success

A valid and pragmatic assessment system allows teachers to collect data regarding both outcome and process variables. **Outcome variables** are the changes in behavior caused by the intervention, or program, such as student game-play performance and skill development. **Process variables** are the elements of an intervention that lead to outcome variables, such as student engagement and teacher performance. Outcome variables are the product of performance (e.g., accuracy or speed). An example of an outcome variable is the number of pins a child knocked down in a bowling activity, which indicates the child's ability to roll a ball to a target from a given distance. Process variables would involve the execution of rolling the ball (e.g., the quality of the roll). Specifically, the child's knee bend, arm swing, and follow-through would be assessed.

Either **quantitative** (i.e., numerical) or **qualitative** (i.e., narrative or categorical) data collection methods can be used to collect assessment data. The first step toward a quality assessment is identifying the indicators of a quality physical activity game intervention. Focusing on both outcome and process variables provides the strongest assessment design. The next steps are to select the measurement approaches and identify data sources. It is valuable to gather both qualitative and quantitative data. Table 8.1 illustrates the differences between the two types of assessment data in terms of purpose, type, collection method, analysis technique, and criteria for rigor. However, this side-by-side presentation is not meant to suggest that one is better than the other. Both have value depending on what the teacher wants to measure through a given assessment plan.

Qualitative approaches to collecting and analyzing data help make sense of what happens in a physical activity game environment and the

---

outcome variables—The changes in behavior caused by the intervention, or program, such as student game-play performance and skill development.

process variables—The elements of an intervention that lead to outcome variables, such as student engagement and teacher performance.

quantitative—Numerical.

qualitative—Narrative or categorical.

Table 8.1 Qualitative Versus Quantitative Assessment Data

Category	Qualitative	Quantitative
Purpose	To make sense of phenomena and their meanings	To measure
Type of data	Text	Numbers
Data collection methods	Interviews, observations, document analysis	Surveys, tests, experiments
Data analysis techniques	Inductive and deductive analysis	Statistical analysis
Criteria for rigor	Trustworthiness, credibility, transferability	Validity, reliability, objectivity, generalizability

meanings children, parents, and teachers assign to what happens (Denzin & Lincoln, 1994). Whereas qualitative approaches involve collecting data in the form of text, quantitative approaches seek to measure what happens in a physical activity game environment. As Creswell and Clark (2007) put it, qualitative approaches are used to collect open-ended data, and quantitative approaches are concerned with closed-ended data.

The two approaches use different data collection methods. Qualitative data are collected from interviews, observations, and document analyses (Patton, 2002), whereas quantitative data are primarily collected via tests, surveys, and experiments. The approaches also differ in how data are analyzed. Data from qualitative collection methods are analyzed inductively (by discovering themes emerging from the data) or deductively (by classifying according to an existing framework). Data from quantitative collection methods use statistical analysis. Together, quantitative and qualitative assessment methods provide markers of children's progress and help teachers modify their games to benefit children while accounting for their individual differences.

This section presents ways to obtain data that indicate whether physical activity games are working in a continuous, practical, and valid manner. Assessments should help teachers see and measure the progress made toward achieving their program outcomes. It is essential to evaluate children's improvement in physical and mental skills, the process through which they reach higher performance levels, and the appropriateness of the teacher's delivery.

Game-Play Performance

The change in performance of individual children is a key learning outcome indicator, particularly in out-of-school programs in which children are rarely grouped by age. Children participating in games in these settings may vary greatly in their motor and mental developmental levels. Such differences

clearly influence an intervention program's effectiveness. For example, consider differences in the starting and ending points of two children. The child who performs well at the beginning of game play will show smaller gains by the end of the program than will the child who finds the game to be initially challenging. The lower initial starting point of the less-able child leaves much room for improvement.

Teacher feedback is critical to motivate both children. Individualized and group teaching strategies must be developed. For example, a child may not be able to demonstrate her ball-shooting skills because she seldom receives the ball from other players. Altering rules will help the teacher evaluate the girl's shooting skills. Remember, however, that considering only performance outcomes in terms of absolute values can have a negative motivational impact on some low-skilled children. Likewise, evaluating only in terms of progress may be frustrating for more skilled children who have less room for improvement. Therefore, relative progress indicators that take into account the starting level of the learner should be used with children who largely vary in skill or physical fitness. Process measures, on the other hand, can reveal children's game knowledge and use of strategy. Recall from chapter 3 the types of game knowledge. Declarative memory underlies knowledge about playing physical activity games, and procedural memory underlies knowledge about how to play physical activity games. Assessing both types of knowledge is critical when students differ in age and abilities.

Skill Development

Measuring children's movement proficiency is essential to program evaluation. On the surface, it would seem simple enough to test children's movement skills. However, the test "must parallel the instructional objectives to really determine skill achievement" (Baumgartner, Jackson, Mahar, & Rowe, 2007, p. 156). Standardized tests such as the Fitnessgram have an important role when many children must be assessed. A weakness of the typical skill battery is that it tends to measure children's skill performance in isolation and, as a consequence, may not paint an accurate picture of how efficiently a child moves in an actual game context. Authentic assessments of motor skill performance are recommended because they challenge the student both to comprehend and to apply essential knowledge and skills in a dynamic, real-world environment.

The importance of using task analyses when developing and teaching physical activity games was addressed in chapter 4. The steps in acquiring game skills can be the basis for assessment as well. A checklist approach, as described later in this chapter, provides a written description of each step required to perform a skill. For example, in the task analysis and checklist presented in chapter 4, four steps were involved in throwing a ball. A child's behaviors at each step can be judged as either acceptable or unacceptable. Importantly, the criteria used should be based on clearly identified actions. Consider the importance of objectivity discussed previously. If several teachers observe a child's actions, their scores for each step of the task analysis should be similar. Thus, teachers need to be very careful in describing what constitutes acceptable behaviors at each stage.

Task analysis checklists used on a regular basis across many days of game instruction show how children progress along the learning curve. At the beginning stages of learning a new game, a child may be able to display adequate performance on only a few of the steps required for competence in the game. However, with proper direct instruction, practice, and feedback, the number of steps performed well will increase, as will the quality of the actions at each step.

Recall that a child's mental engagement is high during the cognitive and associative stages of learning because learning a new skill is so effortful. Although teachers cannot see and measure children's mental activities, they can make educated guesses about their mental involvement based on their actions. Thus, task analysis methods can help them gather both quantitative and qualitative data. For example, the task analysis checklist in figure 4.4b in chapter 4 includes not only the steps involved in task performance, but also descriptions of the quality of the child's actions.

As children become more skilled, game conditions need to be varied to maintain their mental engagement. It is well known that children who have mastered a game may quickly lose interest in it. The task analysis is a formal way for teachers

© kellywegel.com

Children should be encouraged to explore and be creative.

to identify when and how game play should be changed to keep children at their optimal challenge point, or to know when to change to a new game.

Quality Indicators of the Creative Process

As discussed in chapters 6 and 7, one of the teaching strategies that generates cognitive engagement is the exploration and discovery method. With this method, the teacher's role is that of a facilitator who promotes children's creative processes. The same type of instruction may be used both to promote and to assess the creative process. Creative products may range from those that require fine-motor skills (e.g., drawing) to those that require gross-motor skills (e.g., locomotor or object control tasks).

Common drawing tasks thought to measure creative thinking are pencil-and-paper picture construction and completion activities performed in a playful, problem-solving atmosphere. For example, children may be given incomplete figures and asked to complete them in novel ways. Commonly used movement-based creativity tasks for inducing and assessing the creative process in preschool-, kindergarten-, and early elementary school–age children include (1) gross-motor tasks introduced with instructions such as, How many ways . . .? or Can you move like . . . (e.g., a certain animal)? to generate bodily movements, and (2) manipulative tasks introduced by What might it be? or "What other ways . . ? to generate alternate uses of objects (Bertsch, 1983; Torrance, 1981).

What should teachers observe while a child draws or exhibits a gross-motor creativity task? In both cases, there is not a single indicator of creativity to observe; rather, there is a single indicator for each primary dimension of creativity in thinking and moving: flexibility, fluency, and originality.

Consider, for example, the task of going over hurdles discussed in chapter 6. Depending on the hurdle's height and the children's age, motor ability developmental level (balance, leg power), and fundamental motor skills, they will try different solutions. A child who has extensive experience with structured or spontaneous play activities will probably try to step, jump, and hop, whereas a less-skilled child may only try to step. These two children differ in **flexibility**, and the ability to adjust movements as game conditions change.

However, flexibility is only one creativity dimension. In fact, it may be that two similarly skilled children who are both able to use a variety of movement skills (e.g., stepping, jumping, hopping) do not possess the same ability to find variants of each skill. One child might only jump forward over the hurdle and always push off the ground and land on both feet. Another child might jump sideways and push off the ground with either one foot or both feet. A child might only hop forward with the arms held stiffly or swinging to support the leg movement, whereas another child might turn and clap hands while hopping. These children differ in **fluency**, a quality indicated by the range of different solutions applied.

Last, but not least, the third creativity dimension is **originality**, which refers to the ability to generate unique and unusual products or solutions. The uniqueness of a movement solution depends on the game; for instance, in a structured track and field setting, some hurdling and jumping techniques are more common than in recreational settings. Teachers can evaluate originality in these situations by considering how frequently each solution emerges within the educational, recreational, or sport setting.

Indicators of Program Effectiveness

Children's behaviors are complex. Assessing children's movements and their outcomes is indeed informative. However, other aspects of their behaviors can help teachers assess the quality of their instructional methods. They can gather information about their students' social and classroom behaviors from other teachers and from parents. This information reflects how well they control their attention, as well as their degree of impulsivity, level of self-direction, and planning skills. Observing simultaneous improvements in children's behaviors during both physical activity games and classroom settings provide powerful convergent evidence for teacher and program effectiveness.

---

flexibility—The amount of response categories used to adjust movements as game conditions change.

fluency—The range of different solutions that can be applied.

originality—The ability to generate unique and unusual products or solutions.

Student Engagement

Achieving optimal effects on children's cognitive development when teaching physical activity games hinges on two conditions: first, children must be engaged in moderate-to-vigorous physical activity; second, children must be thinking about or be engaged in their actions. Engagement means being attentive; it involves solving movement program. Mental engagement is important because it separates physically active games from mere activity. For example, an adult on a treadmill or stationary bike is seldom mentally engaged in organizing and controlling her muscles because of the exercise's routine nature. A well-designed and well-delivered physical activity game, however, results in a child who is physically active and thinking about various movements and strategies, whether he is playing defense or evading a defender to get open to receive a pass.

Measuring the quality of children's engagement needs to be part of an assessment and evaluation plan. Children can be engaged but not in a developmentally appropriate manner that suitably challenges them. Interventions that are properly presented produce the desired physical and mental outcomes. Interventions that are poorly or incorrectly presented may result in off-task behaviors or frustration, or cause a child to disengage from the game. None of these outcomes promotes children's enthusiasm about participating in physical activity.

Student Enjoyment

An adult who enjoys a game or sport (e.g., cards, golf, tennis, swimming) has acquired a measure of competency in the activity. The enjoyment derived from participating typically increases the likelihood of continued participation. The same is true of children; thus, game enjoyment is a major consideration when evaluating the success of physical activity games. Teachers must monitor the extent to which children enjoy participating in physical activity games so they can create appropriate alterations. Like adults, and probably more so in some cases, children are much more likely to continue their participation in physical activity if they have fun doing it. The natural consequences of their continued participation in physical activity games are increased physical activity and movement competency and improved game skills.

Teacher–Student and Student–Student Interactions

To motivate their students to be physically active, teachers must enjoy interacting with and directing them. This is reflected in conscious and intentional behaviors that energize children's actions. A good teacher connects with students by way of praise or encouragement (Griffey & Housner, 1991), asking questions (Livingston & Borko, 1989), providing feedback on performance (positive, specific, and corrective), and redirecting them when they are off task.

It is important to note, however, that physical activity games are very team oriented. As such, each child influences other children's engagement and activity levels. Student interactions are a critical part of physical activity game assessment. Negative interactions among students, such as arguments, isolation, and criticism, can hamper engagement as much as encouragement, inclusion, and praise can enhance it.

Approaches to and Sources of Data Collection

Once the appropriate game behaviors have been identified, the next step is to determine a data collection approach that provides the most information and is most pragmatic. This can be a very tricky undertaking. Recall that data can be either qualitative or quantitative and that collecting both types strengthens an evaluation.

Although the children themselves provide the main source of data, many other sources are available as well. The following sections describe several sources and methods of data collection. This list is by no means exhaustive; it is intended merely to provide simple and practical data collection examples for assessing game programs. Using the process of **triangulating**, or cross-verifying data from two or more sources, can improve the quality of an assessment plan.

Checklists

Checklists with rubrics provide authentic assessments of children's skill performance. A **rubric** is an evaluation matrix that describes varying levels of quality or achievement for a specific task; it serves as a guide that defines the criteria for a particular performance. An example is shown in table 8.2. Rubrics

triangulation—The process of cross-verifying data from two or more sources.

rubric—An evaluation matrix that describes varying levels of quality or achievement for a specific task.

Table 8.2 Team Game-Play Behavior Assessment Rubric

Category	Criteria
Excellent (E)	Includes teammates in nearly all plays; always listens to teammates when they are talking; constantly offers suggestions to problems; continually uses teammates' names; encourages teammates consistently; plays by rules every time; calls penalties and fouls on self when appropriate.
Very good (VG)	Includes teammates in most plays; often listens to teammates when they are talking; frequently offers suggestions to problems; regularly uses teammates' names; habitually encourages teammates; plays by rules nearly all the time; calls penalties and fouls on self on occasion.
Fair (F)	Sometimes includes teammates; does not speak when teammates are talking; intermittently offers suggestions to problems; sporadically uses teammates' names; irregularly encourages teammates; plays by rules every time; has called at least two penalties or fouls on self when appropriate.
Poor (P)	Isolates self from teammates; ignores teammates when they are talking; never offers suggestions to problems; rarely uses teammates' names; seldom encourages teammates; makes attempts at circumventing rules; has not called more than one penalty or foul on self when appropriate.

serve two important roles: they inform the learner of the standards for assessment, and they provide the teacher with a way to determine the quality of a skill performance rather than just the outcome.

Checklists with rubrics also provide flexibility. A checklist that uses a point system allows the evaluator to select behaviors that are linked to each child's instructional needs. Checklists can be varied as children progress through the stages of learning—cognitive, associative, and autonomous. The items identified for each session help keep them at the optimal challenge point. Across the stages of learning, combining checklists with task analyses

provides a fine-grain assessment of children's physical and mental skills. An example of a game-play skills checklist is shown in figure 8.1.

Systematic Observation

Examining children's behavior before, during, and following a game provides an important indicator of their level of engagement. Methods of measuring physical arousal have improved greatly over the past decade, and many new electronic methods of measuring children's physical activity are available (Ridgers, Stratton, & Fairclough, 2005). Although

Game/Skill Performance Evaluation: Garbage Ball

Name: _____ Date: _____

Game/motor skill	Points earned
Moves without ball	/ 2
When in possession of ball, keeps possession or passes to teammate	/ 1
Attempts a pass OR attempts to dribble	/ 1
Completes a pass to teammate OR dribbles and keeps possession for at least 3 paces	/ 3
Marks an opponent when team does not have ball	/ 1
Is within one step of an opponent when marking	/ 3
Displays at least two communications (verbal or nonverbal) with teammates	/ 2

Perfect score: > 12

Very close: 10-12

Making great progress: 8-9

We'll keep working on it: < 7

Figure 8.1 Game-play skills checklist.

modern technology has produced measurement devices such as accelerometers, pedometers, and heart-rate monitors that provide robust data, particularly for researchers, their use is limited by cost and logistics. Most school (and out-of-school) environments are limited to observational assessment techniques (McKenzie, Sallis, & Nader, 1991).

Systematic observation instruments provide meaningful descriptive data that are easy to obtain and provide essential assessment information. In this section we briefly describe a well-known systematic observation instrument, the academic learning time—physical education (ALT-PE) instrument, which can be easily adapted for use in game assessment.

The ALT-PE instrument was developed to measure the "portion of time in a physical education lesson that a child is involved in motor activity at an appropriate success rate" (Parker, 1989, p. 195). As we have noted repeatedly, out-of-school environments are not physical education classes; however, the content and model of out-of-school instruction often resemble those of a physical education class and, thus, the ALT-PE instrument is quite useful. This instrument is unique in that it measures both cognitive and physical engagement. An example of a modified ALT-PE instrument that physical activity teachers could use is presented in figure 8.2.

Systematic observation instruments are also useful for measuring teacher–student and student–student interactions. One well-known interaction analysis tool designed for physical activity settings is Cheffers' adaptation of the Flanders' Interaction Analysis System (CAFIAS) (Cheffers & Mancini, 1989). Although the training for using this instrument can be lengthy, it provides the ability to code

Adapted ALT-PE Systematic Observation Instrument to Record Student Engagement

Class: _____   Date: _____

Length of observation time: _____ minutes   Time of observation: _____

	1	2	3	4	5	6	7	8	9	10	11	12	13	14	15
Student A															
Student B															
Student C															

	16	17	18	19	20	21	22	23	24	25	26	27	28	29	30
Student A															
Student B															
Student C															

Directions

1. Randomly select three students to observe, and label them Student A, Student B, and Student C.

2. Observe Student A for six seconds.

3. Within the next six seconds, determine engagement (engaged or not engaged) and then select the specific category that best described the student's behavior and record the appropriate code in the box provided in column 1.

4. Repeat process for Student B.

5. Repeat process for Student C.

6. Start again with Student A and record the codes in the next column.

Figure 8.2   Modified ALT-PE observational instrument.

interactions so that any behavior can be categorized as verbal, nonverbal, or both.

Exit Slips

Qualitative measures are particularly useful for verifying the enjoyment children experience from being physically active. Formally asking children about their experiences and perceptions is vital to the assessment of physical activity games. It can be easy for some children in large groups to blend into the environment and become "competent by-standers" (Tousignant & Siedentop, 1983) who do more watching than participating. These children are not usually noticed because they do not stand out and seldom get into trouble. However, teachers should track and assess all children. When physical activity games fail to meet the needs and wants of all children, they quickly lose interest in them.

Although getting anecdotal data from children through an informal question (e.g., Annie, what did you like about that game?) can provide some indication of game effectiveness, there are other, easy ways to get qualitative information from children. The exit slip, for example, can be completed in less than one minute as children leave the learning area (see figure 8.3 for examples). **Exit slips** are short written questionnaires (usually no more than three simple questions) used to determine whether children learned from and enjoyed the activity (Graham, Holt/Hale, & Parker, 2013). For younger children exit slips might use drawing as a means of communicating, or they might present simple drawings that children check or circle to indicate how they felt about the activity. When teachers pose questions in this manner, children's responses are likely to be true representations of their feelings and what they know. The exit slip has the benefit of keeping children's opinions confidential, and therefore, there is less risk of an unpopular opinion resulting in negative social consequences. Even though most children are honest (sometimes more than we want!) when an adult asks them a question, their answers are often vague or stated in a way to ensure that feelings are not hurt. Exit slips can be anonymous or use identifiable information; using both types of slips interchangeably will most likely result in trustworthy data.

> **exit slip**—A short written questionnaire (usually no more than three simple questions) used to determine whether children learned from and enjoyed an activity.

Children Interviews

Exit slips provide a nice way of identifying larger issues regarding the quality of the physical activity game experience that may require attention. They help track trends in the children's knowledge and their game-playing perceptions. When trends are identified, however, they can signal the need for change. Before those changes are instituted, it is a good idea to ask a sample of children about their views of the proposed changes. Questioning children about the physical activity games before or after class can provide a body of rich and robust data about what children are learning and what appeals to them. Asking children about their experiences has two benefits. First, if the questions are correctly posed, their responses can provide a keen representation of what is happening (McCullick et al., 2008) in the program that may not be noticeable through systematic observation. The second benefit is that children have a sense of ownership that is likely to boost their interest in participating.

Interviewing a large number of students is not an easy task, but those data can be obtained! Toward this end, teachers should remember that they do not have to collect all the data. Using other teachers or parent volunteers, for example, is a reasonable approach. As Graham (1995) noted, "it can be effective for someone else to interview students and then anonymously share the findings with the teachers.... the right questions, asked in appropriate ways, have the potential to be extremely useful" (p. 480). This would be especially true for children who feel uneasy about mentioning a negative feeling.

Parent or Guardian Interviews

Collecting trustworthy and credible data from parents is yet another way teachers can triangulate their findings. Through the use of brief, written questionnaires (figure 8.4), e-mailed surveys, or group interviews, teachers can learn a lot about the quality of their physical activity games and their impact on children. Parents can help them determine success by answering questions regarding how often their children refer to the games they play, how many times they have seen or heard their children playing games they have learned, or whether they have detected any differences in their children's physical and cognitive behaviors. A recently developed survey, the Parent Survey on After School Program Satisfaction (PSEP) (Byon et al., 2012), was found to be a reliable predictor of parent satisfaction and willingness to reenroll their child in an after-school program.

Exit Slip

Name: _____

1. Tell me one thing you liked about playing this game. If you did not like anything, tell me what you disliked about it.

2. When playing this game, what are two ways of getting open so you can receive a pass?

3. On a scale of 1 (lowest) to 5 (highest), rate yourself on your effort today.

If you would like to make any other helpful comments, please do so in the space below:

Exit Slip

Name: _____

In the space below, please draw a diagram that shows how a team should be spread out when they have the ball. Use X's to identify the four players on your team and O's to identify the four players of the opposing team.

Figure 8.3 Examples of exit slips.

Parent Questionnaire

Dear Parents:

Please help us gather information on how much of an impact the Frogs 'n Dogs PAGs Program is having on your child's feelings about playing physical activity games. You may choose to remain anonymous or write your child's name in the space provided. This short questionnaire will only take a couple of minutes of your time and will be a great help to us in evaluating our program so we can improve it and make it more beneficial for your child.

Thank you for allowing us to teach your child and taking the time to complete this questionnaire.

Sincerely,
The Frogs 'n Dogs Instructional Team

Child's Name (optional): _____

Please answer the following questions using a scale of 1 (completely disagree) to 5 (strongly agree).

1. My child talks about his/her activities in the Frogs 'n Dogs PAGs Program. Score: ___

2. My child talks about his/her activities in the Frogs 'n Dogs PAGs Program without me asking. Score: ___

3. I have noticed a change in my child's attitude toward physical activity and/or sport. Score: ___

4. I have noticed a change in my child's physical activity levels during non-school time. Score: ___

5. My child feels like the Frogs 'n Dogs PAGs Program is enjoyable. Score: ___

If you would like to comment, please feel free to do so in the space below or on the back of this paper.

Figure 8.4 Parent questionnaire.

Teacher (Deliverer) Data

An evaluation of physical activity games is incomplete without data from the person who teaches them! As the one in the trenches on a daily basis, the teacher can identify issues that may need to be addressed and make small alterations to managerial routines and the physical activity games themselves. To gather these data, teachers need to intentionally reflect on the teaching of physical activity games and record their thoughts as they would in a diary. Most teachers think about their classes in an introspective or reflective way. Putting thoughts to paper on a routine schedule improves the quality of the data. Irregular diary logs may result in a clouded perspective because important information may have been forgotten. On the other hand, reflective and introspective diary logs used over an extended period provide a more trustworthy picture of teachers' feelings. Devoting 15 minutes to writing in and reviewing a journal immediately after teaching or before the children arrive is an easy way to do this. Teachers who are less apt to write down their thoughts may consider using a digital voice recorder to keep an audio log. Consistency is the key.

Individual Differences, Measurement, and Game Development

Perhaps the greatest challenge to teaching physical activity games is accommodating the differences among children. We have already addressed the need for instructional interventions that fit children's abilities and characteristics. The issue of children's differences also arises when assessing their progress in acquiring game skills.

Combinations of Abilities

The study of individual differences has a rich history in the fields of both psychology and physical education. Each child brings to every learning session a unique combination of physical and mental abilities, which are enduring traits linked to genetics, as introduced in chapter 1. At any moment, a child's capacity to learn reflects a blend of many abilities. This composite of abilities explains why certain children learn a game quickly and with little effort. Such children excel in the mental abilities required for the game. However, these same children may have difficulty coordinating their movements in other games. It is important for teachers to identify each child's strengths and weaknesses when creating and introducing games.

Fundamental Movement Behaviors

Part III of this book focuses on developing mentally engaging games for young children (chapter 10) and for older children (chapter 11). We provide two chapters because of the clear age-related differences in children's fundamental movement behaviors. Early childhood (ages 3 to 6) is characterized by the rapid emergence of well-defined movement behaviors and increases in movement control; later childhood (7 to 11 years) is a period of movement-skill refinement. Across time, infants show reflexive movement patterns, young children show slow, immature movement patterns that become increasingly more controlled, and older children show mature movement patterns. Teachers can employ the measurement tools described previously in this chapter to assess children as they shift from exhibiting immature, to mature, to refined behavior. It

is important for teachers to be aware of children's movement behavior development. Understanding when and how these movement behaviors emerge is critical for game development and design. In turn, the games themselves alter and refine children's movements and game play.

Although a detailed overview of children's motor development is beyond the scope of this book, a summary of key observations made by researchers (Gabbard, 2004) is provided. Fundamental movement behaviors that provide the foundation for participating in physical activity games fall into three broad categories: locomotor, nonlocomotor, and manipulative. A rudimentary knowledge of these categories is essential to conducting assessments and then using assessment data to tweak the physical activity games so that they appropriately engage children.

Locomotor Behaviors

The concept of motricity introduced in chapter 1 illustrates the importance of being able to move voluntarily from one place to another. Children develop a wide array of movements, and they use them to physically transport themselves forward, up, and down.

Walking is a complex behavior first seen in infants and displayed by most children by 13 months of age. The skill is fully developed by the age of 4 or 5. Running differs from walking in that it requires the use of leg force to propel the body into space. Unlike walking, in which there is always support from either leg, running includes a phase during which the person does not have direct contact with the ground. Thus, the body is less stable when running than when walking. Most children become proficient at running at the age of 5.

Increases in leg strength and movement control play an important role in jumping, which typically involves a single explosive movement, and hopping, which involves repeated one-foot takeoffs and landings. Many physical activity games involve sprint running, jumping, and hopping, all of which are complex movements that are refined with experience. Hopping, for instance, is typically not seen in children until they are 3 years of age, and it is not performed consistently until 6 years of age.

Nonlocomotor Behaviors

Children must learn to move in environments that change around them. As they bend and twist, they must maintain a base of support and balance. Balance is a very complex phenomenon involving the integration of many sensory inputs. The coupling of vision, which provides information about what is going on in the environment, with vestibular structures, which provide information about what is happening inside the body during movement, is critical for maintaining balance. Likewise, developing muscular strength enables greater movement control and enhanced stability.

Balance can be improved with training and practice. It is interesting to watch the pleasure of young children being swung by their parents. They never seem to get enough of carnival rides that spin, elevate, and drop (perhaps to the dismay of their parents who may no longer be thrilled by disorientation and the queasy feelings that accompany loss of balance).

Consider the spotting technique beginner gymnasts learn to maintain their balance after completing jumps or turns. Spotting requires visually attending to a target at a fixed location, such as a wall, that serves as a reference point and helps the person control her muscles and keep her balance by locating objects around her.

Manipulative Behaviors

Many games involve catching, throwing, striking, and kicking, and children use their hands and feet to perform specific movements. These types of manipulative behaviors are very complex and involve **psychomotor abilities**, which are enduring characteristics that influence the capacity to manipulate and control objects. At the heart of game skills is the ability to time movements with changes in environmental conditions. Catching a ball requires a child to view the speed and size of the ball, judge its speed (the *psych* part of *psychomotor*), and then engage arm and hand muscles to intercept the ball (the *motor* part).

The ability to time, or pace, movements is critical to developing manipulative skills; it is not typically observed in mature form until age 5 or 6. As a result,

> **psychomotor abilities**—Enduring characteristics that influence the capacity to manipulate and control objects.
>
> **selective attention**—A mental process used to both identify important information and block out information that, to the individual, is unimportant.
>
> **divided attention**—A mental process that helps people process and perform several activities at the same time.

a young child's ability to dribble, kick, or strike a ball is not well developed. Although children may show mature throwing movements as young as 6 years old, they do not become proficient until adolescence. This is particularly true for the overhead throwing motion. For some children, often females, this movement is never mastered. Teachers benefit from assessing each child's proficiency level for fundamental motor skills and then documenting changes that occur following their participation in game activities.

Basic Mental Abilities

Many tests have been designed to assess children's mental abilities. Unlike movement measures, which can be seen directly, measures of mental abilities are obtained indirectly through tests. Teachers use tests to infer what children have learned. Learning cannot be seen directly; it occurs somewhere in the brain. In-depth discussions of the development of children's cognition, particularly their executive functions, were presented in chapters 1 through 4. Educators use tests to infer children's learning of such subjects as mathematics, language, and literature. Physical activity game teachers can draw conclusions about children's mental activities by observing their behaviors. The mental abilities that are foundational for participating in physical activity games fall into two broad categories: attention and memory.

Attention

Attention is a word often used in normal conversations. However, researchers have concluded that it is difficult to define. Contemporary scientists suggest that there are three types of attention: selective, divided, and sustained.

Selective attention is a mental process used to both identify important information and block out information that, to the individual, is unimportant. People use all of their sensory systems to gather information from the world around them. Sight, hearing, touch, smell, taste, and movement all provide a picture, or representation, of the world.

Divided attention is a mental process that helps people process and perform several activities at the same time. Adults can drive a car, listen to the radio, and think about what they need to pick up at the store. Children likewise can function in multiprocessing, multitasking environments. Effective behavior is often determined by how well people can use mental energy to accomplish daily routines and chores.

Sustained attention is a mental process that people use to ward off fatigue and help them focus on continuing to perform a task. Children's ability to perform efficiently in a classroom setting tends to decrease with the length of the school day. Classes taught toward the end of the day often require children to overcome the day-long accumulation of mental and physical fatigue and maintain attention to task.

Children's short attention spans are well documented by teachers. Even during the best-planned activities, children's minds inevitably wander. Clearly, in educational settings both children and adults can have difficulty paying attention. Of particular note are children who have disorders of attention, such as attention-deficit/hyperactivity disorder (ADHD). There are three classifications of ADHD: predominantly inattentive, predominantly hyperactive-impulsive, and combined.

Worldwide, attention disorders are the most common psychiatric disorder diagnosed in children,

affecting 3 to 5 percent of school-aged children. Boys are diagnosed with them more often than girls are. Attention disorders are complex, and much debate has arisen concerning their cause and treatment. The prevalence of these disorders is sufficient that teachers should expect a portion of their students to have been diagnosed and be receiving drugs or other forms of treatment.

Teachers need to realize that the behaviors of children with attention disorders are not very different from those of children without such disorders. The defining characteristic is the degree and persistence over time of distractibility, inattention, and fidgeting, and whether these behaviors interfere with learning and social relationships.

Some studies have found that physical activity reduces attention disorders in children. Direct observation of children's class behavior using scales such as the ALT-PE can provide teachers with quantitative data concerning attentional behaviors and how they change during game play.

Memory

Memory provides a way to store experiences and recall them when needed. The role of memory in children's information processing and performance was discussed in chapter 3. Like attention, there are several types of memory, and they are all complex. Children's memory capacity increases with age and experience. However, the memory capacities of children of the same age can differ markedly.

Children diagnosed with **learning disorders** have difficulty listening, reasoning, and performing such academic skills as reading, writing, and solving mathematical problems. These children are not lazy and, in many cases, have average or above-average intelligence. Indeed, many children are aware of their inability to keep up with others and frequently express frustration and act out. Their difficulties stem from the way their brains process

Teachers can observe students during instruction and game play to assess their capacity to pay attention.

sustained attention—A mental process that people use to ward off fatigue and help them focus on continuing to perform a task.

learning disorders—Disorders that make it difficult for children to listen, reason, and perform such academic skills as reading, writing, and solving mathematical problems.

measurement sensitivity—The degree to which changes in performance can be assessed.

information. Teachers who work with children with memory and learning disorders have found that they need to modify learning interventions to help them learn. Qualitative assessments and interviews can provide insights into each child's needs as well as clues as to how changes to instructional methods can help children with learning disorders learn movement-based games.

Assessing Progress

The motor and mental abilities and skills that each child brings to each game session typically change over time. Two factors are responsible for the change: maturation and development. Recall from chapter 1 that maturation reflects the genetically linked changes that occur in mind and body at specific time points. Development reflects changes in mind and body that are caused by experience and learning. A boy's game performance may improve from the beginning to the end of the third grade both because he is growing larger and because of the instruction he receives. Teachers are challenged to determine how much change in a child's behavior is due to their lesson plans and their executions of them.

Many of the assessment tools described earlier in this chapter can be modified to achieve accurate assessments of each child's progress. Modifications can include noting a child's initial entry-level core abilities and ranking the child's abilities relative to others in the class. Of particular importance is **measurement sensitivity**, which is the degree to which changes in performance can be assessed. As an example, consider a child who has difficulty performing a specific step described in a task analysis. It may be that the child is indeed improving on the step, but the criteria used to measure success are too general and do not detail specific subcomponents of the step. Modifying the criteria used to assess the step creates more room for measurable change to occur and allows the teacher to detect and measure improvements in performance. On the other hand, another child may perform virtually all of the steps that make up the game correctly from the beginning. For this child, it would be important to increase the precision of the criteria used to measure each step. Modifying the measurement criteria provides a way of measuring children who perform at the two ends of the normal distribution.

Implications for Educators

Assessment has a connotation that often turns off teachers and students alike. At the forefront of our thinking about teaching children must be the reminder that, if done well, assessment is a vital tool that helps teachers design lessons to increase children's learning. Specifically, in our context assessment can let physical activity teachers know whether what they are doing is working.

Once we remember the contributions of assessment, we must learn the characteristics of quality assessments. Quality assessments are intertwined with instruction, a source of feedback for learners, continuous, conducted in the appropriate context, and marked by clear communication between teachers and students. Furthermore, assessments are most potent when the right measures are used.

This book presents a rationale and process for educators charged with delivering quality physical activity programs to preschool-, kindergarten-, and elementary school–age children. Each game is age appropriate and linked to children's motor and cognitive abilities. Our goal is to describe how and why each game challenges children and promotes their cognitive development. Effective implementation of the games can be verified only through the use of systematic assessment methods.

Furthermore, assessments of both student performance and program effectiveness are necessary. Assessments of children's game-play performance, skill development, and creativity appear to be most essential when determining their progress. Indicators of program effectiveness can be assessed through measures of student engagement, student enjoyment, and teacher–student interaction.

Finally, assessment must be manageable and reasonable. We recognize that assessment can be laborious and might be the reason many have less-than-fond views of it. The use of checklists, systematic observation, exit slips, interviews of children, and parental input are feasible and useful methods of collecting the data needed for making decisions about the direction of a physical activity program. We recognize, of course, that successful teachers are autonomous and create games to meet their needs and their children's needs. With the success of teachers in mind, consider the importance of assessing individual differences and accommodating by task diversification.

© Monkey Business

Integrating Physical Activity Games Into the Home and Community

Sport historians note that in the early 20th century, during the worldwide rise of industrialization and big cities, games and sports provided ways to teach youngsters social responsibility, cooperation, values, and the skills necessary for becoming healthy, productive adults. The role that societies play in promoting the health and wellness of their citizens increased in the mid-20th century. The World Health Organization (WHO), which was created in 1948 by the United Nations, championed the view that health is "a state of mental and social well-being and not merely the absence of disease or infirmity" (Preamble to the Constitution of the World Health Organization, 1946). From the perspective of WHO, physical and mental health is a basic right. More recently, with the rise in health-related diseases related to physical inactivity, many organizations have developed and refined health and physical activity guidelines to help social agencies encourage health-promoting activities.

This chapter focuses on the role of physical activity games within the context of ecological models that examine the influence of a wide variety of people and organizations on children's learning and health behaviors. Children today live in a much different world than that in which their parents and grandparents grew up. The information age and explosion in the use of computers and media has transformed the ways children interact and learn from others. Educators remark on the changes that are taking place in the 21st century. Learning experiences are provided not only during the traditional school day, but also before and after school. The recent findings that well-designed physical activity programs can benefit both physical and mental health have led policy makers to look to physical educators, who play increasingly important roles in teaching children. This chapter discusses ways physical educators can use their specific knowledge and experiences to help parents, families, and communities better connect with children and to give them the support necessary for instilling enduring health-enhancing behaviors.

Ecological Models

Mental and physical health is influenced by many factors. Professionals have attempted to understand the complexities of health behavior in terms of **ecological models**. These models emphasize how multiple factors determine peoples' health-promoting behaviors.

The prototypical ecological model, as depicted in figure 9.1, is based on five interactive levels (McLeroy, Bibeau, Steckler, & Glanz, 1988). Central to the model is the belief that peoples' behavior does not occur in a vacuum. Throughout life, health behaviors are influenced on a personal level by **micro factors** (e.g., family, friends, peers) and on a global level by **macro factors** (e.g., institutions and cultures).

Although ecological models were developed to apply to people across the life span, they are particularly well suited for describing the many micro-level and macro-level factors that influence children's physical activity. The five levels of ecological models are as follows:

- *The individual.* The developing child's behaviors are the result of the blending of nature and nurture; that is, genetic factors and experience. Children's unique personality traits and dispositions set the stage for how they engage in the world and acquire specific behavior patterns and skills. Although children are naturally motivated to move, experiences can modify their motives to be physically active. Youngsters' willingness to engage in play and games is based on rapidly forming self-efficacy perceptions, which are beliefs about performing specific types of games, and outcome expectancies, which are the results that they anticipate. The quickly developing mental capacities of infants and young children influence how they act and evaluate the consequences of their movement actions.

- *Interpersonal relationships.* Infants and young children are totally dependent on the care and support of their parents and families. Older children rapidly establish relationships with friends and those who become **significant others**; that is, people important to their well-being and self-concept. Children learn much from watching their friends, parents, and adults. Further, the support

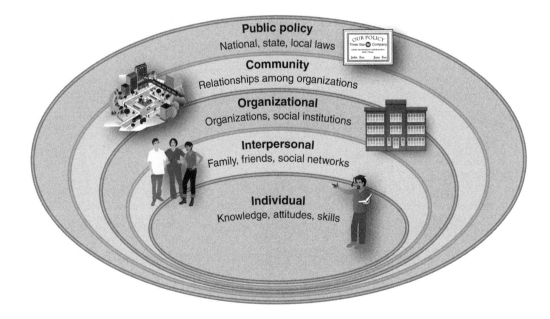

Figure 9.1   Interactive levels of the ecological model.

and inspiration provided by significant others promotes learning.

- *Social institutions.* Schoolteachers provide children with regulations and rules of behavior that are important for success in both their academic and social development. Teachers are uniquely placed to help children acquire confidence and an awareness of their abilities.

- *Community.* Besides schools, children are typically part of communities that may include churches and social organizations. These organizations provide additional sets of rules and expectancies for developing children. As young children develop, increasing numbers of people influence their **self-beliefs**, or their confidence in their abilities or judgments. Children receive considerable, and sometimes conflicting, information about how to think about themselves and how to behave as their social networks increase. Cooperative interorganizational activities are optimal for developing children's physical and mental health.

- *Policy makers.* The schools that children attend and the organizations they are part of follow protocols that are determined by **policy makers**, who are people whose opinions strongly influence the course of events. Policies made at the local, state, and federal levels regulate institutions that influence developing children.

Many factors can influence children's physical activity and, in turn, cognitive growth. Teachers need to be aware of the multiple sources of guidance that affect children's beliefs about engagement in physical activity. Early in life, direct caretakers play key roles in children's experiences. Within a relatively brief time span, however, children's experiences expand rapidly as they become involved in school, community, and church activities.

Coordinated School Health Ecological Model

An influential ecological model that focuses specifically on children's health was introduced by Allensworth and Kolbe in 1987. The coordinated school health model consists of eight components: health education; physical education; school health services; school nutrition services; school counseling, psychological, and social services; a healthy school environment; school-site health promotion for staff; and family and community involvement in school health. The coordinated school health program was adopted by the U.S. Centers for Disease and Control (CDC) and Prevention and has served as the mainstay of the organization's health initiative. The ecological model shown in figure 9.2 depicts one way the coordinated school health program has been formulated (Lohrmann, 2010).

At the center of the model are six sources of knowledge that directly influence children's physical and mental health: health services, health education, physical education, food and nutrition services, counseling psychology and social services, and employee wellness. The model stresses the importance of inhibiting hasty actions, thinking through lifestyle choices, and planning ahead before acting—executive functioning skills. Further removed, but still influencing children's decision making, are governance structures. A unique contributor in the governance structure is a **champion**, a charismatic person who is a strong supporter of a particular innovation. A champion can be either internal to a school or community organization (e.g., principal, nurse, physical educator) or external to it (e.g., university professor, activist parent, member of health agencies), and is typically emotionally tied to a particular method of education. A champion can be successful, however, only to the extent that he or she can collaborate with others who govern the school or community organization. Organizations, particularly long-established ones, are often resistant to change, resulting in champions who try to be innovative losing their motivation and experiencing burnout. Successful champions are often those who are in the right place at the right time.

---

ecological models—Models that emphasize how multiple factors determine people's health-promoting behaviors.

micro factors—Factors that influence health behaviors on a personal level, such as family, friends, and peers.

macro factors—Factors that influence health behaviors on a global level, such as institutions and cultures.

significant others—People important to children's well-being and self-concept.

self belief—A general level of confidence in one's abilities or judgments.

policy makers—People whose opinions strongly influence the course of events at various societal levels.

champion—A charismatic person who is a strong supporter of a particular innovation.

Figure 9.2   Coordinated school health (CSH) program ecological model.

Adapted, by permission, from D.K. Lohrmann, 2010, "A complementary ecological model of the coordinated school health program," *Journal of School Health* 80(1): 1-9. © John Wiley and Sons.

Layered over governance structures are those that provide monetary resources to schools and organizations. Funding for education is tightly linked to changes in economics and the philosophical positions of political representatives. Family and community involvement constitute the outermost layer of the CSH model. Interactions take place at every layer of the ecological model, from the outer layer to the innermost circle.

Whole School, Whole Community, Whole Child (WSCC) Ecological Model

Although the coordinated school health (CSH) model has proven to be an effective way to identify the factors that influence children's health, some

have advocated for changes to the model (Association for Supervision and Curriculum Development, 2007). It has been argued the CSH model can be improved by focusing not only on children's health, but also on education and social outcomes. As a result, the whole school, whole community, whole child (WSCC) model was developed. This model, shown in figure 9.3, builds and expands on the eight components of the traditional CSH model. The additional components emphasize the importance of the social and emotional climate and the physical environment. The overarching theme of the WSCC model is the need to create learning environments that engage children in active participation. The WSCC was developed in collaboration with the CDC and experts in many fields.

Many of the themes discussed in previous chapters are echoed in the WSCC model. The architects

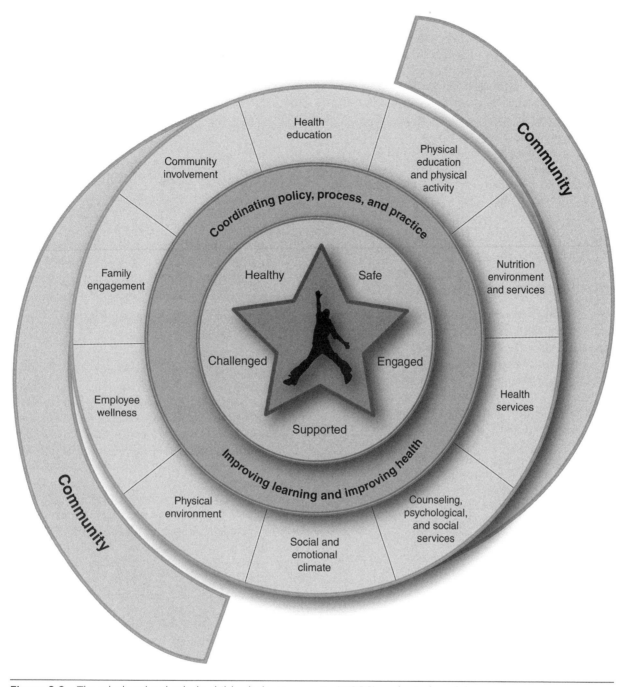

Figure 9.3   The whole school, whole child, whole community (WSCC) ecological model.

Whole child, whole school: applying theory to practice in a community school by Santiago, Eileen; Ferrara, JoAnne; Quinn, Jane. Reproduced with permission of Rowman & Littlefield Education in the format Republish in book via Copyright Clearance Center.

of the model stressed the need for learning conditions that embrace the interplay among each child's mind, body, and spirit. The supposition is that children who feel that they are in safe, trustworthy environments and who are challenged by mentally and physically engaging learning tasks develop the critical thinking skills they need throughout their lives. We too have emphasized the importance

of developmentally appropriate challenges that promote critical thinking, executive processes, and planning.

A central theme of the WSCC model is the view that children benefit most from educational experiences that help them weave together knowledge from multiple sources (e.g., school, family, health services, and community). Proponents of the model assert that schools and communities that prepare children for the future should change from teaching specific content to providing cross-disciplinary learning experiences. Physical activity games can provide a unique context for learning that cuts across the developing child's needs. Of course, we recognize that many other configurations of educational experiences can improve children's cognitive, physical, social, and emotional development. However, as discussed in chapter 1, physical activity is an excellent way to address multiple educational domains.

U.S. Centers for Disease Control (CDC) Guidelines

Using the ecological models as a guide, the CDC has gathered considerable information on people's behaviors and organizational activities. Further, it has developed guidelines to describe ways to prevent disease and improve health. A recent set of guidelines was developed to help teachers and schools facilitate parent, family, and community engagement in children's health and physical activity. Research shows that children who are supported by parents, family members, and those in community organizations are more physically active, perform better academically, and have better social skills than do children who lack support. The complete CDC guidelines can be accessed at www.cdc.gov/HealthyYouth. Three actions are critical to integrating children's physical activity behaviors into the home and community, connecting with parents, engaging parents, and sustaining parents' engagement.

Contributions of Physical Education to Ecological Models

Ecological models reveal micro- and macro-level factors that can influence children's physical activity. Clearly, no single factor can be expected to result in widespread changes in children's levels of physical activity. However, some micro-level interventions can favorably affect not only children but their families and communities as well. Physical activity has long been considered a type of preventive medicine. Indeed, national academic organizations in the United States such as the American College of Sports Medicine have proposed the notion that exercise is medicine (www.acsm.org/access-public-information/articles/2012/01/09/exercise-is-medicine-a-focus-on-prevention).

The worldwide rise in children's obesity in industrialized nations has driven home the importance of daily physical activity at every ecological model level. Policy makers are noting the economic benefits of healthy, physically active children. Community programs to increase children's involvement in play and outdoor activities have increased in number. School administrators who are seeing the contribution of children's exercise and health on academic performance are contemplating changes to physical education and recess times. Families are recognizing the real possibility that the lack of routine physical activity places their children at risk for adult diseases such as type 2 diabetes. Those who participate at the many levels of ecological models are looking to physical educators to develop ways to get children more physically active.

Applying Physical Activity Games to Ecological Models

Ecological models provide frameworks for identifying the roles and responsibilities of those who are accountable for teaching and preparing children to meet the challenges they will encounter as they mature into adulthood. Traditionally, physical educators are tasked with the job of teaching skills that children can use in games or sports across their life spans.

As highlighted in earlier chapters, physical education often does not focus directly on physical activity. Traditional physical educators focus on game skill instruction and very little on moderate-to-vigorous physical activity. In fact, the majority of physical education classes do not promote the levels of physical activity recommended for children. Further, recall that exercise is not the same as physical activity. Exercise programs for children focus on improving their physical fitness. The vast majority of exercise programs are modeled on those used by adults to improve aerobic fitness and muscular strength and endurance. Physical activity is movement that results in the expenditure of energy. Typically, children's exercise programs consist of routines that address intensity, duration, time, and frequency. However, many assert that, particularly with very young children, teachers should look beyond this framework (Dwyer, Baur, & Hardy, 2009; Pesce, 2012).

Physical activity games may be a way to provide children with more than just energy expenditure and fitness enhancement. The level and duration of children's physical activity expended during game play will, in all likelihood, contribute to their physical fitness; however, that is not the main focus. Physical activity games focus on helping children learn to control their bodies to solve problems. They are natural learning experiences that promote positive changes in children's mental abilities, self-confidence, and social skills. Physical activity games do not prepare children to be successful in playing sports; rather, they prepare children to be successful in life.

Research findings described in previous chapters indicate that appropriately trained physical educators who can deliver physical activity game interventions can affect children's cognitive development. Physical educators are uniquely positioned and well suited to develop programs that enhance children's physical and mental skills and contribute to their general health. Reinforcing these skills, however, requires more than what teachers can provide in the few hours they have with children during in- and out-of-school programs. Changing children's health-related behaviors requires input from multiple sources and from all layers of ecological models.

Parent–Child Bonds

Young adults who are expecting their first child often take classes on basic child care. The notion that soon-to-be parents need to learn basic skills in infant and child care and nutrition is well accepted. Less apparent is the fact that young adults may need to be taught how to play games with their children. As emphasized in chapter 7, the ability to teach is not inborn—it is learned. An important role of physical educators within ecological models is to promote bonding within families.

Many parents, with good intentions, surrender the role of teachers of their children to technology or to specialists. Computers and communication devices are a vital part of the 21st century; however, they cannot replace the learning that occurs in natural conditions. Indeed, they can rob parents of opportunities to teach, direct, and guide their children. Consider the advances in automobiles that allow children to wear headphones and watch television. When they are plugged in, their models come from the media, rather than from their parents. The skills that children, adolescents, and adults

Parents and children who spend time being active together are more bonded.

learn from playing computer games are limited to the games themselves; they lack usefulness in solving real-world problems. Playing a two-dimensional simulation of a sport such as bowling has virtually no effect on actual bowling skill.

Also, for multiple reasons, parents have enlisted the services of specialists to prepare their child for sports, arts, and crafts. Again, for better or worse, parents believe that providing special training early in life will increase their children's success. The methods used by child coaches are directed primarily toward early talent identification and training and competition. Children are quickly introduced to deliberate practice, which improves only athletic performance. Under these conditions, practice is a serious undertaking carried out to achieve continued improvement. Practice routines involve repetition and little thought or engagement. Once again, this type of learning has its place, but parents must recognize that it deprives children of opportunities to engage in developmentally appropriate play and games that foster mental and social development. Physical activity games can provide parents with ways to increase quality interactions with their children; through play and games, parents and children can establish enduring bonds (Ginsburg, 2007).

Social Bonds

As children develop, their social networks increase and the first network is the family. Families transfer knowledge from generation to generation via traditions. The skills of elders are recognized by their children and their children's children. Family traditions bind members together. The saying "Blood is thicker than water" conveys the notion that common goals and aspirations are held by family members. Researchers have noted the role that games and sport play in continuing family traditions.

The rules of games and concepts of fair play established on the playing field can mold children's and adolescents' self-concepts. Community youth settings and clubs have long served as centers for health promotion, games, and sport. Physical educators are often called on to lead programs in these settings. Introducing developmentally appropriate physical activity games can link positive experiences to these institutions and promote not only mental development but also lifelong memories—those that, perhaps decades later, will fuel how people guide their own children. This book includes examples of traditional cross-cultural children's games, altered to foster cognitive development.

Some parents do not have the luxury of telling their children to go outside and play. Today, many families live in communities that are not conducive to physical activity. The games described in this book do not require special classes or equipment; they can be performed in limited areas and at low expense. All teachers need is a basic understanding of how physical activity games facilitate mental engagement. Physical educators working with other specialists in community settings can help families restore or maintain the social bonds within families. Pediatricians can play a key role by providing parenting education and advocating for places and programs that ensure child play. According to the American Academy of Pediatrics, pediatricians should educate parents about the importance of free play and the value of participating in physical activities (http://pediatrics.aappublications.org/content/119/1/182.full.html).

Community Bonds

Mental and physical health is reflected in how the developing child accommodates the rules and regulations imposed in the community. Institutions such as schools, churches, and community organizations have rules that sanction appropriate behavior. Often, community events focus on bringing people together (e.g., recreation, games, and sports that promote socialization and not competition). Historically, games and sport have been used to resolve ethnic, religious, and political differences. Indeed, consider that the modern Olympic movement was based on the practice of ancient Greek city-states laying down their weapons and playing on equal terms. There are many other examples of games and sport serving the needs of the community and the common good. Physical educators, because of their unique skills, are well placed to assist community organizers in promoting inclusiveness and stability.

The physical activity games proposed in this book are in line with the recommendations made by the American Academy of Pediatrics to create equal opportunities to play for all children and inclusive practices for economically and educationally disadvantaged children (Milteer, Ginsburg, & Mulligan, 2012). Supervised after-school programs are considered critical for children who live in communities in which unsupervised outside play may be unsafe. Cognitively challenging games such as those described in this book, which can be easily included in supervised after-school programs and taught by nonspecialists, can be integrated into programs of school readiness promotion for low-income children (e.g., Head Start), as well as in out-of-school programs provided by voluntary organizations and foundations. In fact, these games can be employed by a variety of stakeholders, from school educators and parents to community groups and volunteers.

Cultural Influences

The world is rapidly becoming a global community. Patterns of immigration have had profound influences on educational systems. Educators are facing classes of increasing diversity. It is particularly important for physical educators and physical activity specialists to appreciate how heritage and culture determine children's responses to physical activity games and sport. **Culture** is defined as a system of beliefs about the way people interact within a segment of the population. Those who immigrate to a new country bring beliefs and values that reflect their home countries. Once in a new country, immigrants are often faced with the choice of maintaining their **traditional cultures**, the customs and practices handed down from one generation to the next, or embracing **acculturation**, a process of cultural and psychological change (Martinez, Arredondo, Ayala, & Elder, 2008). Family culture can influence how children participate in physical activity games and sports. Girls, and particularly adolescent girls, in certain cultures are discouraged or even prohibited from engaging in leisure-time physical activity (Allender, Cowburn, & Foster, 2006). Children respond favorably to culturally or ethnically tailored physical activity interventions. Changes can be made to make games culturally relevant. Further, researchers have found that children are more active when interventions are delivered by people who look and sound like they do.

Adapting physical activity games to the needs of individual children is particularly challenging for teachers. Effective teaching reflects an understanding of the interrelations that exist among children,

their families, their cultural communities, social institutions, and their greater communities.

21st-Century Schools

Prior to industrialization and the migration of workers to large cities, families were primarily in rural areas. Children learned skills from watching their parents and grandparents and receiving their guidance. For thousands of years, parents have transferred skills directly to their children. The skills of farming, building, hunting, and communicating that were vital for the success of one generation were transferred seamlessly, from father to son and mother to daughter.

With industrialization in the early 20th century, educational systems changed how children were taught. Public education in the United States and Europe has been considered part of the democratic processes and essential for providing equal opportunities to members of society (Laguardia & Pearl, 2009). Since the early decades of the 20th century, classes have been taught in a modular format, with classes for each subject. Further, teaching has been removed from the real world and placed in a controlled context. Scholars of the early 20th century supported this new method of teaching, and, for the time period, it was quite successful for preparing children to be adults in an industrialized world characterized by routine behaviors.

Education in Modern Societies

The schools of the 20th century reflected the growth of stable industries that produced products. Specific skills were required of workers, and schools were designed to meet those needs. Globalization, however, has fundamentally altered the way countries interact. Increased mobility, changes in job creation, and shifts in populations have changed the social structure from the one that existed in the 20th century. The structure of the family has also changed, with single-parent families and fewer stay-at-home parents resulting in an increased need for after-school and community programs. Moreover, the social network provided by extended families has been eroded by mobility and globalization.

Presently, national debates concerning education policy have arisen in the United States. On one side of the debate are those who want to maintain the school structures that have been in place for the past century; on the other side are those who suggest radical change to how children are educated

---

culture—A system of beliefs about the way people interact within a segment of the population.

traditional culture—Customs and practices handed down from one generation to the next.

acculturation—A process of cultural and psychological change.

(Lawson, 2009). The main theme of researchers who study educational policy is that modern schools need to change and adapt to the way the world has changed. Predictions of the effects of globalization, mobility, and changes in employment opportunities have led to recommendations concerning the role of schools and the preparation of future generations for the world they will live in.

Teaching In- and Out-of-School Programs

Preschool and after-school programs have played an increasing role in providing access to physical activity, art, and recreation opportunities. Indeed, policy researchers have noted the change from the traditional focus on education from kindergarten through high school (K-12) to education from preschool to the undergraduate degree (P-16), a type of cradle-to-career system (Lawson, 2012). A program that began in 1998 in the United States called 21st-century community learning centers provides federal funds to support preschool, after-school, and summer pro-

grams for low-performing schools in disadvantaged areas serving approximately 1.2 million children (U.S. Department of Education, 2010). Preparing children to meet the rapidly changing social and employment needs that will exist a decade or more in the future is a challenge for educators in general and physical education teachers in particular.

Some policy analysts have targeted the changing role of physical education in the 21st century (Lawson & Lawson, 2013). Traditionally, teachers specialize in particular areas—science, mathematics, reading, or physical education. Although there are benefits to specialization, it hinders the types of cross-disciplinary work that can affect children's levels of physical activity. Echoing the principles of the ecological models, we maintain that gains in children's physical activity can be realized when teachers accept a team approach in encouraging activity throughout the day using both in-school and out-of-school programs. In addition, the roles and prominence of physical educators will likely play a larger role in the near future by working in school-community partnerships.

© kellywegel.com

Learning cannot be confined to the school day; learning must be supported by quality teaching from all the adults in a child's life.

Physical educators who have specialized knowledge about teaching methods need to share their expertise with paraprofessionals, parents, and community organizations. The success of physical activity games depends on how they are taught. Keeping children on the learning curve demands teacher involvement and direct instruction, guidance, and feedback, as well as teaching strategies that promote problem solving, discovery, and creativity. Good teaching is not simple, and it requires more than organizing children's activity schedules. In-school, preschool, after-school, and community program teachers need adequate instruction in teaching methods. Addressing this need is consistent with the ecological models; however, out-of-school and community settings pose unique challenges for 21st-century teachers because teachers in these settings are less likely to receive instruction in these teaching methods.

New Roles for Physical Educators

Innovations are required to reconfigure physical education in extended-day, after-school, and community-based youth development and sport programs (Lawson, 2009). Traditionally, university teacher training programs have provided content knowledge and specialized training in methods of teaching in school settings. Federal, state, and local initiatives in the United States are changing the landscape of children's educational opportunities. Private-sector, market-driven program providers are functioning in many out-of-school organizations. Contemporary physical educators are being called on to assist in not only providing instructional services to children but also training providers to implement instructional programs. Successful physical education teachers can adapt teaching methodologies to new instructional environments.

Firm connections between schoolteachers and those who provide physical activity interventions in after-school and community-based settings are crucial. The concept of physical activity game playing stressed in this book is based on multidisciplinary research findings. The fidelity of the game interventions must be maintained by sharing instructional methods with those working in different environments or contexts.

> **translational research**—The uptake, implementation, and sustainability of research findings within standard care.

The RE-AIM model (which stands for reach, effectiveness, adoption, implementation, and maintenance) provides one way to appreciate the need for transdisciplinary approaches to instituting physical activity games in preschool and after-school programs. **Translational research** can be defined as the uptake, implementation, and sustainability of research findings within standard care (Estabrooks & Glasgow, 2006). For the past five decades, much of the basic science research conducted worldwide has been performed in university and national laboratories. Basic science is built on the belief that researchers' discoveries will answer specific questions about natural phenomena. From the 1960s to the 1990s, federally funded research in the United States led to many advances that had the potential to help humankind. The transfer of knowledge from research laboratories to the real world followed a linear pathway model, which assumed that teachers, practitioners, clinicians, and policy makers would discover and adopt new programs on their own.

Although great advances have been made in some areas, the transfer of research on exercise and physical activity to real-world applications has been lacking. In response, a different approach, referred to as the relationship model, was recommended in the mid-1990s. Successful translational work was seen as a knowledge exchange among multiple sources based on collaborative interpersonal and social relationships. For translational projects to flourish and succeed, input from individuals, organizations, and broader networks is needed—the process must be transdisciplinary (Estabrooks & Glasgow, 2006).

The general RE-AIM model developed by Glasgow and colleagues (2004), an approach to translational research that takes ecological and contextual factors into account, is composed of five components:

- *Reach:* The number of children and parents expected to participate. This component addresses several issues. For example, if there is a specific target population, will people in that population benefit from the program? A physical activity program for children in lower socioeconomic areas would need to take steps to ensure that children can attend.

- *Effectiveness:* The impact of the intervention on participants' quality of life. Interventions should have clearly stated outcomes that limit adverse events and unintended consequences. The benefits gained by children should be obvious.

- *Adoption:* The success of a program based on the number of schools or organizations that adopt it. A physical activity program created for children in before- or after-school programs may be perfectly designed, yet to succeed, it needs the support of administrators and school personnel.
- *Implementation:* How consistently the program is delivered and the time and cost of the intervention. The success of a physical activity intervention is determined by the quality of its teachers and the consistency of instruction across sites and days.
- *Maintenance:* The degree to which the program maintains participants' adherence and becomes institutionalized.

Using the RE-AIM framework is a useful way to plan and implement a physical activity program for children. It highlights factors critical to the initiation, execution, and maintenance of any translational research project. The relationships shown in figure 9.4 reveal the multiple linkages within the ecological models that underlie the implementation of a quality physical activity intervention.

Implications for Educators

Education is part of a democratic philosophy. However, the resources to fund it are linked to economic and political factors. During times of economic growth, the funding of educational programs occurs without much debate; however, when economies slow, fewer resources are available and discussions concerning educational priorities increase among policy makers. Historically, the core instructional domains of science, mathematics, and reading have been maintained in schools when economic resources lag. Education in the arts and physical education, on the other hand, tends to receive less support and fewer resources. A longstanding perception is that physical educators are a weak link in the overall educational process.

This perception has changed over the past decade as researchers have revealed the importance of physical activity on children's developing bodies and minds and as an intervention to promote physical and mental health and prevent obesity and disease (Physical Activity Guidelines, 2008). National and international funding sources in the United States are beginning to support translational research, which makes the results of basic laboratory studies applicable to real-world conditions. Multidisciplinary collaboration is a central theme in translational research. Many social problems are viewed as too complex to be resolved by a single specialization. In universities, it is becoming increasingly important for teacher educators to prepare the next generation of physical educators for working in a changing landscape in which the specialized skills and knowledge of physical education can be applied in many settings.

Worldwide, government, private, and community organizations are changing the way they

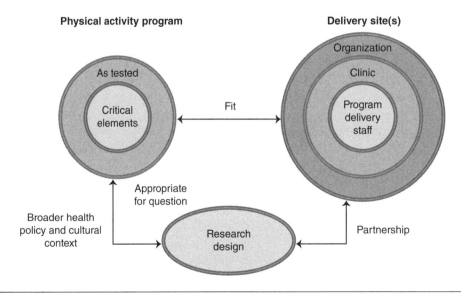

Figure 9.4 Simplified systems model of physical activity translational research.

Reprinted from *American Journal of Preventive Medicine*, Vol. 31(4S), P.A. Estabrooks and R.E. Glasgow, "Translating effective clinic-based physical activity interventions into practice," pgs. S45-S56, copyright 2006, with permission of Elsevier.

allocate resources to researchers and practitioners who focus on children's physical and mental health. Governments allocate funds to support research and programs that promote the general welfare of their people. Historically, research has been categorized as either **basic research**, which focuses on accumulating facts about humans and the world, or **applied research**, which focuses on solving practical problems. Researchers apply for grants that are reviewed by committees, and those determined to have merit are funded. Usually, government grants are provided to answer very specific, basic science questions. Funds for applied research studies and programs in the United States are typically provided to regional and state agencies to support community programs. Community agencies or groups such as the YMCA and Boys and Girls Clubs submit proposals to state or regional officials for evaluation and support. Currently, many preschool, after-school, and summer programs obtain support for teachers and staff through regional and state agencies.

Private foundations also provide support for programs that address social needs. Also, the role of industry in funding educational physical activity promotion programs for young people is emerging. One response to the alarming rise of obesity and physical inactivity at pediatric age is that businesses are increasingly engaged in promoting health-enhancing sport and physical activity initiatives as offshoots of their policies of corporate social responsibility. The important message from the changes taking place worldwide is that the discipline of physical education is poised to receive an extreme makeover and play a central role in emerging 21st-century educational policy.

> **basic research**—Research focused on accumulating facts about humans and the world.
>
> **applied research**—Research focused on solving practical programs.

Part III

Creating Effective Physical Activity Games

The final part of this book consists of two chapters; one shows games for preschool- and kindergarten-age children (3 to 6 years), and the other shows games for elementary school–age children (7 to 11 years). Alterations and modifications to spark children's engagement and learning are described for each game. These chapters also explain how to present games to children who differ in age and developmental level. Guidance concerning the application of physical activity games in preschool and after-school settings is also provided.

The aim of this book is not to merely provide a set of games to promote mental and motor develop-

ment; detailed explanations of how to teach them effectively are also presented. For each game, we explain why it works in the light of what we know about the nature and development of cognition. This promotes a deeper understanding of the particular executive functions, motor abilities, and skills that are challenged by each game and how new game rules and conditions alter these challenges. With this knowledge, teachers can create games and game alterations themselves. Teaching quality physical activity games to promote cognitive, physical, and social development is not simple or easy, but the rewards are immense.

Physical Activity Games
for Preschool- and
Kindergarten-Age Children

The level of motor development in preschool- and kindergarten-age children has declined over the past decades. This lag in movement capacity has led to calls for renewed attention to the quality of physical activity experiences, free play, and structured physical activity. This chapter focuses on quality physical activity games for children of this age.

Movement-based learning is very important during the preschool and kindergarten years (ages 3 through 6). The challenge for educators is to closely align learning experiences with young children's developmental levels in terms of both fundamental movement skills and mental functions. It is important to recognize that although fundamental movement skills and executive functions are linked,

they have different developmental trajectories. This represents a clear challenge for the educator, but it is one that can be overcome.

The games presented in this chapter promote, in an age-appropriate way, the development of both fundamental movement skills and executive functions that ensure adaptability and self-regulation in social and educational settings. They also facilitate the natural shift from parallel play, which is common in 2- and 3-year-olds, to social play and group games, which emerge in 4-year-olds.

This chapter provides (1) a brief background on the components of physical activity games necessary for facilitating the transition from play to games, (2) an explanation of how the games are related to SHAPE America guidelines (preschool) and standards (kindergarten) for the physically literate child, and (3) examples of developmentally appropriate games and game alterations to promote cognitive development. Also provided are the mental and motor demands of the movement games.

Moving From Play to Games

From infancy to early childhood, children progressively move from exploration and deliberate play to the deliberate practice of games. Exploration increases when children become comfortable with their settings and the people around them. Recall from chapter 4 that deliberate play is an end in itself, an activity performed for its own sake that is characterized by flexibility and positive enjoyment. Play is freely chosen, pleasant, symbolic, and engaged in either physically or psychologically, or both (Huges, 2010). Deliberate practice, on the other hand, is targeted, task-centered training that involves instruction. Games are organized activities in which there are rules and a goal (typically, winning the game). Developmentally, playing games with rules tends to be common after about 6 years of age, whereas simple play is more frequent in 2- to 6-year-olds. The transition from play to games and from unstructured to structured activities is an important developmental step. To facilitate this transition in the preschool years, teachers must offer learning experiences that maintain the essential features of play, but move toward organized, goal-oriented activities. The games proposed in this chapter move along this path.

Pretend Play

The games in this chapter contain features of the symbolic, or pretend, play activities that dominate at the preschool age (Smith & Pellegrini, 2008). Children who pretend give objects or actions meanings that are different from what they really are. Sociodramatic play, introduced in chapter 7, is social pretend play that has a story line involving sustained role taking and an understanding of others' intentions. It is common among children around 3 years of age. Game rules that promote cognitive development can be embedded in a make-believe environment characterized by imaginary roles and scenes. The imaginary world gives children the opportunity to mix story lines and contribute to the shaping of the story.

Discovery Play

The games in this chapter are open-ended and only partially structured, which gives children some freedom to make decisions. The games do not require that children reproduce predetermined movement patterns demonstrated by the teacher; rather, they promote the discovery of one or more solutions by the children to increase their mental engagement. As discussed in chapters 6 and 7, games can be taught using either the exploration and discovery method or the direct instruction method, or a combination of the two (Siedentop & Tannehill, 2000).

Games That Challenge Executive Functions

As noted in chapter 1, children's core executive functions emerge at different points in time, starting early during the preschool age. Thus, all of the executive functions are already present in preschool children to some degree. This chapter provides examples of movement games that increase the efficiency of these executive functions and promote children's ability to control their thoughts and actions.

The games proposed here reflect the three principles of mental engagement introduced in chapter 6: (1) contextual interference, (2) mental control (stopping, updating, and switching), and (3) discovery. The games and game alterations that we propose serve only as examples; teachers can create their own and change them to meet the needs of the children they teach. To do so, they must be aware of the abilities required for game performance not only in the motor domain, but also in the mental domain.

Each game description in this chapter highlights the mental and motor abilities required as well as changes that can challenge those abilities to a higher degree or introduce additional challenges not present in the basic version of the game. Alterations include those that can be made within a game or between games or while moving from one version to another. Each game includes three versions to provide variability in the mental challenge.

We focus on game alterations that progressively increase mental effort and specifically train executive functions. As noted in chapter 2, generating mental effort does not depend so much on the type of movement skills children perform. What matters is the complexity of movement coordination and the demands on thoughtful action. The proper balance of variation within a game and between games establishes and maintains an optimal challenge point for each child and challenges executive functions. Searching for the cognitively optimal challenge point is crucial for the success of the game, because executive functions must be continually challenged to promote improvements. Children who are not challenged do not gain in executive functioning.

Games can be varied by doing the following:

- Changing the motor demands by adding movements or increasing their coordinative difficulty
- Altering the rules to make the game more challenging
- Changing game intensity or duration, or both
- Altering the roles children play to maximize group effort
- Shifting the structure of the game to encourage problem solving and divergent discovery

How Games Are Featured and Presented

According to typical developmental progression (Gallahue & Cleland, 2003), the games presented here are characterized by the following:

- Limited or no equipment
- Limited rules with only one or two easy or slightly more complex strategies
- A focus on single skills or simple combinations of motor skills
- Playability by one person or a small group with a low level of competition

The game presentation format throughout chapters 10 and 11 is consistent. Each game is introduced, key instructional points are made, and strategies for keeping children on the learning curve are provided. The setup is as follows:

- Teacher Essentials and Explanation Points. This section describes content and the arrangements of tasks, their sequencing, and how to structure the learning environment.
- Challenges Posed. This section covers issues of instructional flow and flexibility that influence when and how to alter the game.
- Small Modifications and Moving On. This section suggests small changes to games to adjust children's physical and cognitive engagement.

- Zooming Into the Game. This section presents an analysis of the mental and motor abilities required for game performance.
- Game Breakdown. This section provides a user-friendly breakdown of the games, including equipment, skills needed, rules, and questions that can be used to promote mental engagement ("teaching through questions" strategies).

Connecting Games for Preschool- and Kindergarten-Age Children to SHAPE America Standards

In chapter 7 we emphasized the importance of creating games that meet international guidelines and standards of quality physical activity and physical education for children. Recently, the American Alliance for Health, Physical Education, Recreation and Dance (AAHPERD), including the National Association for Sport and Physical Education (NASPE), which had published authoritative statements, guidelines, and standards for children's physical activity, has been reorganized and renamed the Society of Health and Physical Educators, or SHAPE America. The document "Active Start: A Statement of Physical Activity Guidelines for Children From Birth to Five Years" outlines guidelines and information for teachers, parents, and other caregivers of children. The games for preschool- and kindergarten-age children presented in this chapter are aligned with the "Active Start" guidelines, as listed here:

- Guideline 1: Preschoolers should accumulate at least 60 minutes of structured physical activity each day.
- Guideline 2: Preschoolers should engage in at least 60 minutes—and up to several hours—of unstructured physical activity each day, and should not be sedentary for more than 60 minutes at a time, except when sleeping.
- Guideline 3: Preschoolers should be encouraged to develop competence in fundamental motor skills that will serve as the building blocks for future motor skillfulness and physical activity.
- Guideline 4: Preschoolers should have access to indoor and outdoor areas that meet or exceed recommended safety standards for performing large-muscle activities.

- Guideline 5: Caregivers and parents in charge of preschoolers' health and well-being are responsible for understanding the importance of physical activity and for promoting movement skills by providing opportunities for structured and unstructured physical activity.

The above guidelines are not prioritized in a particular order.

Reprinted from National Association for Sport and Physical Education, 2009, *Active start: A statement of physical activity guidelines for children from birth to age 5* (Reston, VA: NASPE).

The games in this chapter, which are based on principles of variability of practice, are in line with guideline 3 for preschoolers, which recommends promoting the development of competence in fundamental motor skills that will serve as the building blocks for future motor skillfulness. Guidelines 1 and 2 recommend that young children accumulate at least 60 minutes of structured physical activity and engage in at least 60 minutes of unstructured physical activity each day. The games in this chapter have the potential to modify the physical activity of young children. Their focus on deliberate play promotes spontaneous activity that can be performed in many environments. When playing these games in the context of structured physical activity, children may engage in elements of spontaneous play by creating their own story lines. Conversely, they may later use these experiences in unstructured physical activity contexts. Thus, these games should facilitate the flow between spontaneous and deliberate play in unstructured contexts and deliberate practice in structured contexts.

The games for preschool- and kindergarten-age children in this chapter also reflect SHAPE America's (2014) National Standards for Physical Education that apply to kindergartners, as follows:

- Standard 1—The physically literate individual demonstrates competency in a variety of motor skills and movement patterns.
- Standard 2—The physically literate individual applies knowledge of concepts, principles, strategies, and tactics related to movement and performance.
- Standard 3—The physically literate individual demonstrates the knowledge and skills to achieve and maintain a health-enhancing level of physical activity and fitness.
- Standard 4—The physically literate individual exhibits responsible personal and social behavior that respects self and others.
- Standard 5—The physically literate individual recognizes the value of physical activity for health, enjoyment, challenge, self-expression, and/or social interaction.

The standards are not prioritized in a particular order.

Reprinted from Society of Health and Physical Educators, 2014, *National standards & grade-level outcomes for K-12 physical education* (Champaign, IL: Human Kinetics).

Table 10.1 is a game finder for this chapter that connects aspects of each game to the SHAPE America standards for physical education.

Table 10.1 Game Finder for Preschool- and Kindergarten-Age Children

Game	Page	Performance outcomes (preschool)	Performance outcomes (kindergarten)
GAMES HIGHLIGHTING CONTEXTUAL INTERFERENCE			
The Pied Piper	142	• Alternates slow and fast movements and travels forward and sideways, changing directions in response to a signal or obstacle using a variety of locomotor skills (standard 1). • Holds a rule in mind and behaves according to this rule, properly switching between two actions (standard 2). • Engages in short, frequent bouts of moderate-to-vigorous physical activity, alternating with short breaks, while playing the games (standard 3). • Follows directions given to the class for an all-class activity and is able to use space safely, avoiding collisions (standard 4). • Enjoys self-expression in various make-believe roles loaded with diverging emotions (standard 5).	• Reacts to unpredictable changes in the environment and adapts the direction and speed of movements according to those changes, using a variety of locomotor skills (standard 1). • Holds a rule in mind that involves more than two action alternatives, and is able to use them properly in response to various signals (standard 2). • Engages in progressively longer game phases characterized by moderate-to-vigorous physical activity (standard 3). • Displays first forms of prosocial behavior, focusing not only on game participation, but also on responsibility for others (freeing teammates) (standard 4). • Does not back out of play; enjoys fluctuating between competition (tagging) and cooperation (freeing) and accepts risk (being caught) (standard 5).
The Piper and the Mice	144		
The Chameleon	145		
Rock, Paper, Scissors	147		
Fly, Frog, and Snake	149		
The Bigger Tags the Smaller, and the Smaller Tags the Bigger	151		
GAMES EMPHASIZING MENTAL CONTROL			
The Statues Game: One, Two, Three . . . Star	153	• Alternates locomotor skills (walking, running) and quick stopping in response to signals (standard 1). • Is able to inhibit prepotent responses and stop moving according to the game rule (standard 2). • Engages in short, frequent bouts of moderate physical activity, alternating with short breaks, while playing the games (standard 3). • Accepts the teacher's decision when the decision is disadvantageous (e.g., being sent back to the starting line) (standard 4). • Enjoys self-expression in various make-believe roles and is able to assume a variety of parts, empathizing with animals or objects (standard 5).	• Demonstrates contrasts between slow and fast and forward and backward motion and various body positions in response to signals (standard 1). • Holds a rule in mind that involves more than two action alternatives, and is able to use them to move or stop properly in response to various signals (standard 2). • Engages in progressively longer game phases characterized by moderate-to-vigorous physical activity (standard 3). • Learns competition to succeed in the game and cooperation to find solutions in pairs (standard 4). • Interacts with others to overcome the challenges of motor problem-solving tasks, and appreciates the differences between own and others' solutions (standard 5).
One, Two, Three . . . Star or Moon	155		
One, Two, Three . . . Star or Moon or Sun	157		
Crazy Traffic Lights	159		
My Clock Is Late	161		
The Magic Hoop and the Stick of Contrary	163		
GAMES HIGHLIGHTING DISCOVERY			
The Cobweb and the Little Spiders	165	• Explores ways to solve simple gross-motor problems and alternate uses of objects using simple locomotor and manipulative skills, respectively (standard 1). • Inhibits habitual, more common responses in favor of less-usual movement strategies (standard 2). • Engages intermittently for short periods of time in moderate physical activity (standard 3). • Exhibits respectful physical contact when using the teacher's body to cope with motor problem-solving tasks (standard 4). • Enjoys self-expression in various make-believe roles and appreciates differences between own and others' solutions (standard 5).	• Achieves competence in finding and executing original and pertinent movement solutions using a variety of gross-motor (locomotor) and fine-motor (manipulative) skills (standard 1). • Develops strategies to move creatively both when the environment is stable and when it progressively changes (standard 2). • Engages intermittently for progressively longer periods of time in moderate physical activity (standard 3). • Works in pairs to find simple forms of cooperative solutions in a stable or slowly changing environment (standard 4). • Copes with fear (e.g., of climbing) and interacts with others to overcome the challenges of motor problem-solving tasks (standard 5).
The Moving Cobweb and the Little Ladybugs	167		
The Fable of the Magic Cobweb	169		
Photo Album	171		
Picture of Courage	173		
Movie of the Animal World	175		

Games Highlighting Contextual Interference

The games in this section are tag games. What makes them unique is that children play them by alternating tagger and taggie roles. The game conditions do not allow children to repeat tagging and avoidance movement sequences. These conditions generate contextual interference and promote the use of repetition without repetition. As discussed in chapter 6, the principle of contextual interference is applied when game demands are not fully predictable and children must assume more than one role (usually two at this young age). Given the situation uncertainty, children cannot repeat a solution and therefore must repeat without repeating; that is, they must solve the problem many times in many ways. Most of the games in this section require only a safe, open space. Some require a few small tools or easy, self-made equipment.

The Pied Piper

In symbolic, sociodramatic play, children often play the roles of friends or foes. This game gives children the opportunity to experience these roles in a playful situation. The game promotes contextual interference because children must shift between approach and avoidance behaviors, according to whether you are exhibiting the characteristics of a friend (with happy facial expressions and opening your arms to invite them to come closer) or a foe (with evil facial expressions and moving as if to tag them and inducing them to run away).

Teacher Essentials and Explanation Points

Explain that you are the pied piper, a person who can bewitch and capture mice with the magic sound of your flute. Demonstrate by walking around and pretending to play lovely music with a flute and ask the children to follow you silently as bewitched mice. Then stop, and explain that you are sometimes a good piper who loves mice and sometimes a bad piper who wants to catch them. Explain that you can suddenly turn toward them either showing a lovely smile and opening your arms to hug all of them, or showing an angry face and trying to tag them. Then start playing. To challenge their cognitive ability to switch between approach and avoidance behaviors, turn toward them at variable time points and randomly alternate the roles of hugging friend and catching foe.

The Pied Piper game teaches children complex response inhibition.

Challenges Posed

During short breaks between game phases, ask the children how many ways they tried to run away (see the questions in the Game Breakdown section). Even though very young children may not answer your questions, they will reflect on them and probably show how they behaved. This will help you point out that there were many ways to avoid being caught and that they did not always repeat the same solution. Also, use the breaks to remind children that they must pay attention while running ("Keep your eyes open") to avoid colliding with one another, both when hugging and when running away.

Small Modifications and Moving On

When all children have demonstrated that they can adhere to the game rules, you can introduce the following change. When you suddenly turn toward the children, you can say, "Hug Susan!" or "Catch Randy!" indicating a child to be hugged or tagged, respectively. This enhances the situational uncertainty; the rule is the same, but the running direction in space is different each time, according to the child you indicate to be hugged or tagged. Be mindful of choosing children who have moved apart from the group to bring them back into the group.

Zooming Into the Game

This game addresses the mental domain (i.e., executive functions) by having two roles for you and two movement behaviors for the children (approaching and hugging versus avoiding and running away). The children must hold two responsibilities in mind, which challenges their working memory store. It corresponds, in scientific research, to the challenge posed by simple working memory tasks that require the child to hold information in mind over time. Also, the two roles fluctuate unpredictably during the game, requiring children to perform an ongoing action (following the piper) and then switch to either of two actions (approaching or running away). This involves response inhibition and mental shifting. It corresponds, in scientific research, to the challenges posed by complex response inhibition tasks (which require the child to hold a rule in mind, respond according to this rule, and inhibit another response) and by response shifting tasks, which require that the child build an arbitrary stimulus–response set (teacher turns/child approaches) and then shift to a new stimulus–response set (teacher turns/child runs away).

This game addresses the motor domain (i.e., coordinative abilities) by challenging perceptual–motor adaptation (response orientation, reaction time). In fact, children must react to changes in the environment that are rather unpredictable and adapt the direction and speed of their movements according to those changes. The game alternates among vigorous physical activity (when the piper turns and starts tagging), moderate activity (when the piper walks slowly around), and breaks (when the piper turns and invites hugs).

Game Breakdown

This is a physically, cognitively, and emotionally activating game that involves fundamental locomotor skills (walking and running). Children experience fluctuations between two actions that are loaded with emotions (approaching and hugging or avoiding and running away).

Equipment

A 30-student class requires only a safe, open space.

Skills Needed

- Locomotor skills: walking, running
- Safe travel in space, chasing, fleeing
- Reading facial expressions and body communications

Rules

1. When you are walking around playing a virtual pipe, children must follow you in a line.
2. When you stop walking and turn to the children, they must recognize your facial expression and react accordingly (approach for a smile, or run away for an angry face).

Questions

- How did you try to escape?
- How did you turn to keep me in sight?
- How often did you change direction?

The Piper and the Mice: Who Tags Whom?

Tagging games are among the most common cross-cultural movement games (Dienstmann, 2008). In the more common version of a tag game, the tagger is identified in advance and does not change out of the role until the end of the game. In this variation of the story, the pied piper is less predictable and may behave in several ways. When turning toward the children, you can (1) smile and open your arms to hug the mice, (2) show an angry face and start tagging, (3) look deadpan (i.e., show no expression), or (4) appear scared. In the first and second cases, the rule is the same as in The Pied Piper game (approaching and hugging or avoiding and running away); in the third case, the mice must freeze in place, and in the fourth case, they must tag the scared piper.

Teacher Essentials and Explanation Points

Explain that the pied piper is not always able to bewitch the mice with flute music. When you turn and look at the mice without expression, they must freeze in place; when you look scared, it means that the mice are no longer bewitched and can tag you. Explain and add the third and fourth alternatives sequentially only after the children have played the first two alternatives correctly. Before starting the game, demonstrate the four facial expressions and ask children what they see and what they should do when they see each expression or gesture. If they understand the rules and remember the four alternatives, begin the game. To challenge their cognitive ability to switch rapidly between behaviors, turn toward them at variable time points, and choose your roles randomly.

Challenges Posed

As in The Pied Piper game, provide short breaks between game phases and ask children how many ways they tried to tag you or avoid being caught. Ask some of them whether they want to show what they did. Use the breaks also to remind children that they must pay attention to those around them while running to avoid collisions.

Small Modifications and Moving On

When all children have demonstrated that they can adhere to the rules, you can create small groups and assign the role of the piper to a child in each group. From what you observed in the previous phases of the game, choose children who were best able to maintain the four stimulus–response alternatives to act as pipers.

Zooming Into the Game

This game addresses the mental domain (i.e., executive functions) by confronting the children with more complex rules comprising three and then four movement solutions (approaching, avoiding, stopping, and tagging) that they must hold in mind. This represents a higher challenge for the working memory store than that posed by The Pied Piper game. The novelty lies in the fact that children must alternate the roles of tagged and tagging mice according to the piper's expression and action. This response shifting task is more challenging than that of The Pied Piper game. In fact, children must shift not only between two alternatives (teacher turns/child approaches, or runs away), but among further alternatives (teacher turns/child freezes in place, or tags).

The motor domain demands (i.e., coordinative abilities) are similar to those of The Pied Piper game except that the increased number of alternatives challenges fast perceptual–motor adaptation abilities and particularly reaction time.

Game Breakdown

This game is physically, cognitively, and emotionally activating and requires basic locomotor skills. Children alternate among several actions that are loaded with emotions (approaching and hugging, avoiding and running away, chasing, or freezing). The emotional component of this cognitively challenging game renders the game enjoyable. Most important, children learn to interpret the emotions of others and react to them properly, which is a relevant life skill (empathy).

Equipment

A 30-student class requires only a safe, open space.

Skills Needed

- Locomotor skills: walking, running
- Safe travel in space, chasing, fleeing
- Reading facial expressions and body communication

Rules

1. When you are walking around playing a virtual pipe, the children must follow you in a line.
2. When you stop walking and turn to the children, they must recognize your facial expression and react accordingly by approaching, running away, running toward, or stopping.

Questions

- How did you try to escape?
- How did you turn to keep me in sight?
- How often did you change direction?
- What pose were you in when you froze in place?
- Was it easier for you to run away from the piper or to try tagging him? Why?

The Chameleon

The Pied Piper story can be transformed into the story of a chameleon (you) who can assume the aspects of many animals. In this game you move around followed by the children. You can change into a different animal every time you turn toward the children. Also, the children pretend they are animals. There are four alternatives: (1) you are a bird that either calls its little birds to a hug or tries to catch butterflies; (2) you are a frog who wants either to hug its little frogs or catch crickets; (3) you are a snake who wants either to hug its little snakes or catch frogs; (4) you are an eagle who either calls its little eagles to a hug or tries to catch rabbits.

Teacher Essentials and Explanation Points

First, tell the children that you can transform yourself into various animals. Start the game with the first two animal roles (bird and frog) and add the third (snake) and the fourth (eagle) sequentially. Explain that you will start moving around imitating an animal and asking the children to follow you silently. However, they must pay attention because you can suddenly turn and tell them that you are looking for your baby animals to hug them, or that you are hungry and looking for animals to capture. Demonstrate this rule with a child; for each animal role you play, tell the child, "I am now a bird and you are my baby bird" while opening your arms, or "I am now a bird and you are a tasty butterfly" while reaching out to tag him. Explain that he must approach you while imitating the movements of a baby bird or run away from you while pretending to be a butterfly. Then you can start the game with all the children. To challenge their readiness, turn toward them at variable intervals and alternate your roles randomly (bird, frog, snake, eagle), looking either for your baby animals or for food.

Challenges Posed

As in the previous games, provide short breaks between game phases and ask children to explain and show the many ways they tried to tag you or avoided being caught. This promotes reflection on their actions. Remind children that they must pay attention to the others while running.

Small Modifications and Moving On

To modify this game, you can ask children what additional animal roles they would like to play. You can add a new rule when the children are playing the role of prey and are running away from you (the predator) by having them try to surprise you by running around behind your back and tagging you before you tag them. If one of them succeeds, you must assume the role of a new animal.

Zooming Into the Game

This game addresses the mental domain (i.e., executive functions) by confronting the children with several options that challenge their working memory store. Different from The Piper and the Mice game, there are only two and not four possible responses to your behavior: hugging or avoiding being caught. However, cognitive effort is enhanced because children do not know in advance how they will have to behave in response to your transformation into a bird, frog, snake, or eagle. In fact, you say only at the very last minute whether you are a lovely animal looking for your baby animals or a hungry animal looking for dinner. Also, the game challenges contextual interference when you pretend to be a lovely parent frog or a hungry snake. In both cases, the children must pretend to be frogs, but behave in different ways: nearing and hugging in the first case, and running away and avoiding being caught in the second case.

In the motor domain (i.e., coordinative abilities), the challenges are similar to those of the previous games, but the difficulty level for the children varies depending on the roles you assume. When you play the role of the bird or frog, the game is easier, because the motor pattern performed when either approaching or moving away is the same (flapping wings as either baby birds or butterflies). Analogously, when you play the role of the frog, children hop both as approaching baby frogs and as fleeing crickets. In contrast, in the case of the snake, when children are baby snakes, they must approach creeping; when they are fleeing frogs, they must hop. In the case of the eagle, when children are baby eagles, they approach running and flapping their wings, whereas when they are rabbits, they run away on all fours.

Game Breakdown

This physically, cognitively, and emotionally activating game requires children to use alternate fundamental movement patterns to perform two actions (approaching and avoiding).

Equipment

A 30-student class requires only a safe, open space.

Skills Needed

- Locomotor skills: walking, running, jumping
- Nonlocomotor skills: creeping, "all fours" locomotion
- Safe travel in space, chasing, fleeing
- Coping with alternating positive and negative emotions

Rules

1. When you are walking around, the children must follow you in a line silently.
2. When you stop and turn to the children saying what animal you are and whether you want to hug your babies or eat little prey, the children must react accordingly, selecting both the appropriate behavior (approaching or avoiding) and the movement pattern of the animal they are pretending to be.

Questions

- How did you try to escape?
- How did you turn to keep me in sight?
- How often did you change direction?
- Did you sometimes move as the "wrong" animal (a bird when you had to be a frog)?
- Did you make more mistakes when approaching to hug, or when escaping?
- Did you hop in the same or a different way when you had to be a frog approaching for a big hug or avoiding being caught by a predator?

Rock, Paper, Scissors: The Tagged Tagger

Rock, Paper, Scissors is a tagging game that does not provide stable roles. Each child may both tag and be tagged: the rock wins against (or tags) the scissors, but is tagged by the paper; scissors tag paper, but are tagged by the rock; and paper tags the rock, but is tagged by the scissors. This game requires self-made equipment (colored cards with drawings); its modifications require a few small tools.

Teacher Essentials and Explanation Points

To start, prepare a card for each child that has a drawing of a rock, paper, or scissors. Children can paint their own cards and hang them around their necks. To better identify the three objects, use different background colors. Then demonstrate the three roles by using a movement-based pretend game: paper-children use their arms to envelop the rock-children; scissors-children close and open their arms to virtually cut the paper-children; and rock-children show resistance to the cutting of the scissors-children by squatting with their arms around their knees to assume the form of a round rock. Make sure the children are clear that paper-children should tag rock-children, but avoid scissors-children, and so forth. Tell them they are caught when touched by a tagger. Once tagged, a child must squat down. Let three children play once as an example for all. Then let all the children play, first speed-walking rather than running. This is a good way to help young children learn to play tag, because initially, most of them cannot move safely in open space when chasing or fleeing. This game phase should be played only until all children understand the main rule, because it excludes less-able children. Those who need exercise most are excluded early and must remain physically inactive (squatting) for a longer time than their higher-fit and more-skilled mates. Once they all understand the rules, explain the next rule: a caught child may be freed if a child playing the same role (i.e., with an identical card) frees her by touching. Again, have a smaller group (six children, two for each role) play a trial phase. Thereafter, all children play.

Turn a classic hand game into a fun tag game for kids in Rock, Paper, Scissors.

Challenges Posed

Considering the children's young age, limit directives and give only enough feedback to maintain the game and encourage the players to free other players with cards identical to theirs; this ensures that caught children resume play. Provide short breaks between game phases to let children reflect on what they did to avoid being caught and to tag and catch others. Also, the breaks can be used to remind children to pay attention while running, lest they collide with others. In fact, the major safety issue in tag games is the risk of children colliding with others because they often pay attention only to the child they want to catch or avoid. The rule that a child is considered caught when simply touched reduces the collision risk.

Small Modifications and Moving On

Many traditional tag games have spaces where children can stop safely and not be caught. These places, often called home base or the safety zone, give children the opportunity to have a self-paced break, which reduces the physical and emotional load of the game and gives them time to observe the game and reflect without time pressure before resuming play. This is a useful modification to make when you observe several children who cannot adhere to the rules. Safe places can be identified by hoops on the floor. To increase the game's cognitive demands, the hoops can be the same three colors used for the rock, paper, and scissors cards. Children can stop safely only within a hoop that is the same color as their card. For kindergarten children, you can further enhance the cognitive demands by allowing them to stop safely only within a hoop that is a different color from the child's card, or introduce a time limit for standing in the safe zone.

Zooming Into the Game

This game addresses the mental domain (i.e., executive functions) by providing two roles (tagger and taggie) that the children must hold in mind, thereby challenging working memory. Also, the roles of tagger and taggie fluctuate unpredictably during the game, requiring children to inhibit an ongoing action (tagging) to switch to another type of action (avoiding being tagged) in response to an approaching child; this makes this a response shifting task.

Tag games address the motor domain (i.e., coordinative abilities) mainly by challenging coordination under time pressure and, particularly, fast perceptual–motor adaptation abilities (response orientation, reaction time). In fact, children must react to changes in the game that are rather unpredictable and adapt the direction and speed of their movements according to those changes. Tag games alternate bouts of moderate-to-vigorous physical activity (MVPA) with breaks. Being caught and waiting to be freed so they can pop up to resume play gives children a brief rest. These pauses are naturally tuned to children's fitness levels: a low-fit child will feel tired early and probably decelerate and be caught. The pause also provides time to observe and learn game roles and rules.

Game Breakdown

In this game, mental effort is generated by the fact that each child may both tag and be tagged according to the roles played as rock, paper, and scissors. Children experience fluctuations between two actions (chasing and fleeing) that are loaded with emotion. The game also trains forms of prosocial behavior (freeing and being freed) and promotes the learning of competition (tagging) and cooperation (freeing) (Lafont & Winnykamen, 1999).

Equipment

Needs based on a 30-student class:

- Safe, open space
- Self-made equipment: cards in three colors with drawings, one for each child
- A few small tools (six hoops)

Skills Needed

- Locomotor skills: walking, running
- Safe travel in space, chasing, fleeing, dodging

Rules

1. Paper-children tag rock-children, rock-children tag scissors-children, and scissor-children tag paper-children.

2. Children are caught when touched by a tagger and must squat down.

3. A caught child is free when touched by a child playing the same role.

Questions

- How did you try to tag or escape from other children?

- Did you pay more attention to tagging or avoiding being caught?

- How did you turn to keep taggers in sight?

- How often did you change direction?

- How often did you try to free children who were the same (rock/paper/scissors) as you?

Fly, Frog, and Snake: The Tagged Tagger

An enjoyable variation of the Rock, Paper, Scissors game for kindergartners is one similar to that proposed by Kubesch and Walk (2009). The story is built on the concept of the food chain. Near a pond a snake is looking for dinner. It finds a frog, which, in turn, aims to eat a fly. The fly has seen the snake and wants to annoy the snake to amuse itself. The basic premise is the same as in the Rock, Paper, Scissors game: a circular relationship exists among the fly, frog, and snake. However, this game also presents new alterations to provide additional cognitive demands. It requires no equipment apart from self-made colored cards with drawings of a fly, a frog, or a snake.

Teacher Essentials and Explanation Points

To start, prepare a card for each child that has a drawing of a fly, frog, or snake. Children can also paint their own cards and hang them around their necks. To better identify the three animals, use different background colors. Then demonstrate the three roles by using a movement-based pretend game: flies annoy snakes by moving around the snake-child and touching it with one finger repeatedly, frogs eat flies opening and closing their arms as a big mouth around the fly-child, and snakes eat frogs in the same way. Tell them they are caught when touched by a tagger. Once tagged, a child must squat down. A caught child may be freed if a child with an identical card frees him by touching.

This game differs from Rock, Paper, Scissors in that only half of the children start the game; the other half stand around linked in pairs. The pairs represent the safe place; a child cannot be caught when in a pair. However, when a child joins a pair to avoid being tagged, the child at the other end of the pair (i.e., the child not being touched by the child seeking refuge) must leave. The leaving child must rapidly compare his card with that of the tagger to determine whether he must tag or avoid being tagged. If they have the same animal card, they may run away separately in search of prey. Before starting the game, let eight children (four free players and four linked in two pairs) demonstrate the roles and rules once for all children. Then let all children play, first using a speed-walk pace to help them learn the rules and how to move safely in open space with low time pressure.

Challenges Posed

Limit directives and feedback during the game, although do encourage children to join pairs several times and to free playmates with the same animal card, to ensure that all children have an opportunity to break from a pair and resume play. Compared to Rock, Paper, Scissors, there is less need for breaks because half of the children are motionless during the game. Children who adhere to the rules could be appropriate targets for questions during the breaks. At this young age, questions should not be general; rather, they should be very concrete (e.g., "Jeff, how did you try to avoid being caught by Matthew at the start of the game?").

Small Modifications and Moving On

For kindergartners and older children, a further rule may be added: a child who wants to join a pair to escape being tagged cannot join a pair if the child who must leave has the same card as the child joining the pair. Furthermore, children may imagine a fantastic world in which flies grow to enormous sizes and develop such wide mouths that they can eat frogs; frogs, in turn, develop such long stomachs that they can swallow snakes without chewing; and snakes develop honey mouths that attract big flies. This is an example of dramatization and movement-based role playing, but you should prefer ideas suggested by children. When the new roles and rules have been learned, the tag game can be started.

Zooming Into the Game

This game may seem easier than Rock, Paper, Scissors, from a mental domain (i.e., executive function) perspective, because the number of taggers is halved and children can evade by joining pairs that are standing around. This may reduce the overall time pressure, but working memory and shifting ability are challenged. In fact, children must hold in mind one more rule (i.e., if a new child joins the pair, the child on the other end must leave, even though the child did not join her directly) and decide what to do after comparing their own animal role with that of the free player who was just tagging.

In terms of the motor domain (i.e., coordinative abilities), the Fly, Frog, and Snake game is similar to Rock, Paper, Scissors, except that fast perceptual–motor adaptation abilities are challenged to a lesser degree because of the lower number of free players and, therefore, potential taggers. Also, the possibility of stopping in a safe place gives children more frequent, mainly short, breaks between activity bouts. This reduces the need for you to provide breaks.

Game Breakdown

This tagging game for children of kindergarten age has circular tagging roles similar to those of Rock, Paper, Scissors. The additional rule that children may join pairs of children who stand around as safe places—but the external child must leave—enhances mental effort. Also, joining pairs under time pressure to avoid being caught does not allow children to choose a preferred friend for joining; this will contribute enhancing familiarity with most mates.

Equipment

Needs based on a 30-student class:

- Safe, open space
- Self-made equipment: cards in three colors with drawings, one for each child

Skills Needed

- Locomotor skills: walking, running
- Safe travel in space, chasing, fleeing, dodging

Rules

1. Snakes tag frogs, frogs tag flies, and flies tag snakes.
2. Children are caught when touched by a tagger and must squat down.
3. A caught child is free when touched by a child playing the same role.
4. A child who joins a pair of children (i.e., safe place) cannot be tagged, but the child at the other end of the original pair must leave.

Questions

- How did you try to tag or escape from other children?
- How did you turn to keep taggers in sight?
- Did you pay more attention to tagging or avoiding being caught?
- How often did you change direction?
- How did you try to avoid being caught by Matthew at the start of the game?
- When you were tagging Jane, who joined Tim to be saved, did you pay attention to the card of John, who had to leave the pair, to understand if you must tag him or escape from him?
- How often did you try to free children who were the same (fly/frog/snake) as you?

The Bigger Tags the Smaller, and the Smaller Tags the Bigger

In this game for children of kindergarten age, animal roles vary during the game. Children receive cards in one of two colors, without any drawings of animals on them, to hang around their necks. You have numerous cards in the same two colors, but your cards have drawings of big and small animals. The basic rule of this game is that the bigger animals tag the smaller ones. The novelty of the game is that it requires a form of inhibition termed **interference control,** which is the ability to select task-relevant information and filter out irrelevant, distracting information. This is difficult when the irrelevant information attracts attention more strongly than the relevant information does. In this game, interference control is required when the relative size of the animal drawings on two players' cards and their size in reality are inconsistent (e.g., a big drawing of a mouse and a small drawing of an elephant). This game requires easy, self-made equipment (colored cards for children and colored cards with drawings for you).

Teacher Essentials and Explanation Points

To start, provide each child with a card in one of two colors to be hung around the neck. Then explain that they must pay attention to the animals drawn on your two cards. If on your yellow card there is an elephant and on your blue card a mouse, then the yellow children are taggers. After a short break, restart the game showing either the same cards or two new cards and reversing the association between the color and the animal and therefore the tagger and taggie roles. Once tagged, a child must squat down and is freed only when touched by a child with the same color card. Let a few children play once as an example for the rest of the group. When all children understand the rules and behave accordingly, explain that you are a fairy or a wizard who can reduce or enlarge the size of animals and make an elephant smaller than a mouse and a mouse bigger than an elephant, or a giraffe shorter than a dog and a dog taller than a giraffe. Then, introduce new inconsistent cards, showing, for instance, a large drawing of a mouse and a small drawing of an elephant. Remember, however, to explain that only the size of the animal in real life is important, not how big it is drawn on the card.

> **interference control**—The ability to select task-relevant information and filter out irrelevant, distracting information. This is difficult when the irrelevant information attracts attention more strongly than the relevant information does.

Challenges Posed

Limit directives and feedback, and use breaks during which children can recover and reflect on the game. As in previous tag games, let all children play, first using a speed-walk pace to help them learn the rules and how to move safely in open space with low time pressure. To reduce the collision risk, during the breaks recall the rule that a child is considered caught when simply touched and use frequent reminders ("Remember to keep your eyes open").

However, in this game the fairy or wizard is the pacemaker who controls repetition and change, because roles change depending on the cards you show during the breaks. To enhance contextual interference progressively, vary the association of animals with the card colors. First do it regularly and then more randomly. To help children deal with inconsistent cards, before starting the game, show them the cards and ask them whether they have already seen an elephant in the zoo, circus, or elsewhere (to help them understand what you mean by *real size*).

Small Modifications and Moving On

With kindergarten-age children, you may decide, at a given point, to reverse the rule and have the smaller animals tag the bigger ones. This rule change requires the ability to shift between mental sets, because it is a sort of **reverse categorization task** (i.e., one that requires the use of complex response inhibition). When you introduce this new rule (small animals are taggers and big animals are avoiders), first use only consistent cards (big elephant drawing and small mouse drawing) to avoid cognitive overload. Only when children have learned the new rule should you use the inconsistent cards to stimulate interference control.

Zooming Into the Game

In this game the mental domain (i.e., executive functions) is stimulated by the addition of inconsistent cards. Children must learn and hold in mind the new rule of ignoring the size of the drawings and concentrating on the size of the animals in real life. The inconsistent cards generate interference and promote interference control. To choose the proper role of tagger or taggie, children must suppress the interference generated by the misleading size of the animal drawings and concentrate on the size of those animals in reality.

This game addresses the motor domain (i.e., coordinative abilities) mainly by challenging coordination under time pressure and, particularly, fast perceptual–motor adaptation abilities (response orientation, reaction time). In fact, children must react to changes in the game that are rather unpredictable and adapt the direction and speed of their movements according to those changes. Tag games alternate bouts of MVPA with breaks. Being caught and waiting to be freed and resume play gives children a brief rest. These pauses are naturally tuned to children's fitness levels: a low-fit child will feel tired early and probably decelerate and be caught. The pause also provides time to observe and learn game roles and rules.

Game Breakdown

This tagging game for children of kindergarten age alternates between tagging and taggie roles. Children are attributed animal roles that vary during the game at a pace that you define. As compared to the previous tagging games, additional interference is generated by how you use the drawings of animals to determine who tags whom.

Equipment

Needs based on a 30-student class:

- Safe, open space
- Self-made equipment: cards in two colors without drawings, one for each child, and eight cards in the same two colors with large and small drawings of two animals

Skills Needed

- Locomotor skills: walking, running
- Safe travel in space, chasing, fleeing, dodging

> **reverse categorization**—A task that requires complex response inhibition. For instance, children sort big blocks into big buckets and small blocks into small buckets; then do the reverse.

Rules

1. The basic rule of this game is that the bigger animals tag the smaller ones.
2. Each child has a card in one of two colors without any drawing of an animal. Children whose cards have the same color as the card of yours that bears the drawing of the bigger animal take the tagger role.
3. Once tagged, a child must squat down and is free only when touched by a child with the same color card.
4. If you show inconsistent cards (e.g., a large drawing of a mouse and a small drawing of an elephant), children must consider only the size of the animal in real life to understand whether they must tag or avoid being tagged.

Questions

- How did you try to escape?
- How did you turn to keep taggers in sight?
- How often did you change direction?
- How did you try to avoid being caught at the start of the game?

Games Emphasizing Mental Control

Recall from chapter 6 that different types of games challenge different aspects of mental control. Stopping games challenge simple and complex response inhibition behaviors. Updating games challenge the use of simple and complex working memory. Switching games require the use of response shifting and attention shifting.

The Statues Game: One, Two, Three . . . Star

This game and the two that follow apply the task of stopping. The Statues Game is a popular children's game with various names across the globe. In Italy it is called One, Two, Three . . . Star; in France it is called One, Two, Three . . . Sun; and in Mexico it is called One, Two, Three . . . Pumpkin. It is a great game for progressively increasing executive and motor coordination demands. The teacher or a child is the curator and stands at one end of the play area; statues (the remainder of the children) are at the far end behind a starting line. The object of the game is for a statue to tag the curator, thereby becoming the curator and resetting the game. Statues can move freely toward the curator as long as the curator's back is turned, but must freeze in place when the curator faces them. Statues that are caught moving by the curator are sent back to the starting line. This game requires only a safe, open space.

Teacher Essentials and Explanation Points

To start, explain that you are the curator and the children are statues. Explain that statues usually do not move because they are made of stone. Tell them that they are magic statues that can move when the curator isn't looking, and that they are free to race toward you when your back is turned and you are counting loudly "One, two, three." However, they must freeze in position when you, at any time after calling "three," turn around to face them and shout "star." Emphasize that they must pay attention, because if you catch them moving and not being as still as a statue, they will have to go back to the starting line. Also explain that the first child who touches you wins and becomes the curator for the next round.

Challenges Posed

Between games, ask children to explain how they avoided being spotted while moving. Prompt them with questions that help them reflect on when and how they stopped (see the questions in the Game Breakdown section). Also, ask how they behaved when they came very close to you. Older players often stand right behind the curator without touching, only to touch as soon as the curator turns around to count. These children are exhibiting the ability to delay a response. If children do not discover this strategy on their own, you can promote this kind of inhibition by recommending that they not touch you until you start to turn your back.

Small Modifications and Moving On

Require children to stop in a specific pose. Children who are caught either moving or stopping in the wrong pose are sent back to the starting line. However, you must not fully define and above all not demonstrate the pose in order to promote to some extent the discovery learning described in chapter 6 and applied in the section of "Games Highlighting Discovery" later in this chapter. For instance, you can ask "Stop on all fours" or "Stop on one foot" without demonstrating a predefined pose, for the children to find out the pose they can reach fastest (when you call "Stop on all fours", squatting down with hands on the floor or assuming belly-down poses on all fours is easier and faster for children running forwards than belly-up poses on all fours). The need to stop in a partially defined pose is a task constraint that makes it more difficult for children to show off their skills.

Another modification is to have children play in pairs and add a rule that requires pairs to stop in a way that conceals one of the children behind the other. This modification requires children to control both their own and their partners' movements and positions, adding to the rule to alternate going and stopping according to the signals given by the curator (i.e., go/ no-go rule).

With beginners, always maintain the same turning and shouting speed. As they become increasingly familiar with the game, you can increase the difficulty by chanting "One, two, three . . . star" at varying speeds or saying it so fast that it is impossible for players to move at all. You can also chant "One, two, three" slowly or at varying speeds and shout "star" rapidly, or any combination you like.

Zooming Into the Game

This game challenges a specific executive function in the mental domain: the inhibition of prepotent responses, which are responses that are difficult to be refrained. Particularly, it represents a complex response inhibition task (stopping): the children must hold a rule in mind and respond according to this rule (going when the curator is counting and stopping when the curator shouts "star") and inhibit a prepotent response (continuing to move when the curator turns because of the desire to tag quickly).

In the motor domain (i.e., coordinative abilities), running in response to a go signal and stopping on a no-go signal creates a discrimination reaction time task that challenges fast perceptual–motor adaptation ability, as well as fast motor control ability (to freeze in position). The game alternates bouts of MVPA with breaks.

Game Breakdown

This game challenges the executive function of response inhibition, or stopping. Its basic version may be easily used with children as young as 3 years old. It is a useful way to progressively increase executive and motor coordination demands. The modification requiring that children move in pairs and stop with one of them concealing the other promotes cooperative and creative searches for solutions.

Equipment

A 30-student class needs only a safe, open space.

Skills Needed

- Locomotor skills: walking, running
- Safe travel in space

Rules

1. Children are free to race toward you when your back is turned and you are counting loudly, but they must freeze in position when you turn to face them and shout "star."
2. Any child you catch moving and not being as still as a statue has to go back to the starting line.
3. The first child who reaches and touches you wins and becomes the curator for the next round.

Questions

- Did you stop at a given number, or just when I started to turn around?
- What pose were you in when you stopped?
- How did you behave when you came very close to me?

One, Two, Three . . . Star or Moon

In an Australian variant of The Statues Game, called London, the curator can either spell out London or shout "London Bridge fell down" before turning. In the first case, children have to freeze in a standing position; in the second case, they have to sit or at least not be standing when the curator turns around. The Statues Game may be modified by adding a further freeze condition that is coupled with a requirement to freeze as either a star or a moon, when you count "One, two, three" and then call out either "star" or "moon." Children who are caught either moving or stopping in a position different from the one you called out are sent back to the starting line.

Teacher Essentials and Explanation Points

To start, explain that you are the curator and the children are statues. Explain that statues usually do not move because they are made of stone. Tell them that they are magic statues that can move when the curator isn't looking, and explain that they are free to race toward you when your back is turned and you are counting loudly "One, two, three." However, they must freeze in position when you, at any time after calling "three," turn around to face them and shout "star" or "moon." Emphasize that they must pay attention, because if you catch them moving and not being as still as a statue in the star or moon pose you have called out, they will have to go back to the starting line. Also explain that the first child who touches you wins and becomes the curator for the next round.

This game differs from The Statues Game in that, when you turn, you can call out either "star" or "moon" and the children must stop in a pose representing either a star or the moon. To help them determine how a star or moon may be represented, let them play in a preliminary explorative phase in which they try to find as many ways as possible to assume star or moon poses. By doing this, you promote to some extent the discovery learning described in chapter 6 and applied in the section of "Games Highlighting Discovery" later in this chapter. At the end of this preliminary phase, you must identify with the children some star and moon poses the majority of them converge on. Those will be the valid poses for the children not to be bent back to the starting line.

Challenges Posed

Between games, ask children to explain how they avoided being spotted while moving. Prompt them with questions that help them reflect on when and how they stopped (see the questions in the Game Breakdown section). Also, ask how they behaved when they came very close to you. Older players often stand right behind the curator without touching, only to touch as soon as the curator turns around to count. These children are exhibiting the ability to delay a response. If children do not discover this strategy on their own, you can promote this kind of inhibition by recommending that they not touch you until you start to turn your back.

Add questions regarding the many ways they found to represent a star or the moon during the preliminary explorative phase and how many they used during the game. They will discover on their own that, under time pressure, they all traded richness of pose solutions for speed, using only the easiest solution so they could stop in time.

Small Modifications and Moving On

During a preliminary discovery phase, you can ask children to explore in pairs how many ways they can assume star and moon poses. Begin the game by asking children to move in pairs and freeze in a star or moon pose together. Because you have added a new responsibility, you should reduce the speed at which you chant "One, two, three . . . star (or moon)" and keep it constant and predictable across trials.

Zooming Into the Game

In terms of the mental domain (i.e., executive functions), this game challenges the ability to inhibit prepotent responses. Moreover, the addition of an alternative challenges the ability to hold information in working memory (assuming a star or moon pose based on what you call out).

In terms of the motor domain (i.e., coordinative abilities), the presence of two stimulus–response associations (star call/star pose, moon call/moon pose) generates a choice reaction time task that challenges fast perceptual–motor adaptation ability. The demands on fast motor control are higher than in the previous game, because this variation requires alternating motor skills (walking or running) and stopping positions (standing or sitting in different poses) under time pressure. Also, this game alternates bouts of MVPA with breaks.

Game Breakdown

This is a variation of the game One, Two, Three . . . Star, and as such, also challenges the executive function of response inhibition, or stopping. This alteration adds a rule that requires children to stop in a position representing a star or the moon. This requirement increases the need for fast motor control. The extent to which fast motor control is challenged depends on the difficulty of the star and moon poses you select with the children at the end of the preliminary explorative phase in which children discover how many poses they can assume to look like a star or the moon.

Equipment

A 30-student class needs only a safe, open space.

Skills Needed

- Locomotor skills: walking, running
- Nonlocomotor skills: bending, twisting, balancing
- Safe travel in space

Rules

1. Children are free to race toward the curator when his back is turned and he is counting loudly, but they must freeze in a star or moon pose when the curator turns around to face them and shouts "star" or "moon."
2. Any child caught moving or being as still as a statue but not in the appropriate star or moon pose, has to go back to the starting line.
3. The first child who reaches and touches the curator wins and becomes the curator for the next round.

Questions

- Did you stop at a given number, or just when I started turning around?
- What pose were you in when you stopped?
- How did you behave when you came very close to me?
- How many ways did you find to represent a star or the moon before starting the game?
- How many star or moon poses did you use during the game?

One, Two, Three . . . Star or Moon or Sun

The previous game can be altered by including a third alternative to a star or the moon: the sun! Should you shout "sun," the children must not stop, but continue moving. If you shout "star" or "moon," they must freeze in a pose that represents a star or the moon based on what you shouted. Remember that you can introduce a preliminary exploratory phase in which the children try to find as many star or moon poses as possible and then you select with them those poses that will be considered valid for playing the game.

Teacher Essentials and Explanation Points

To start, explain that you are the curator and the children are statues. Explain that statues usually do not move because they are made of stone. Tell them that they are magic statues that can move when the curator isn't looking, and explain that they are free to race toward you when your back is turned and you are counting loudly "One, two, three." However, they must freeze in either a star or moon position when you turn around to face them and shout "star" or "moon." To help them determine how a star or moon may be represented, have them play in a preliminary explorative phase to find as many ways as possible to assume a star or moon pose. By doing this, you promote discovery learning, as you can recall from chapter 6 and see as applied to further games in the section of "Games Highlighting Discovery" later in this chapter. At the end of this preliminary game phase, you must clearly identify with the children some star and moon poses to be considered valid. Different from when you shout "star" or "moon," if you call out "sun" after counting "One, two, three," they can continue moving. Explain that as long as the sun shines, the magic statues can continue moving. Under the hot rays of sunshine, children cannot be frozen in place. The sunshine gives the statues a power you cannot counteract. Also explain that the first child who touches you wins and becomes the curator for the next round.

Challenges Posed

Between games, ask children to explain how they avoided being spotted while moving. Prompt them with questions that help them reflect on when and how they stopped (see the questions in the Game Breakdown section). Also, ask how they behaved when they came very close to you. Older players often stand right behind the curator without touching, only to touch as soon as the curator turns around to count. These children are exhibiting the ability to delay a response. If children do not discover this strategy on their own, you can promote this kind of inhibition by recommending that they not touch you until you start to turn your back.

Add questions regarding the many ways they found to represent a star or the moon during the preliminary discovery learning task and how many they used during the game. They will discover on their own that, under time pressure, they all traded richness of pose solutions for speed, using only the easiest solution so they could stop in time. Focus in particular on whether they were able to continue moving when you turned and shouted "sun" or whether they first stopped in place and then restarted.

Small Modifications and Moving On

You can set this game under the sea instead of in the sky. Instead of "star," "moon," or "sun," you may shout "starfish," "balloon fish," or "crayfish." When you call out either starfish or balloon fish, children must freeze in place and represent the appropriate fish. In the case of the crayfish, children should continue moving, but they should move as a crayfish would—backward toward the starting line until you turn your back and restart counting. This alteration adds to the two previous alternatives (of either stopping or moving forward) a third alternative of moving backward.

Zooming Into the Game

This game addresses the mental domain (i.e., executive functions) by challenging the ability to inhibit prepotent responses more than the previous statues games do. In those games, the rule was that after the count, which was a go signal for the children to move toward the curator, the next word would be a stop signal, regardless of the position they froze in. In contrast, in the present alteration, the word called out after the count might be a second go signal ("sun"), indicating that children may continue moving. As a consequence, the tendency to continue moving will be stronger, and the inhibitory function for suppressing it when "star" or "moon" are called out will be challenged at a higher degree. Also, adding a new alternative (to continue moving when "sun" is called) requires children to hold more information in their working memory.

In terms of the motor domain, the addition of a further stimulus–response association enhances the difficulty of the choice reaction time task and therefore the demands on perceptual–motor adaptation (reaction) ability. Also, this game alternates bouts of MVPA with breaks. Moreover, the game alteration "under the sea" introduces higher demands of response orientation and balance, since when children are allowed to move, they must alternate direction and speed (running forward when the curator calls "one, two, three . . ." and walking backward when he shouts "crayfish").

Game Breakdown

This is a further variation of the basic One, Two, Three . . . Star game, and as such, also challenges the executive function of response inhibition, or stopping. The addition of the option to continue moving challenges the ability to react or inhibit a reaction at a higher degree, and the affective commitment is correspondingly strong.

Equipment

A 30-student class needs only a safe, open space.

Skills Needed

- Locomotor skills: walking, running
- Nonlocomotor skills: bending, twisting, balancing
- Safe travel in space

Rules

1. Children are free to race toward the curator when her back is turned and she is counting, but they must freeze in a star or moon pose when she turns around to face them and shouts "star" or "moon."
2. Any child caught moving or being as still as a statue, but not in star or moon pose, has to go back to the starting line.
3. If the curator shouts "sun" instead of "star" or "moon," the children may continue moving toward her.
4. The first child who reaches and touches the curator wins and becomes the curator for the next round.

Questions

- Did you stop at a given number, or just when I started turning around?
- What pose were you in when you stopped?

- How did you behave when you came very close to me?
- How many ways did you find to represent a star or the moon before starting the game?
- How many star or moon poses did you use during the game?
- Were you able to continue moving when I turned and shouted "sun," or did you first stop in place and then restart?
- If you stopped when I turned and shouted "sun," did you restart because you saw other children restarting, or because you remembered that the sun is hot and cannot freeze you in place?

Crazy Traffic Lights

The Statues Game is also known as Red Light/Green Light. This game, which primarily requires inhibitory ability, may be the starting point to develop a new game that challenges another aspect of inhibition—interference control—and challenges the function of switching to promote cognitive flexibility. The first and second phases of the game do not address interference. In the first phase, the children can move around freely when you call out "Green light, go" and must immediately stop when you call out "Red light, stop." In the second phase, you do not give a verbal instruction, but issue a visual color signal by holding up either a green or a red object. The third phase introduces interference. You give a verbal and a visual signal simultaneously, but in some cases they are contradictory (i.e., you call out "Go" but hold up the red object, or call out "Stop" but hold up the green object). The children must behave according to the color signal, not the verbal signal. The game requires open space and one red and one green small object.

Teacher Essentials and Explanation Points

At the outset explain that you are a traffic officer. Ask the children to move freely around when you shout "Green light, go" and to stop immediately when you call out "Red light, stop." To reinforce stopping immediately, praise the children who stop the soonest. When you see that they have learned the rule, take a break and explain that you are now a traffic light. Indicate that when you hold up a green object, they can move; when you hold up a red one, they must stop. When they understand the rule, pause to explain that you are now a broken traffic light, doing the opposite of what you should be doing. Demonstrate by saying "Go" as you raise the red object and saying "Stop" as you raise the green object. Explain that they are to ignore what you say and instead obey the lights you hold up (the red or green objects). To integrate the characteristics of symbolic play and make the game more enjoyable, ask the children to move around while pretending to drive a car. They can also make car sounds when moving or stopping or pretend to turn a steering wheel.

Challenges Posed

Provide a further break within the third (interference) phase of the game by asking the children how they managed not to be confused by the misleading verbal instructions (see the questions in the Game Breakdown section). One strategy they may offer is that they watched your hands for as long as possible while moving around. This strategy, although good, often results in distracting attention from the control of their own and others' movements and risks collisions. Therefore, reminders are needed ("Remember to keep your eyes open").

Small Modifications and Moving On

For kindergarten-age children, the demands on inhibitory ability and cognitive flexibility may be enhanced by requiring them to deal with reverse categorization (stopping for green and moving for red). Explain to the children that they are now driving a car on the moon, where the traffic rules are reversed: moon drivers move with red lights and stop with green lights. The cognitive effort is higher when the misleading information that children must ignore is reinforced by consistent verbal and visual information (e.g., you shout "Go" while raising the green object, but children must stop). You can also vary the children's movements and their stop positions by having them pretend that they are much lighter because they are on the moon. They can build on what they learn by playing the Photo Album and Movie of the Animal World games, described later in this chapter. These require actions such as moving on all fours and stopping on both feet and one hand, or moving only on one foot and stopping on both hands and one foot.

Zooming Into the Game

This game challenges all three core executive functions in the mental domain. In fact, in the first game phase, children must hold a rule in mind and respond according to this rule (to move in response to a given signal and to stop in response to another signal), inhibiting the tendency to continue moving. This is a complex response inhibition task. In the second game phase, children must learn a new rule (simple working memory task) and switch from the previously learned rule (to pay attention and react to a verbal signal) to the new rule of paying attention and reacting to a visual signal. This is an attention shifting task. Finally, in the third game phase, they must actively suppress the tendency to react to the voice signal that draws attention from the color signal to which they must react. This phase challenges children's interference control, which is the ability to ignore pop-ups.

In the motor domain (i.e., coordinative abilities), the demands are analogous to those of the previous statues games: the presence of two stimulus–response associations (green light/go, red light/stop, or the reverse association) generates a reaction time task that challenges fast perceptual–motor adaptation ability. Moreover, there are demands on response orientation because there is no given run direction. Also, this game alternates bouts of MVPA with breaks.

Game Breakdown

This game for children of preschool and kindergarten age is based on the popular red light/green light game, which challenges the executive function of mental shifting, or switching. Mental effort is generated and cognitive flexibility is challenged by changing rules and varying the associations applied to stimuli and the ways children must respond to them. Furthermore, this game and its alterations introduce another aspect of inhibition—interference control: you simultaneously give a verbal and a visual signal that are sometimes contradictory. The make-believe story elicits emotional involvement.

Equipment

Needs based on a 30-student class:

- Safe, open space
- One red and one green small object

Skills Needed

- Locomotor skills: walking, running
- Safe travel in space

Rules

1. When you play the role of a traffic officer and say "Green light, go," the children can move freely around. When you call out "Red light, stop," they must stop immediately.
2. When you pretend to be a functioning traffic light and hold up a green object, the children can move, but when you hold up a red one, they must stop.
3. When you pretend to be a broken traffic light, the children must ignore what you say and react instead to the color of the object you hold up.

Questions

- How many times did you follow my voice and forget to pay attention to the color?
- What are some things that helped you not be tricked by the voice trap?

My Clock Is Late

This game is not an alteration of the previous Crazy Traffic Lights game, but a different example of how the principle of mental control may be applied, introducing the requirement to update information held in the working memory store. Recall that the principle of mental control is an umbrella term that includes stopping, updating, and switching. Specifically, the present game consists in **delayed imitation**, that requires both stopping and updating. It involves a task in which a child imitates a movement pattern, but after a time delay. In this game, also tailored to improve your students' coordination, you stand in front of them and perform predefined movement patterns they must imitate. The coordination sequence is as follows: (1) clap hands four times, (2) hop in place four times, (3) hop to make a complete rotation four times, and (4) alternate squatting and standing up two times each. To introduce the principle of delayed imitation, do not have the children start moving when you do; rather, have them start clapping when you start hopping; then hop in place when you start turning and so on.

This activity may be played best with the use of appropriate music that helps children maintain the right movement rhythm.

Teacher Essentials and Explanation Points

Before applying the principle of delayed imitation, children must learn to perform the coordination pattern. To facilitate motor learning, the cognitive load may be reduced by using a progressive **part practice,** which involves practicing the sequence in segments until each is learned before progressively adding the parts together. For instance, children may first learn to alternate clapping four times and then hopping in place four times by imitating your movements. Before adding new segments, introduce delayed imitation.

To explain the principle of delayed imitation, ask the children to pretend that they are clocks and that you are an absent-minded clockmaker who sets each clock delayed. Render this make-believe phase enjoyable by moving their arms as if they were clock hands. Hereafter, you can restart the coordination task with the clapping sequence, but tell the children that they cannot move yet because they are late clocks. Give a verbal signal ("Clap now") to prompt them to start the clapping sequence as you start the hopping sequence. When you return to the clapping sequence, call out "Hop now" so the children start their hopping sequence. In other words, while you are clapping, the children are doing nothing; when you hop, they begin clapping. When you return to clapping, they start hopping. Practice until they can perform the delayed imitation without verbal cues. After a break, demonstrate the next part of the sequence (hopping while turning and alternating squatting and standing) and teach these new parts through imitation, without adding the delayed imitation requirement for hopping and clapping. When they can perform the whole sequence, you can reintroduce the clockmaker theme and apply the principle of delayed imitation to the whole sequence of four different movement types.

---

delayed imitation—Imitating a movement pattern, but after a time delay.

part practice—Practicing a sequence in segments until each is learned before progressively adding the parts together.

Challenges Posed

During breaks, ask children how they managed to not imitate your movements and how they behaved as late clocks. Ask whether they watched what other children were doing or tried to follow your verbal cue (see the questions in the Game Breakdown section).

Small Modifications and Moving On

To simplify this activity or make it more difficult, you can modify the complexity of the movements, the number of repetitions of each movement, and the number of movements within the sequence. Preschool-age children should practice this activity in its easiest form (e.g., alternating eight repetitions of only two easy movement patterns involving either arm or leg movements). With kindergarten-age children, you may progressively enhance interlimb coordination demands (e.g., adding arm movements to the hops in place), reduce the number of repetitions (from eight to four to two), and add new movements to the sequence (from two to four different movement types).

Zooming Into the Game

In the mental domain (i.e., executive functions), this game involves both the ability to inhibit habitual responses (simple response inhibition) and the ability to update and manipulate information being held in mind (complex working memory). On the one side, children must inhibit the habitual tendency to immediately imitate your movements. On the other side, they must hold the observed movement pattern in working memory. After a delay, they can perform that movement and remove it from the working memory store, but must hold in mind the next movement pattern you are executing. This means that they must continuously update the information held in working memory.

Help students work on their motor control and balance with coordination sequences that include movements such as hopping, turning, and standing up from a squatting position.

In terms of the motor domain (i.e., coordinative abilities), this activity challenges precise motor control abilities and particularly the ability to combine movements and control balance (especially when turning while hopping).

Game Breakdown

The degree of complexity of this game may be tailored to children's age and skill level as indicated in the section Small Modifications and Moving On. This game applies the principle of delayed imitation: children learn a sequence of coordinated movements by imitating you, but they perform the sequence in a delayed fashion. The pretend-play features of this activity elicit emotional involvement.

Equipment

Needs based on a 30-student class:

- Safe space
- Music with an appropriate tempo and clearly identifiable rhythm

Skills Needed

- Locomotor skills: hopping
- Nonlocomotor skills: turning
- Rhythm reproduction skills

Rules

1. Children learn a movement sequence made up of progressively increasing segments through immediate imitation.
2. Children, pretending to be clocks that have been set delayed by an absent-minded clockmaker, imitate your movements in a delayed fashion.

Questions

- Did you sometimes look at what other children were doing?
- Did you listen to my voice to remember what you had to do next?

The Magic Hoop and the Stick of Contrary

This game is derived from movement experiences proposed by Mezzetti-Pantanelli and Maiello (2001) for preschool- and school-age children. It is adapted here to promote creativity and challenge the function of complex response inhibition. Therefore, this game is not an alteration of the previous Crazy Traffic Lights and My Clock Is Late games, but an example of how the principle of mental control may be applied and joined with the principle of discovery and creativity that dominates in the next section of games. Recall that the principle of mental control is an umbrella term that includes stopping, updating, and switching and that creativity broadly builds on all these components. Its novel aspect is the alternation of imaginative imitation and **anti-imitation**. Anti-imitation is a form of complex response inhibition in which children make gestures that are the opposite of the one made by the teacher. To render anti-imitation more enjoyable for children at this age, this game has the characteristics of make-believe play. Children do not imitate your movements, but the movements of an object you are holding, pretending that they are that object. The first phase of the game is exclusively an imaginative imitation, in which children try to interpret the movements of the object (the magic hoop) you are holding and manipulating. The second phase, which alternates imaginative imitation and anti-imitation, involves your holding a new object (the stick of contrary) in several changing positions (e.g., horizontal, vertical, close to the floor, high over your head). After a given imitation time, children are asked to assume a position opposite to the one in which the stick is held. This game requires open space and small tools such as hoops, sticks, or ropes. Also, using an appropriate music helps children take the role of the moving object, following its tempo and rhythm.

Teacher Essentials and Explanation Points

To start, explain that the hoop you hold in your hands is a magic hoop: when it starts moving, the children should imagine that they have become hoops and not resist the temptation to move as the hoop moves. Then, start a music sequence and begin moving the hoop slowly while standing in front of the children. Vary the tempo and rhythm of your own movements and move the hoop in as many ways as possible (e.g., roll it on the floor, hold it at a right angle to the floor and bounce it, hold it parallel to the floor and turn around with it, twirl it with your fingers). After a break, exchange the hoop for a stick and repeat the activity. After the children have learned to imitate the stick, take a break and introduce the anti-imitation phase of the game. Explain that the stick is silly. Sometimes it likes obedient children, so they must therefore move as the stick moves. Sometimes, however, it likes disobedient children, so they must do the opposite of what it does. For instance, when the stick is held upright, the children must lie down; when the stick lies on the floor, the children must stand up. To challenge response inhibition, alternate your requests for anti-imitation ("Now do the opposite") with imitation trials.

Challenges Posed

After the magic hoop game phase but before starting the instructions for the stick of contrary phase, ask children how many ways they found to roll, bounce, and turn as the hoop, and ask them to show you again how they moved. During the game, children play alone and concentrate on the hoop's movements and their own imitations of its movements. These questions give them a chance to compare their solutions to others' solutions. The children come to appreciate that there are many ways to interpret a moving object. After they have played the stick of contrary game

anti-imitation—A form of complex response inhibition in which children make gestures that are the opposite of the one made by the teacher.

phase, ask them (as you did in the My Clock Is Late game) whether they concentrated on what other children were doing or on the movements of the silly stick.

Small Modifications and Moving On

To simplify the stick of contrary game or make it more difficult, you can change the number of positions and movements that children must respond to with anti-imitation. For kindergarten-age children, you may add further alternatives by having them turn to the right when the stick is turned to the left, squat when it is held overhead, and stretch toward the ceiling when the stick is close to the floor. Moreover, children may then take the lead in this game: you can create small groups of three children each in which group members alternate taking the lead. Also, the leading child may have two sticks that she can move simultaneously in the same or a different way, also crossing them to promote social interaction between the imitating children.

Zooming Into the Game

The imitation and anti-imitation phases are characterized by various cognitive demands in the mental domain (i.e., executive functions). The imitation phase is an open-ended task requiring imagination and creativity. The anti-imitation phase challenges the ability to hold a rule in mind (performing a gesture or adopting a position opposite to that of the stick), respond according to this rule, and inhibit the strong desire to imitate (complex response inhibition).

In terms of the motor domain, the demands on coordinative abilities and motor skills depend largely on how you move the object and how children interpret the object movements. The intensity depends on the tempo and rhythm you set: the music should alternate between lower and higher tempos to provide rest from high-intensity bouts.

Game Breakdown

This game is ideal for children of preschool and kindergarten age because of the use of imaginative imitation, which challenges motor creativity (motor creativity is central to the next group of games). The anti-imitation phase, which may be best for kindergarten-age children, challenges inhibition and cognitive flexibility. The request to take the role of an object rather than a living being challenges empathy in an unusual way.

Equipment

Needs based on a 30-student class:

- Safe space
- Music that alternates between lower and higher tempos to provide rest from high-intensity bouts
- 10 small tools (e.g., sticks, hoops, ropes)

Skills Needed

- Nonlocomotor skills: creeping, turning, rolling, etc.
- Rhythm reproduction skills
- Imaginative skills and motor creativity

Rules

1. Imitation phase: Children pretend they are the object you are holding and move as the object is moved.
2. Anti-imitation phase: Children must do the reverse of what the silly stick does. For instance, when the stick is held upright, the children must lie down; when the stick lies on the floor, the children must stand up.
3. Alternate series of imitation and anti-imitation trials to challenge response inhibition.

Questions

- How many ways did you find to roll, bounce, and turn as the hoop?
- Laura, can you show me again how you moved to imitate a rolling hoop?
- How many of you moved the way Laura did?
- Did you find other ways to bounce like a hoop than the way Terry did?

Games Highlighting Discovery

The games presented in this section are symbolic games that apply the principles of divergent discovery, repetition without repetition, and creativity presented in chapter 6. Movement-based creativity tasks for children of preschool and kindergarten age are (1) gross-motor tasks introduced by instructions such as "How many ways . . .?" and "Can you move like . . ." (e.g., animals)?, aimed to generate multiple original bodily movements, and (2) manipulative tasks introduced by "What might it be?" or "What other ways . . .?", which generate ideas about alternate uses of objects (Bertsch, 1983; Torrance, 1981). As noted in chapters 6 and 7, the key teaching strategies for promoting motor creativity are using open-ended tasks, providing the opportunity for free exploration with a variety of appropriate cues, and creating a climate that both supports children's creative process and allows them to integrate their own thoughts.

The games in this section require safe, open space. Some require a few small objects or a music player. One involves climbing and requires landing mats.

The Cobweb and the Little Spiders

Like the Magic Hoop and the Stick of Contrary game, this game is derived from movement experiences proposed by Mezzetti-Pantanelli and Maiello (2001) for preschool- and school-age children. It has been adapted to make use of the principles of discovery learning and creativity. The story deals with a spider parent (i.e., you) who builds a cobweb by means of an elastic band anchored at your wrists and ankles. The children are newborn spiders who explore the cobweb by going in and out of it in several ways. They may hug you and lean against your body for support as they go through the cobweb. You can praise them when they find new ways to go through the web (divergent discovery) so that they go through more times (repetition . . .) while exploring different ways to do so (. . . without repetition). The search for novel solutions to the same task promotes creativity. This activity requires no equipment apart from a long elastic band.

Teacher Essentials and Explanation Points

Explain to the children that they will pretend to be newborn spiders. They should first squat and wrap their flexed legs with their arms to create a round form and then slowly stand up and stretch out their arms and legs and move around on all fours as if coming out of a cocoon. Anchor an elastic band at your wrists and ankles and assume a spider-in-cobweb position (e.g., getting down on one knee with arms stretched and open). Explain that the cobweb is a beautiful house with many entrances and exits to discover. Promote divergent discovery by asking, "How many passageways can you find?" and "How many ways can you find to go through the web?" Explain that you are a lovely spider parent who likes helping kids, and that they can use your arms, legs, and body as support as they go through. They can hug you to rest when they are tired. After indicating the start of the story, the goal, and the task conditions, let them explore as long as they engage in and enjoy this activity.

Challenges Posed

Do not indicate where and how to go through the web, because doing so promotes imitation and convergent discovery. To help children understand that there is not just one correct solution, refrain from making judgments about their performance, but only praise novelty: as long as different solutions are pertinent, they are all equally good, regardless of whether a solution is simpler and another one is more complex or sophisticated. Provide feedback only if a child repeatedly uses the same way to go through at the same point of the cobweb (e.g., "Try to go through another way" or "Try to go through here again, but move in another way"). Provide short breaks between exploration phases to let children reflect on how many ways they found and what way they liked best, as well as to remind them that they can go through only one at a time to avoid colliding with others and destroying the cobweb.

Small Modifications and Moving On

You can add novel stimuli in the environment and change the task to promote creativity and encourage children to search for new solutions. To create a new condition, you can predict that an approaching storm has destroyed the cobweb and it has to be rebuilt. You then assume a new position. This generates new challenges for the children. Another change could be allowing children to go through the cobweb in pairs and help each other. At such a young age, most of them will merely go through hand in hand without cooperating to find a novel solution. However, during a break, you can prompt reflection on their actions by asking whether it was easier or more difficult or more or less enjoyable going through the cobweb in pairs than one by one.

Zooming Into the Game

The question "How many ways . . . ?" promotes the creative search for solutions, which challenges executive functions in the mental domain. After the children have gone through the web in the easiest and most common ways, encourage them to explore more original solutions. Recall from chapter 6 that originality in movement is strictly linked to the ability to inhibit habitual motor responses (i.e., simple response inhibition). To generate novel solutions, children also need to monitor the information in working memory to remember what solutions they have already tried and avoid repeating them (i.e., complex working memory). Also, the ability to shift between mental sets is required: for instance, the association between a stimulus (your flexed leg) and a response (creeping under it) must be broken to create a new solution. In this case you can change the part of your body the children must creep under (e.g., an arm), or a child can change the movement she uses while going under your flexed leg (e.g., rolling).

In terms of the motor domain (i.e., coordinative abilities), children do not need to perform highly precise movements, and fast coordination is not required at all. You can increase the demands on coordinative abilities by applying the modifications indicated in the section Small Modifications and Moving On.

Game Breakdown

This game makes use of the principles of discovery learning and creativity and is broadly tailored for children of preschool and kindergarten age. The game modification allowing children to go through the cobweb in pairs promotes cooperation.

Equipment

Needs based on a 30-student class:

- Safe space
- Long elastic band

Skills Needed

- Locomotor skills: walking, hopping
- Nonlocomotor skills: rolling, creeping, climbing
- Imaginative skills and motor creativity

Rules

1. Children must go in and out of the cobweb many times (repetition . . .), while exploring different ways to do so (. . .without repetition).
2. Children may lean against the spider parent's body for support as they go through the cobweb.

Questions

- How many ways did you find to go through the web? Can you find one more way?
- How many passageways did you find? Is there another way to go through?
- Can you move in another way when you try to go through again?
- Was it easier or more difficult, or more or less funny, going through the cobweb in pairs or rather one by one?

The Moving Cobweb and the Little Ladybugs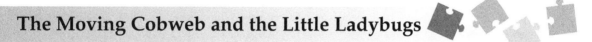

This variation of the Cobweb and the Little Spiders game involving a group of little ladybugs adds new roles and rules that alter cognitive, motor, and social interactions. The ladybugs' goal is to bring home precious stones (little balls) located at the other end of the play area. To bring them home safely, they must get through the cobweb of an evil spider (you) several times and every time in a different way. The little ladybugs may not touch the spider, which sometimes moves its arms and legs. Thus, the basic task is the same as in the previous game in that children may not repeat their solutions. In this game, however, the task is more precise and time constraints are greater to create more of a challenge. This activity requires only a long elastic band and small balls or other objects.

Teacher Essentials and Explanation Points

To begin, anchor the elastic band at your wrists and ankles and assume a spider-in-cobweb position (e.g., getting down on one knee with arms stretched and open). Then introduce role playing and ask the children to pretend to be little ladybugs. They may try moving on all fours and flying around and moving silently when they are near the evil spider. Before starting the game, explain that the goal is to bring home all the precious stones by carrying them through the cobweb. Remind the children that the spider sometimes sleeps, but sometimes wakes up and moves its arms and legs; it may even leave its position to build a new cobweb in another place. Demonstrate by moving your arms and walking to another place. Thereafter, explain that they must not touch the spider because it would be angered. Furthermore, if the little ladybugs do not go through the cobweb in a different way each time, the spider will catch them because it remembers where and how they went through the last time. Promote divergent discovery by asking, "How many passageways can you find" or, "How many ways can you find to go through?" After they have performed a solution ask, "Can you find one more way?" Play the game until the children have brought all the balls home.

Challenges Posed

Similar to the previous game, the promotion of divergent discovery requires that you refrain from judging children's performance. Limit your directives and feedback as much as possible, and give feedback only when a child repeats solutions. You can approach this game in a sociodramatic, playful fashion by pretending to capture the ladybugs that touch you as they go through the web. Provide short breaks between exploration phases to give children time to reflect on how many paths and different ways of moving they found to avoid being caught.

Small Modifications and Moving On

When the spider's movements generate new cobweb forms, the children have new challenges that require new solutions. However, this also generates time pressures that limit the creative process. Therefore, you should initially perform only slow, repetitive, and highly predictable arms movements. Gradually add less predictable and random movements of your whole body. If you create a new cobweb on a climbing structure, allow children to go both over and through the cobweb to stimulate the exploration of climbing solutions. As in the previous game, a further modification is to allow children to go through the cobweb in pairs, helping each other along the way.

Zooming Into the Game

In this game the mental domain (i.e., executive functions) is challenged by the evil spider that catches the ladybugs who try to go through twice in the same way; this renders more imperative the search for novel solutions. As in the previous game, this creative process challenges all three core executive functions: inhibiting habitual, more common responses (response inhibition); updating information about how the child has already gone through the cobweb (working memory); and associating different motor responses with changing spider positions (mental shifting).

In the motor domain (i.e., coordinative abilities), the need to coordinate movements precisely and rapidly is greater than in the previous game. In fact, precise motor control abilities are required to avoid touching the still spider, whereas precise perceptual–motor adaptation abilities are required to avoid being touched when the spider moves.

Game Breakdown

This variation of The Cobweb and the Little Spiders game also makes use of the principles of discovery learning and creativity and is broadly tailored for children of preschool and kindergarten age. Children practice avoidance behaviors and cooperation within a sociodramatic play situation in which they enact the relationship between prey and predator. The game modification that allows them to go through the cobweb in pairs promotes cooperation.

Equipment

Needs based on a 30-student class:

- Safe space
- Long elastic band
- Small balls (one for each child)

Skills Needed

- Locomotor skills: walking, hopping
- Nonlocomotor skills: rolling, creeping, climbing
- Manipulative skills: grasping, reaching
- Imaginative skills and motor creativity

Rules

1. Children must go through the cobweb many times (repetition . . .), while finding different ways to do so (. . . without repetition) to bring small balls to the far end of the play area.
2. Children may not touch the spider's body as they go through the cobweb.

Questions

- How many ways did you find to go through the web? Can you find one more way?
- How many passageways did you find? Is there another way to go through?

- Can you move in another way when you try to go through again?
- Was it easier or more difficult, or more or less funny, going through the cobweb in pairs than one by one?
- How could you avoid touching the evil spider when it was moving its arms?

The Fable of the Magic Cobweb

In this game, the cobweb is magic and you are a spider fairy or wizard who can transform people into animals (little spiders and ladybugs) and animals into magic people who can also transform objects. The novelty is that only cooperative solutions that involve pairs of children (one spider and one ladybug) are allowed. Children therefore discover solutions that are not possible when they act individually. Again, the goal is to go through the cobweb several times in different ways. If a spider and a ladybug find at least five ways to go through the cobweb while maintaining body contact with and helping each other, the spider fairy or wizard rewards them by transforming them into magic children and giving them a stick. Magic children can transform the stick into anything that looks like a stick, such as an umbrella, a witch's broom, or a horse (Mezzetti-Pantanelli & Maiello, 2001).

This pretend game comprises two movement-based creativity tasks. The first is the search for different ways to go through the cobweb. This task is introduced by the instruction, "How many ways . . .?", as in the previous game, but there is the added criterion that children must perform cooperative solutions. The second movement-based creativity task is the search for alternate, unusual uses of the stick. This is introduced by the question, "What might it be?" This activity requires a long elastic band and sticks or other small tools (e.g., jump ropes) that are appropriate for alternate uses, as well as self-made equipment (colored cards with drawings).

Teacher Essentials and Explanation Points

First, help children prepare cards with a drawing of a spider or a ladybug and hang them around their necks. If pairing up is hindered by the fact that there are more children wishing to be spiders than those who desire being ladybugs (or vice versa), set the rule that after the first half of the game time the children building a pair must exchange their role. Tell them that they must then pretend that you are a fairy or a wizard spider who transforms them into little spiders or ladybugs. Children get their cards just when you as a wizard have transformed them. Anchor the elastic band at your wrists and ankles and assume a spider-in-cobweb position (e.g., getting down on one knee with arms stretched and open). Before starting the game, explain that the goal of the game is to go through the cobweb at least five ways so that you can transform the little spiders and ladybugs into magic children. Explain that little spiders and ladybugs are friends and are allowed by the spider to go through the cobweb in pairs. Only spider–ladybug pairs (and not spider–spider or ladybug–ladybug pairs are allowed, since ladybugs may go through the cobweb without being caught only if accompanied by a spider. The spider–ladybug pairs may never lose body contact while moving through the web and may not touch the cobweb. Promote divergent discovery by asking, "How many passageways and ways to go though can you and your friend find together?" and, after they have performed one solution, "Can you find one more way?" After indicating the start of the story (where they have to go while linked together), the goal (finding at least five pathways and modes to go through so they can be transformed into magic children), and the constraints (they may not touch the spider or lose body contact with each other), let the children play the game until all of them have completed the cobweb phase and been transformed into magic children. Then give each child a stick and ask, "What might the stick be?" Remind them that they are magic children who can transform the stick into anything else that looks like a stick.

Challenges Posed

Refrain from judging children's performance and give feedback only when children repeat the same solution. Because the novelty of this game is the search for cooperative solutions while working in pairs, during short breaks you can ask such questions as "How can you help your little spider or ladybug friend go through the cobweb while passing over the spider's leg?"

Small Modifications and Moving On

You can add novel stimuli to this game and change task requests. In the first example (going through the web), you can promote exploration and enhance the challenges to motor control and adaptation abilities by asking the children to go through in pairs and maintain body contact using a new part of the body on each trial (for instance, the most common hand-in-hand contact cannot be used twice). As the spider, you can increase the time constraint by making slow movements that might lead to contact if children are not quick enough. Another modification might involve giving the children new objects instead of sticks (e.g., cords or hoops) and asking them, "What might this be?" For example, children can pretend that ropes are reins on a horse.

Zooming Into the Game

As in the previous games, the search for divergent solutions is a creative process that challenges all three core executive functions in the mental domain: response inhibition, working memory, and mental shifting.

In terms of the motor domain (i.e., coordinative abilities), the demands on precise perceptual–motor adaptation abilities are higher than in the previous games, because children must finely control their movements and adapt them to the movements and perturbations generated by their partners while avoiding touching the cobweb.

Game Breakdown

This variation of the Cobweb and the Little Spiders game makes use of the principles of discovery learning and creativity for children of preschool and kindergarten age. This pretend game comprises two movement-based creativity tasks. The first is the search for different ways to go through the cobweb in pairs. The second is the search for alternate, unusual uses of small objects. The second task further promotes divergent discovery and creativity.

Equipment

Needs based on a 30-student class:

- Safe space
- Long elastic band
- Small tools (e.g., jump ropes) appropriate for alternate uses (one per child)
- Self-made equipment: cards in two colors with drawings, one for each child

Skills Needed

- Locomotor skills: walking, hopping
- Nonlocomotor skills: rolling, creeping, climbing
- Manipulative skills: grasping, reaching, manipulating
- Imaginative skills and motor creativity

Rules

1. Children must go through the cobweb many times (repetition . . .), while finding different ways to do so (. . . without repetition) linked in pairs. Once they have gone through the web five different ways, the spider fairy or wizard transforms them into magic children.

2. Children may not lose body contact with each other or touch the spider's body as they go through the cobweb in pairs.

3. Children must try alternative uses of the small tool they receive after completion of the go-through task.

Questions

- How many ways did you find to go through the web? Can you find one more way?
- How many passageways did you find? Is there another way to go through?
- Can you move in another way when you try to go through again?
- Was it easier or more difficult, or more or less funny, going through the cobweb in pairs than one by one?
- How could you avoid touching the evil spider when it was moving its arms?
- How many passageways and ways to go through did you and your friend find together?
- How did you help your little spider or ladybug friend go through the cobweb while passing over or under the spider's leg?
- What might it (the stick or rope) be?
- How many different ways to use it (the stick or rope) did you find?

Photo Album

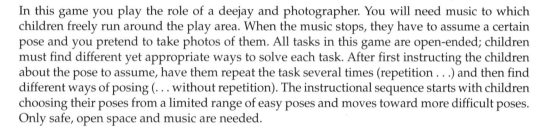

In this game you play the role of a deejay and photographer. You will need music to which children freely run around the play area. When the music stops, they have to assume a certain pose and you pretend to take photos of them. All tasks in this game are open-ended; children must find different yet appropriate ways to solve each task. After first instructing the children about the pose to assume, have them repeat the task several times (repetition . . .) and then find different ways of posing (. . . without repetition). The instructional sequence starts with children choosing their poses from a limited range of easy poses and moves toward more difficult poses. Only safe, open space and music are needed.

Teacher Essentials and Explanation Points

Begin by telling the children that you are a deejay who will start and stop the music. When you start the music, the children can run freely around the play area in any direction. When you stop the music, they must stop immediately because you are now a photographer and want to take photos of them. Before starting the music, tell them the pose they must assume when the music stops and encourage them to think about this pose while they are running to the music. The instructional sequence for the poses is as follows:

1. Both hands and both feet (all fours)
2. Both feet and one hand
3. Both hands and one foot
4. One hand and one foot
5. One foot

Each pose should be repeated several times, as long as the children find it enjoyable. After they have performed each pose in the sequence above multiple times, ask them to pose at every stop in a new position of their choosing, explaining that to complete your photo album, you need as many photos as possible and each one must be unique. At this point, the children do not need to follow the sequence any longer, but are only requested to assume every time a pose never assumed yet. This is because after having systematically explored different ways to realize each pose of the sequence, they should be able to switch between poses with novel ideas.

Challenges Posed

As with all games in this section, avoid demonstrating, refrain from judging children's performances, and give feedback only when a child repeats a solution during the free-pose period, saying, "Uh-oh, remember to pay attention! I have already taken this photo!" You can prolong the breaks during posing and promote children's imagination by asking such questions as, "What are you posing as?"

Small Modifications and Moving On

The more repetitive part of the activity, running to the music, may be varied to promote the development of a broader range of fundamental motor skills by alternating running with galloping, hopping, or skipping.

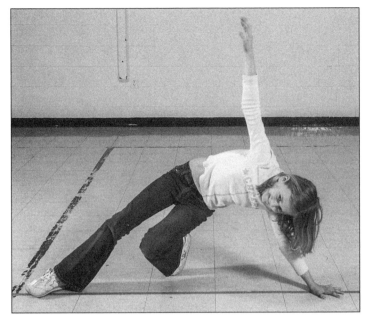

Children get to be physically active and creative in the Photo Album game.

You must match the skills performed with the children's age and developmental level, because the age range for measurable qualitative changes is earliest for running, followed by galloping, hopping, and skipping. To further promote the search for new cooperative solutions in the free-pose period, encourage children to find poses requiring two people or perhaps a small group of three or four.

Zooming Into the Game

The question "How many ways . . .?" promotes the creative search for solutions and challenges all three core executive functions of the mental domain: response inhibition, working memory, and mental shifting.

Stopping for photos addresses the motor domain (i.e., coordinative abilities) by making progressively increasing demands on precise motor control ability and static balance. Also, this game alternates bouts of MVPA with breaks.

Game Breakdown

Because it is composed of open-ended tasks, the game makes use of the principles of discovery learning and creativity. Children have an opportunity to appreciate differences in the outcomes of the same problem-solving process.

Equipment

Needs based on a 30-student class:

- Safe space
- Music with varying tempos and rhythms

Skills Needed

- Locomotor skills: running, galloping, hopping, skipping
- Rhythm reproduction skills
- Imaginative skills and motor creativity

Rules

1. When the music starts, the children run freely around the play area.

2. When the music stops, they must immediately stop and assume a pose for a photo.

3. The instructional sequence for the poses is (1) all fours, (2) both feet and one hand, (3) both hands and one foot, (4) one hand and one foot, and (5) one foot.

4. Every time the instruction (e.g., "Stop on all fours") is repeated for more than one trial, at every stop the children must respect the instruction, but assume a new pose (for instance belly-up or belly-down on all fours).

5. When the instructional sequence is completed (many times on all fours, then many times on both feet and one hand, finding novel ways to do it, etc.), children can freely choose the type of pose, but excluding all poses they have already assumed.

Questions

- What are you posing as?
- How many ways did you find to pose on all fours (on both feet and one hand . . .)?
- What were you thinking about while you were running?
- Did you sometimes look at what other children were doing?

Picture of Courage

This game merges the characteristics of the Photo Album game with those of a movement experience proposed by Mezzetti-Pantanelli and Maiello (2001). Again, you play the role of both a deejay and a photographer. The novelty is that pictures of courage are taken. When the music stops, children must assume a new pose on a climbing structure. As in the Photo Album game, the instructional sequence starts with easy poses and moves toward more difficult ones. This game requires open space, a climbing structure, and safety mats.

Teacher Essentials and Explanation Points

Begin by telling the children that you are a deejay who will start and stop the music. When you start the music, the children can run freely around the play area in any direction. When you stop the music, they must climb the structure slowly and carefully (to avoid falling) until they reach their preferred height and then stop in a pose because you are now a photographer and want to take photos of them. Before starting the music, tell them the pose they must assume when the music stops and encourage them to think about this pose while they are running to the music. The instructional sequence for this game is to hold a pose on the climbing structure using the following sequence:

1. Both hands and both feet
2. Both feet and one hand
3. Both hands and one foot
4. One hand and one foot
5. Hands only

As in the Photo Album game, all steps of the sequence must be repeated several times each with the children climbing to their comfort height and assuming the requested pose in a different way every time, so that you can take a novel photo of their courage. After completion of each pose of the sequence every time, the children may freely choose a new pose.

Challenges Posed

As with all games in this section, avoid demonstrating and judging the children's performances. Give feedback only when a child repeats a pose she has assumed previously. Use the breaks during posing to remind children to pay attention while climbing. To promote their imagination, ask, "What are you posing as?"

Small Modifications and Moving On

During the activity phases using music, you can have children alternate walking with various motor patterns (galloping, hopping, skipping), according to their age and developmental level.

Zooming Into the Game

As in the previous games, the search for divergent solutions is a creative process that challenges all three core executive functions in the mental domain: response inhibition, working memory, and mental shifting.

Stopping for photos addresses the motor domain (i.e., coordinative abilities) by making progressively increasing demands on precise motor control ability and static balance. This game also challenges climbing skills. The game alternates bouts of moderate physical activity with breaks.

Game Breakdown

This game is composed of open-ended tasks that make use of the principles of discovery learning and creativity and is tailored for children of preschool and kindergarten age. Children also have the opportunity to cope with the fear of climbing and height thanks to the playful characteristics of this experience.

Equipment

Needs based on a 30-student class:

- Safe space
- Climbing structure
- Safety mats

Skills Needed

- Locomotor skills: walking
- Nonlocomotor skills: climbing
- Rhythm reproduction skills
- Imaginative skills and motor creativity

Rules

1. When the music starts, children move freely around the play area.
2. When the music stops, they must climb to a comfortable height and hold a pose on the climbing structure according to the instruction.
3. The instructional sequence for the poses is (1) both hands and both feet, (2) both feet and one hand, (3) both hands and one foot, (4) one hand and one foot, and (5) hands only.
4. Every time the instruction (e.g., "Hold yourself at the climbing structure with both hands and both feet") is repeated for more than one trial, at every stop the children must respect the instruction, but assume a new pose (for instance climbing pose with front or back to the climbing structure).
5. When the instructional sequence is completed finding novel ways to do it (many times with both feet and both hands, then many times with both feet and one hand, etc.), children can freely choose the type of pose, but excluding all poses they have already assumed.

Questions

- What are you posing as?
- How many ways did you find to pose holding yourself with both hands and both feet (with both feet and one hand…)?
- What were you thinking about while you were walking?
- Did you sometimes look at what other children were doing and at what height they climbed?
- Did you try to climb higher?
- Did you try novel poses at higher or lower height?

Movie of the Animal World

This game merges some characteristics of the Photo Album game with features of pretend play. You play the role of both a deejay and a filmmaker. The novelty is that children are not requested to assume poses. Instead, they are instructed to move creatively, finding novel ways to deal with the tasks you propose as you pretend to film a movie. In the game phases with music, children either run or walk, to alternate moderate and vigorous bouts of physical exercise. When the music stops, children must move according to your instruction. After an exploration phase without a story line, you can promote divergent discovery by telling a fable in which certain animals must move around in different worlds and change their movements as they enter new worlds. This game requires safe, open space, and its modifications require equipment such as benches and small obstacles (e.g., cones, hoops, jump ropes) for children to pass over or under.

Teacher Essentials and Explanation Points

Begin by telling the children that you are a deejay who will start and stop the music. When you start the music, the children can run freely around the play area in any direction. When you stop the music, they must continue to move, but in a way you have told them ahead of time. Before starting the music, tell them the way they will have to move when the music stops and encourage them to think about it while they are running to the music. Following is the sequence of ways to move when the music stops:

1. On both hands and both feet
2. On both feet and one hand
3. On both hands and one foot
4. On one hand and one foot
5. On one foot

As in the Photo Album game, all steps of the sequence must be repeated several times. Ask the children to change their way of moving each time the music stops so that you can record new scenes for the movie. When they have explored many ways to move around, in accordance with your requests, you can start the new phase of the game by posing this question: "Can you move like (the name of an animal)?" To promote the search for different ways to behave as a horse, for example, create imaginary scenarios such as a horse that is very tired after galloping a long way, is very happy because it has found a friend, has an injured leg, or must go through a forest or cross a river.

Challenges Posed

Avoid demonstrating and judging the children's performance, and give feedback only when a child repeats movements he just performed ("Please pay attention! I have already recorded this scene!"). While children are exploring ways to move (e.g., on all fours), ask, "What animal are you?" In this way you prepare them for the following make-believe phase of the game when you say, "Now let's move like (the name of an animal)!"

Small Modifications and Moving On

You can alternate the performance of motor skills in the music phases according to the age and developmental level of the children. In the creativity phases when the music stops, you can encourage children to find solutions that require them to work in pairs. Also, you can promote the development of fundamental motor skills by changing your requests. For example, you can ask them to go under equipment (e.g., a bench) in a different way each time. This promotes the exploration of movement types (e.g., going on all fours, rolling, creeping). You can also ask them to step or climb over benches and obstacles using different parts of the body (on all fours, on both feet and one hand, on both hands and one foot, on one hand and one foot, or on only one foot). This develops the skills of climbing, balancing, and jumping down from heights. For safety, ensure that benches and obstacles are adequate and stable and surrounded by mats.

Zooming Into the Game

As in the previous games, the search for divergent solutions is a creative process that challenges all three core executive functions in the mental domain: response inhibition, working memory, and mental shifting.

In the motor domain (i.e., coordinative abilities), the progression of problem solving starting on all fours (step 1) and ending on only one foot (step 5) involves progressively increasing demands on precise motor control ability and dynamic balance. The game alternates bouts of moderate and vigorous physical activity.

Game Breakdown

This game is composed of open-ended tasks that make use of the principles of discovery learning and creativity and is tailored for children of preschool and kindergarten age. To generate a story line and help children discover solutions, you can use the teaching strategies introduced in chapter 7 (checklists, forced relationships, analogies, attribute listing). The instructional sequence starts with easy movements and moves toward more difficult movements. The make-believe environment of the fable enhances children's emotional commitment.

Equipment

Needs based on a 30-student class:

- Safe, open space
- Benches, small obstacles (e.g., cones, hoops, jump ropes) for children to pass over or under, and safety mats

Skills Needed

- Locomotor skills: walking, running, hopping
- Nonlocomotor skills: creeping, climbing
- Rhythm reproduction skills
- Imaginative skills and motor creativity

Rules

1. When the music starts, children move freely around the play area.
2. When the music stops, they must move according to the tasks you propose as you pretend to film a movie.
3. The instructional sequence for the movements are (1) on all fours, (2) on both feet and one hand, (3) on both hands and one foot, (4) on one hand and one foot, and (5) on one foot.

4. Every time the instruction (e.g., "Move on all fours") is repeated for more than one trial, the children must respect the instruction, but move differently.

5. In the following pretend-play phase with storyline, the children pretend moving as animals with different characteristics moving in different environments, alone or in couples.

Questions

- Can you move like (the name of animal)?
- What animal are you?
- How many ways did you find to move on all fours (on both feet and one hand . . .)?
- What were you thinking about while you were running?
- Did you sometimes look at what other children were doing?
- Did playing in pairs help you find new ways to move like (the name of animal)?

Implications for Educators

This chapter outlined physical activity games for preschool- and kindergarten-age children that promote cognitive development. They do so by challenging their executive functions in playful and age-appropriate ways according to the three principles of mental engagement: contextual interference, mental control, and discovery. To help teachers analyze the games and generate new games on their own, we have explained why and how each game works. We focused on the mental and motor coordination demands of the games, because they strongly influence the mental effort necessary for playing them. However, we have also indicated some social-emotional aspects of the games, because executive function training is more effective when embedded in emotionally and socially challenging experiences (Diamond & Lee, 2011). We are convinced that the games in this chapter translate into practice the "whole child" perspective on physical education (NASPE, 2011).

Physical Activity Games for Elementary School–Age Children

Many of the conditions that can affect teaching success are uniquely attributable to elementary school–age children. Their physical activity patterns and mental abilities differ from those of preschool- and kindergarten-age children. Further, the conditions that make games intellectually challenging vary widely. Modifying games to challenge children cognitively can be a daunting and demanding task, even for accomplished teachers. This chapter provides physical activity games for elementary school–age children that promote their cognitive development.

Games That Challenge Executive Functions

Similar to the games for preschool- and kindergarten-age children described in chapter 10, the games presented in this chapter fall into three categories: games that highlight contextual interference, games that emphasize mental control, and games that promote discovery. Six games are provided in each category, and emphasis is placed on explanation, potential challenges, and how the games can be modified. All game versions are presented in a user-friendly format.

Connecting Games for Elementary School–Age Children to SHAPE America Standards

Like the games in chapter 10, the games in this chapter align with and contribute to the attainment of SHAPE America's (2014) National Standards & Grade-Level Outcomes for K-12 Physical Education, as listed here:

- Standard 1—The physically literate individual demonstrates competency in a variety of motor skills and movement patterns.
- Standard 2—The physically literate individual applies knowledge of concepts, principles, strategies, and tactics related to movement and performance.
- Standard 3—The physically literate individual demonstrates the knowledge and skills to achieve and maintain a health-enhancing level of physical activity and fitness.
- Standard 4—The physically literate individual exhibits responsible personal and social behavior that respects self and others.

- Standard 5—The physically literate individual recognizes the value of physical activity for health, enjoyment, challenge, self-expression, and/or social interaction.

The standards are not prioritized in a particular order.

Reprinted, by permission, from Society of Health and Physical Educators, 2014, *National standards & grade-level outcomes for K-12 physical education* (Champaign, IL: Human Kinetics).

Furthermore, games presented in this chapter are in line with the current Appropriate Instructional Practice Guidelines (National Association for Sport and Physical Education [NASPE], 2009), which represent "expert consensus about important appropriate and inappropriate practices observed frequently in elementary school physical education" (p. 2). That is, the games help children develop the skills, knowledge, and desire to enjoy a lifetime of physical activity through the participation in physical activities appropriate for their developmental levels. Table 11.1 shows how each game addresses specific learning outcomes for children in grades 1 and 2 and in grades 3 through 5.

Table 11.1 Game Finder for Elementary School–Age Children

Game	Page	Student expectations and performance outcomes (grades 1 and 2)	Student expectations and performance outcomes (grades 3 through 5)
GAMES HIGHLIGHTING CONTEXTUAL INTERFERENCE			
Hop, Pop, and Tag	182	• Hops, gallops, jogs, and slides using a mature pattern (S1.E1.1). • Differentiates between strong and light force (S2.E3.1b). • Accepts personal responsibility by using equipment and space appropriately (S4.E1.1). • Accepts responsibility for class protocols with behavior and performance actions (S4.E2.2). • Describes positive feelings that result from participating in physical activities (S5.E3.1a).	• Travels showing differentiation between sprinting and running (S1.E2.3). • Uses various locomotor movements in a variety of small-sided practice tasks (S1.E1.4). • Applies simple strategies and tactics in chasing activities (S2.E5.3a). • Applies simple strategies and tactics in fleeing activities (S2.E5.3b). • Participates with responsible behavior in a variety of physical activity contexts, environments, and facilities (S4.E2.5a). • Exhibits etiquette and adherence to rules in a variety of physical activities (S4.E5.4). • Describes and compares the positive social interactions when engaged in partner, small-group, and large-group physical activities (S5.E4.4).
Team Pop-Up	183		
Popper Ball	185		
Hoopla	187		
Guardian Hoopla	189		
Hands-Free Hoopla	191		
GAMES EMPHASIZING MENTAL CONTROL			
Team Bowling	193	• Throws underhand using a mature pattern (S1.E13.2). • Differentiates between strong and light force (S2.E3.1b). • Travels demonstrating a variety of relationships with objects (S2.E2.1b). • Responds appropriately to general feedback from the teacher (S4.E3.1). • Accepts specific corrective feedback from the teacher (S4.E3.2). • Recognizes that challenge in physical activities can lead to success (S5.E2.1).	• Throws underhand to a partner or target with reasonable accuracy (S1.E13.3). • Combines traveling with manipulative skills for execution to a target (S1.E1.5c). • Applies movement concepts to strategy in game situations (S2.E3.5a). • Recognizes the type of throw, volley, or striking action needed for various games and sport situations (S2.E5.5c). • Recognizes the role of rules and etiquette in physical activity with peers (S4.E5.3). • Analyzes various physical activities for enjoyment and challenge, identifying reasons for a positive or negative response (S5.E3.5).
Super Team Bowling	195		
Goalie Bowlie	197		
Garbage Ball	198		
Bountiful Ball	200		
Mega Garbage Ball	202		
GAMES PROMOTING DISCOVERY			
Trash Can Polo	203	• Strikes a ball with a long-handled implement, sending it forward, while using proper grip for implement (S1.E25.3). • Varies time and force with gradual increases and decreases (S2.E3.2). • Follows teacher directions for safe participation and proper use of equipment without teacher reminders (S4.E6.1). • Recognizes the role of rules and etiquette in teacher-designed activities (S4.E5.2). • Discusses personal reasons for enjoying physical activities (S5.E3.1b).	• Combines traveling with the manipulative skills of dribbling, throwing, catching, and striking in teacher-designed small-sided practice-task environments (S1.E26.4). • Combines striking with a long implement with receiving and traveling skills in a small-sided game (S1.E25.5b). • Applies the concepts of direction and force to strike an object with a long-handled implement (S2.E3.5b). • Recognizes the type of throw, volley, or striking action needed for various games and sport situations (S2.E5.5c). • Exhibits etiquette and adherence to rules in a variety of physical activities (S4.E5.4). • Applies safety principles with age-appropriate physical activities (S4.E6.5). • Describes the positive social interactions that come when engaged with others in physical activity (S5.E4.4).
Four-Team Pillow Polo	205		
21 or Bust	207		
Speedy Swappers	209		
Grid Runners	211		
Doorway Tag	212		

Games Highlighting Contextual Interference

The games in this section highlight the principle of contextual interference. As described in previous chapters, the key to creating contextual interference and increasing mental engagement lies in how the activities are interspersed within the game. Contextual interference can be created in many tag games. The amount of contextual interference children experience can be controlled by making only small changes in rules, boundaries, and modes of traveling.

Hop, Pop, and Tag

Adapted from Dienstmann 2008.

Games have evolved in all cultures as adaptations of games played by earlier generations. This game and its variations are adapted from a game called Pop-Up Tag (Dienstmann, 2008); it requires no equipment and only open space. Its subsequent alterations require some inexpensive equipment. This game is a different take on the traditional game of tag; it provides additional challenges. Students may have trouble performing the game at first, but they will quickly learn to focus on key elements.

Teacher Essentials and Explanation Points

Begin by explaining that any child may tag any other child; no child is "it." This rule immediately provides some contextual interference because there is usually a person (or several people) who must be avoided in most tag games. Tell the children that this game condition may conflict with how they might have played tag in the past. Once tagged, they must squat down and may pop up to resume play only when someone else tags their tagger. Point out that they should watch carefully the person who tagged them. Make sure students understand that they may tag anyone throughout the game; students often mistakenly believe that they are in competition with their initial tagger, chasing that one person throughout the game. For example, if person A tags person B, person B must wait for person C to tag person A before popping up to resume play. A player may tag several opponents before being tagged. A tagged player may not tag anyone else while squatting. Encourage children to be honest and good-natured about close calls. For example, they can decide who has been tagged by playing a quick game of rock, paper, scissors.

Challenges Posed

Because you want the game to proceed in short but vigorous bouts, provide small breaks between bouts as needed. These short breaks serve several purposes:

- They give children a brief rest.
- They give children the opportunity to gradually learn the game and apply strategies they have implicitly or explicitly learned.
- They allow you to pose challenges to children that they must confront.

Instinctively, many inexperienced teachers want to give children feedback about what they are doing and what they need to improve. Although easy to provide, directives do little to stimulate mental engagement. Rather than direct, you can suggest the importance of communication among tagged players during the short breaks and then give the group a directive such as, "Raise your hand to share your ideas about how you can keep from being tagged in the first place." If there is no response, call on a child you saw use a strategy—whether he seemed to realize it or not. Pose additional questions later on that relate to the two roles each player assumes during the game, such as, "What things do taggers need to be aware of, and why?" and, "If you've been tagged, what things should you be aware of, and why?" Although both questions may not prompt many answers, asking them is a way to suggest things children should be thinking about when playing the game.

As with all games, make sure the play environment is uncluttered and safe, that the children understand the rules of tagging, and that they keep their eyes open and stay alert. You can accomplish this by stressing classroom rules, which should be both clearly posted and properly taught.

Some responsibilities require a more trained teaching eye, especially if you want to promote cognitive functioning. One strategy is to focus on the children who are adhering to the rules. Although fair play is essential, focusing exclusively either on the children who are bending or breaking the rules or on those who are playing by the rules may not be the best plan. However, the children who are playing properly and successfully, *and* following the rules, are those who are using strategies. These children could be targets for your questions during breaks.

Small Modifications and Moving On

If children are playing safely, try shrinking the play area slightly—to make avoiding taggers more difficult. You can try varying children's movement patterns as well. You might start out by having the children speed-walk or run, and then change the mode of travel to skipping, hopping, or galloping. Once children have demonstrated an understanding of the rules and objectives, you can think about altering the game.

Game Breakdown

This game requires very little in the way of equipment or complicated motor skills.

Equipment

A 30-student class requires only a safe, open space.

Skills Needed

- Safe travel in general space
- Chasing, fleeing, and dodging

Rules

Players may tag several opponents before being tagged. As the game progresses, suggest the importance of communication among tagged players.

1. Any player may tag any other player throughout the game.
2. Once tagged, a player must squat and wait for someone else to tag her most recent tagger.
3. If players tag each other at the same (or nearly the same) time, they play rock, paper, scissors to determine who squats.
4. A tagged player may not tag anyone else while squatting.

Questions

- How can you keep from being tagged in the first place? Describe a strategy.
- What does a tagger need to be aware of—other taggers? tagged people? Why?
- What does a tagged person need to be aware of—other taggers? tagged people? his last tagger? Why?

Team Pop-Up

Adapted from Dienstmann 2008.

Team Pop-Up challenges children to be aware of more than just their own survival. The two teams need to be differentiated via the use of pinnies (a type of jersey or shirt). Remind students that they are responsible for helping those on their team and are not working against one another.

Teacher Essentials and Explanation Points

Begin by having all of the players on one team put on pinnies of the same color to differentiate them from those of the other team, who are not wearing pinnies. Explain clearly that the taggers are wearing pinnies and chase only children who are not wearing pinnies. As before, tagged children may only pop up when someone else tags their last tagger. Point out that they should watch carefully the person who tagged them. A tagged player may not tag anyone else while squatting. Encourage children to be honest and good-natured about close calls. For example, they can decide who has been tagged by playing a quick game of rock, paper, scissors. When all the players of one team are tagged, the game is over.

Like Hop, Pop, and Tag, the children's understanding of the game is enhanced by playing it a few times. To start, it might be helpful to have the children walk to tag players. After one or two short bouts to

Pinnies help children keep track of their teammates in Team Pop-Up.

illustrate the game, and as children gain experience with the basic mechanics, you can institute changes to make the game more challenging for both teams.

Challenges Posed

During the short breaks between games or at other times that seem appropriate, you can address the notions of evasion and team support. Children should be able to answer such questions as, What can you do to avoid the other team? Should teammates work together as a group and spread out to tag opponents? and Why (or why not) might this be a good plan? By the end of the second or third game, you can ask a child to name a responsibility she has as a member of a team. You might ask more advanced children to share their insights with one another and discuss how one team can gain an advantage over the other.

In this game, the number of possible taggers has been reduced by half from the game Hop, Pop, and Tag. On the surface this may appear to make the game easier, because a player without a pinnie has only to avoid someone wearing a pinnie. However, the added responsibility of tagging people on the other team who have tagged a teammate provide more things to consider than in Hop, Pop, and Tag. Children will likely need to play multiple games before remembering to avoid being tagged while trying to tag others. During the first trial of Team Pop-Up, you may need to stop the game, remind the children of the rules, and perhaps physically demonstrate a situation before having them resume play.

Small Modifications and Moving On

Try splitting children into more than two teams per play area (or combine play areas, but make sure every team is easily identifiable). Make sure there are enough players on each team to keep any team from losing too easily. Try changing the play area size to further increase the challenge. You might begin by having the children speed-walk before moving to running; this slows the game down and enables children to get a better feeling for how it is played. After a while you can change the mode of travel to skipping, hopping, or galloping.

Game Breakdown

Once again, almost no equipment is needed. Just remember to have pinnies for half the class and adequate space.

Equipment

Needs based on a 30-student class:

- Safe, open space
- Pinnies (one color, enough for half the class)

Skills Needed

- Safe travel in general space
- Chasing, fleeing, and dodging

Rules

1. Players with pinnies may only tag players on the other team (without pinnies).
2. Once tagged, players must squat and wait for someone else to tag their most recent tagger.
3. If players tag each other at the same (or nearly the same) time, they play rock, paper, scissors to determine who squats.
4. A tagged player may not tag anyone else while squatting.

Questions

- What can you do to avoid the other team?
- Should teammates work together as a group or spread out to tag opponents?
- What is one responsibility you have as a member of your team?
- Can one team gain an advantage over the other? How?

Popper Ball

Adapted from Dienstmann 2008.

Popper Ball extends the games of Hop, Pop, and Tag and Team Pop-Up by introducing manipulative motor skills to the chasing, fleeing, and dodging actions. Although it might not occur to them at first, children soon begin to understand that throwing and catching balls with their teammates is essential for success.

Teacher Essentials and Explanation Points

Begin by having all of the players on one team put on pinnies of the same color to differentiate them from those on the other team, who are not wearing pinnies. Then give all of the players of one team, except one, small balls they can hold in their hands. Explain that all of the players on one team may tag any of the players on the opposite team. When a child holding a ball is tagged, she must give it to her tagger and then squat. She may pop up to resume play only when someone else tags her tagger. A tagged player may not tag anyone else while squatting. Play continues in rounds of 60 to 120 seconds. The objective is to see how many balls the original team possesses at the end of each round. Teams swap starting with ball possession between rounds.

Encourage children to be honest and good-natured about close calls. For example, they can decide who has been tagged by playing a quick game of rock, paper, scissors.

Challenges Posed

In this game, children need to think about how they can retain possession of balls as a team. Not everyone on the team has a ball; one person is always without one at the start of the game. One thing you may need to ask the children is, "What are two ways to keep a ball safe or in your team's possession during play?" The directions for Popper Ball intentionally do not mention the strategy of passing the ball to a teammate before being tagged. This is done so the children have to ask whether this is allowed, or simply discover it on their own. Leading questions such as, "Does everyone on your team have a ball at the start?" and, "How do teams keep possession of the ball in other sports, such as basketball and soccer?" may help children realize the value of passing the ball. Conversely, possession of the ball also has implications for the defense, or the chasing team. Try to avoid focusing solely on the team with the ball, but also prompt the entire class by asking questions such as, "Should you always chase after a person holding a ball?" "Why would you chase opponents who don't have a ball?" and "Why would you not chase opponents who don't have a ball?"

Adding balls and requiring children to keep possession of them make this the most complex version of the original game. Some children focus on ball possession and forget the rules from the previous two versions of the game. Watch them carefully to make sure they remember the strategies they learned during previous play, such as tagging people who have tagged teammates and paying attention to the person who tagged them so that they know when they are free to pop up and resume play. Once most students are consistently displaying the appropriate game-play behaviors, you can concentrate on the type of passes they use and determine whether you need to demonstrate some easy ways to pass balls to teammates.

Small Modifications and Moving On

Undoubtedly, the size and type of ball or object could be changed. A mix of footballs, basketballs, playground balls, tennis balls, and beanbags will increase the contextual interference the children experience, because they have to be manipulated in different ways.

Game Breakdown

Balls that are easy to throw and catch are the only new equipment needed for Popper Ball. Such balls are usually pretty easy to find; even tennis balls can be used.

Equipment

Needs based on a 30-student class:

- Pinnies (one color, enough for half the class)
- Gator Skin (or similar) balls (enough for half the class, minus one)

Skills Needed

- Safe travel in general space
- Chasing, fleeing, dodging

Rules

1. A player holding a ball must hand it to her tagger.
2. Players may only tag players on the other team.
3. Once tagged, a player must squat and wait for someone else to tag his most recent tagger.
4. If players tag each other at the same (or nearly the same) time, they play rock, paper, scissors to determine who squats.
5. A tagged player may not tag anyone else while squatting.

Questions

- What are two ways to keep a ball safe or in your team's possession during play?
- Does everyone on your team have a ball at the start? What does that mean for keeping possession of a ball? (Think passing!)
- Should you always chase after a person holding a ball? Why chase opponents without a ball?

Hoopla

Another physical activity game highlighting the principle of contextual interference is Hoopla. In each of the three versions presented in this section, children must gather and protect objects that are considered theirs. In each successive version, however, the aim and process of gathering and protecting objects is noticeably altered from the previous version.

Teacher Essentials and Explanation Points

Separate students into four teams with no more than four students per team. For larger classes the number of teams can increase as space safely allows. Place four different objects (e.g., ball, beanbag, Frisbee, poly spot) in each team's hula hoop. The goal of the game is for each team to get all four of the same object in its hoop. Place each team's hoop a few feet (about a meter) from each corner of the play area to allow for a balance of offense and defense at each hoop.

Divide the play area into quadrants using small cones. Inform the children that there are four teams and that each one is trying to recover as many of its objects from other teams' hoops as possible. It is important that you show the children what the game is like after describing it, because play tends to be chaotic once the game begins. On your signal, each team is to retrieve only a certain color object from each hoop, returning each object to its own hoop (i.e., the blue team gets blue objects from other hoops for its own hoop) for safekeeping. It is helpful if each team wears the same color pinnies or flags for team identification. The strategy is to get only objects of their team's color and to gather only one object per person at a time. Children are likely to ask whether they can guard their own team's hoop. Let them know that there is no reason to guard their hoop because there is nothing anyone can do to keep objects from being removed. As in previous games (and perhaps all of the games in this text), mandating speed-walking rather than running for the first couple of games is a good idea. Children can easily bump into each other in this game, and speed-walking reduces the chances of injury in addition to helping children see how the game is played. Additional rules are that players may only retrieve objects of their team color;

Children sort objects by color in the fun game of Hoopla.

and players may not throw, kick, or pass objects to teammates. If you want to give the children an option of having a defender, you can do so. Just be sure to show the children what a defender does and how s/he can keep someone from stealing an object. A defender is allowed to tag someone who has an object in their hand. If the person stealing the object is tagged, s/he has to replace the object in the hoop before venturing out again for more objects.

Challenges Posed

The following problems and questions are typically posed by children, but usually not without some prompting. Ask children the following questions to help them verbalize the strategic challenges of the game. It is very important to avoid presenting questions with dichotomous, or either–or, answers. A helpful approach is to pose all questions as directives. The following examples engage children so they can perform higher-order cognitive functions that improve their game play:

- Tell me what good teamwork looks like (i.e., spreading out or sticking together).
- Explain how important communication is in this game.
- With all that is going on during the game, it can be hard to communicate. Share some ways you and your team communicated.
- Tell me what three things would help make a team successful in this game.

Children have to be mindful of multiple targets and threats in the form of both invading opponents and opponents they have to dodge as they attempt to retrieve objects. Balancing an attack across a wide play area is difficult for children. Being aware of the number of other teams' objects that remain in a team's own hoop is also an aspect of the game that affects how aggressively a team must attack. If no children can articulate the importance of this, let them try one more game before telling them about this issue.

Children usually fail to use any coherent strategy the first or second time they play Hoopla. This inevitably leads team members to attack the same hoop. When this happens, labor is unevenly distributed, and gathering all the objects quickly is difficult. Once the game ends and before another one begins, it helps to ask, "Is it easier to get all the objects you need when everyone goes to whichever hoop they want, or should each person be responsible for one hoop?" An excellent follow-up question would be "Why?"

If a team realizes that the fastest child (usually the one with the longest stride) should be responsible for collecting objects from the farthest hoop, stop and highlight this strategy.

Small Modifications and Moving On

Allow teams to play until one team collects all the objects of its assigned color. If one team dominates the first game, pause between games to discuss effective attacking strategies.

At any time you may implement Zoo Hoopla, a slight modification. Call out the name of an animal (e.g., tiger, elephant, frog, crab), and have the children travel in a way that mimics that animal's movement. There is no one correct way of moving, so children should be given time to explore creative solutions. However, frogs do not run on all fours like tigers; make sure the children are reasonable with their imitations!

Give children 30 to 60 seconds to perform as each animal so they can explore moving in different ways. Remember that each movement presents its own challenges to playing the game. Getting the children to verbalize those challenges is crucial. Children are likely to complete rounds of the first game quickly, so look for children to exhibit the ability to invade areas and return objects to their team's hoop quickly and with a considerable level of cooperation and coordination.

Make the defender optional. Ask students the first question in the Challenges Posed section after a round or two, giving teams the opportunity to explore the game with and without a dedicated defender.

Some students may try to pass stolen objects back to their home hoop by tossing them to the defender. Allow this strategy initially, and then explore why it may or may not be a good strategy during a pause for questions.

You may also choose to place cones around each hoop and prohibit defenders from stepping inside the cones.

Game Breakdown

Hoopla requires more equipment than the previous three games do. The good news, however, is that the objects can be anything as long as they are the same color as three other objects.

Equipment

Needs based on a 30-student class:

- Four hula hoops
- Objects of four colors, 15 or more per color (balls, beanbags, flags, etc.)
- Colored pinnies or flag belts for team identification
- 10 or more cones

Skills Needed

- Safe travel in general space
- Chasing, fleeing, dodging

Rules

1. Teams decide on a target object before each round begins. Teams may end up choosing the same target item; this is OK, because it adds to the challenge of the game.
2. Players may steal only one item at a time.
3. Each team must have a defender at its home hoop (although the defender must stay outside of the coned area, if you decide to use them).
4. If the defender—and only the defender—tags an opponent, the opponent must go back to his home hoop (and, if holding an item, return it to the defender).

Questions

- What is the advantage of having a defender? What is the disadvantage?
- How can you get your target objects if another team is trying to get the same objects?

Guardian Hoopla

Guardian Hoopla is an invasion game that includes aspects of tagging. Whereas Hoopla offered children a high degree of freedom and enjoyment based on accomplishing a task without being threatened by other players, Guardian Hoopla challenges them to be more cautious and cognitively engaged during play. Students spend time working both individually and as members of a team to both gather objects and protect objects from other teams.

Teacher Essentials and Explanation Points

In this game, players retrieve objects and return them to their hoops, but the difficulty is increased through the introduction of defensive players who can hinder attackers. Incorporating defenders adds a physically demanding element to game play—chasing, fleeing, and dodging while attempting to meet an unrelated objective (stealing objects).

To start, create four teams and assign each team a particular color; then divide the play area into four quadrants (one for each color). Explain that the object of the game is for each team to retrieve all objects of its color from the other teams' hoops. Depending on your class size, you should make sure that each quadrant's hoop contains three to five objects per color except for that team's color. Before beginning, show the students an example of a team's hoop; students can then help reset objects in the hoops after each round.

Guardian Hoopla is similar to Hoopla; the main difference is that teams now have defenders who can tag invading players from other teams, which sends them back to their own hoops. If, for example, a green player retrieves a green ball from the blue team's hoop and is tagged by a blue player within the blue area, the green player returns the green object to the blue team's hoop. The green player must then immediately return to the green area before re-attacking another team's hoop.

Challenges Posed

When discussing strategies and tactics, you must now present dilemmas that focus on both offensive and defensive elements. Have children discuss, just among their own team members, strategies for defending against attackers. Ask them whether the team should designate a certain number of attackers and defenders, whether more or fewer of one type of player helps or hurts a team, whether attackers should work alone or in groups, and whether there might be better places to attack first.

Eventually allowing children to defend their own quadrant requires them to make better planning decisions. They must be aware of their opponents' positions and initiate attacks when they are not paying attention. Planning an attack also requires planning an escape after retrieving an object. Players must also focus on defending against attackers from other teams. If all blue players abandon their quadrant, other teams will have little difficulty gathering objects. Therefore, teammates must cooperate. This requires that they discuss who will fill the roles of attacker and defender. Without clear communication among teammates, teams do not succeed.

A player is only safe from taggers in her own quadrant. No player may guard the team's hoop, though (defenders must stay a certain distance from their own hoops—you will need to decide these boundaries and mark them by putting hoops behind a line or inside a ring of cones). Although children will understand this rule, it takes a while for them to implement it. One possible reason for this is that the idea of not guarding is counterintuitive to children. In many of the games they play and watch, a defensive team is trying to keep another team from meeting its objective. In terms of social development, we know that territoriality is a component of the egocentrism prevalent in elementary school–age children. This game requires that they act contrary to this urge, so you will need to be on the lookout for children who appear to be instinctively guarding their hoops.

Small Modifications and Moving On

Teams should play until one team collects all the objects of its assigned color. Reaching this goal may be difficult at first because of the added defensive (i.e., tagging) element. Losing an object after being tagged requires children to be persistent in trying to gather all objects of an assigned color. Team members could struggle to cooperate with each other and, as a result, be unable to form and communicate offensive and defensive strategies. If this is the case, pause the game and have a group discussion about ways to improve each aspect (e.g., assigning roles, having a captain who directs others, having defenders who cover certain zones within their quadrant), or let teams brainstorm. You may consider changing the mode of travel (e.g., as in Zoo Hoopla, in which players move like animals; see the description in Hoopla).

If possible, combine play areas (e.g., two halves of a gym or two areas if outside) to form four larger quadrants with more students per team. Defensive and offensive strategies may change with larger quadrants and more teammates. Increase the number of objects per color in each hoop accordingly. With a play area smaller than a typical basketball court, you may decide not to divide the area into quadrants. In this case, have the children play the game like Hoopla with the only difference being that teams try to get objects of their team's color.

Game Breakdown

The equipment needed for Guardian Hoopla is no different from that needed for Hoopla. Only some rules have changed.

Equipment

Needs based on a 30-student class:

- Four hula hoops
- Objects of four colors, 15 or more per color (balls, beanbags, flags, etc.)
- Colored pinnies or flag belts for team identification
- 10 or more cones (to identify quadrants)

Skills Needed

- Safe travel in general space
- Chasing, fleeing, dodging

Rules

1. Players are safe from taggers only in their home quadrants.
2. If tagged in another team's quadrant, a player must return to her home quadrant.
3. If tagged while holding a stolen object, a player must return it to the hoop from which she stole it.
4. Players may retrieve only one item at a time of the color assigned to them.
5. Defenders must stay an arm's length from the hoop they are defending.

Questions

- Should attackers spread out or try to attack one zone at a time?
- Should a team have more attackers or more defenders? Why?
- What three things make a team successful in this game?

Hands-Free Hoopla

Hands-Free Hoopla involves pairs of children and fosters the generation of creative solutions to a familiar problem. Removing the tagging element of Hoopla and Guardian Hoopla allows children to focus on cooperation, which plays a critical role in determining how well pairs perform throughout the game.

Teacher Essentials and Explanation Points

Hands-Free Hoopla is markedly different from the previous two games. To start, create four teams and assign each one a particular color; then divide the play area into four quadrants (one for each color). Gather all objects into a central space of each play area. With players in their own quadrants, explain that the goal is to transport objects to other teams' hoops. The twist is that they may not use their hands. Have them start at their home hoops. Explain that when you give the stop signal, the team whose hoop contains the fewest objects wins!

The task in this game is to pick up an object of any color and deposit it in another team's hoop. However, children must work alone—initially—to transport objects, and they must do so without using their hands. The aim of the game is to discover the most efficient ways to move the objects.

Children may not move an object while it is on the ground (i.e., no kicking, nudging, sliding). To make the game more challenging, stop play after the first round (or two, depending on whether children make quick work of the initial format) and have children work in pairs. The same rules apply, although one pair on each team (teams must designate this pair and strictly adhere to this rule) may transport one object at a time of the team's color back to the central hoop from its team's hoop in a hands-free fashion. If children exhibit creativity and understand the strategies needed for succeeding, you could have them move like animals in pairs while transporting objects without using their hands.

Challenges Posed

Problems and questions are likely to arise when playing this game. You can help children come up with solutions by saying, "Which parts of your body might be easier to use than others?" "Are there other ways to travel besides walking or standing upright?" and "Try to use a different way of moving objects (e.g., with feet, on head, on back, on belly)."

The most immediate problem is figuring out a practical and reliable way to transport objects without using their hands. Children will likely exhibit a good deal of creativity at first, trying elbows, backs, hips, and legs. However, once a couple of children find an effective way to carry objects, other children are sure to mimic it. A second problem lies in the fact that the goal of the game is for a team to have the fewest objects of its own color at the end of the game. Children will be tempted to carry any object to another team's hoop, although the alert child will realize the benefit of carrying her own team's objects to other hoops!

Small Modifications and Moving On

You can modify the game by assigning certain roles to students. Depending on class size, each team may have one or two returners, and the remaining team members could be spreaders. Start the game with two objects in each team's hoop and the rest of the objects in the central space. Returners may transport objects from their own hoops back to the central space, while spreaders continue to scatter objects from the center to other teams' hoops. The game is still hands-free; between rounds, encourage students to demonstrate to the class new ways of carrying objects.

Additionally, you may further limit the ways players may transport objects between rounds (e.g., from hands-free to hands- and arms-free).

Game Breakdown

Nothing is new in the way of equipment and skills needed for this game. You could give teams (or players) other objects to help them transport objects (e.g., Lummi sticks to use as chopsticks).

Equipment

Needs based on a 30-student class:

- Four hula hoops
- Objects of four colors, 15 or more per color (balls, beanbags, flags, etc.)
- Colored pinnies or flag belts for team identification
- 10 or more cones (to identify quadrants)

Skills Needed

- Safe travel in general space
- Chasing, fleeing, dodging

Rules

1. Players may carry only one object at a time.
2. Players may not kick, slide, sling, or toss objects.
3. Players must work alone in transporting objects.
4. Players must place objects inside other teams' hoops.

Questions

- Should you place objects in the same hoop every time? How do you decide?
- What are some keys to success?
- What are some reliable ways to carry objects? Why is this important?
- Do you always have to travel upright? What about crawling, rolling, or crab-walking?

Games Emphasizing Mental Control

This section presents six games that focus on the principle of mental control. Because sport is such a prevalent aspect of society that crosses cultural boundaries and unites people from a variety of backgrounds and experiences, it follows that teaching sport-related activities to children is a critical component of their formal learning. Because sports come in a variety of forms, deciding which ones to teach can often be a tough task for educators. However, many of the skills used in one sport carry over to others. The principle of mental control is nearly universal among sports and games. The games and their progressive alterations outlined in this section foster the development of mental control in children.

Team Bowling

Team Bowling may not sound like a game requiring even moderate physical activity. However, this game not only elicits some vigorous physical activity, but also requires more complex skills found in sports such as basketball, soccer, and most notably, team handball.

Teacher Essentials and Explanation Points

Similar to team handball in many respects, Team Bowling involves the use of rolling, passing, and shooting skills to knock down an opposing team's pins. As in the sport of team handball, players face ball-handling, running, and shooting limitations. Teams can range from five to seven players (depending on class size and the space available), and the shooting line should be roughly 10 to 15 feet (3 to 4.6 m) from the pins. Each team has five to seven pins. Play areas look roughly similar to team handball courts (see figure 11.1) and have two teams of up to seven players each. One team per play area wears pinnies. As in traditional bowling, students try to

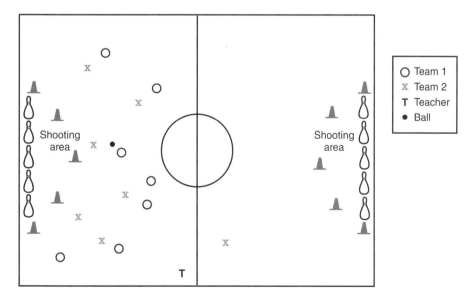

Figure 11.1 Activity map for Team Bowling.

knock down pins. However, in Team Bowling students are on teams and try to knock down the pins of the opposing team. To start, cluster the pins relatively close together.

You will need to clearly outline the rules. We recommend that you use a rules sheet (as may be used in golf) in the form of a poster or slide that can be hung or projected onto the gym wall to remind children of the rules. The rules require all players to roll handballs along the ground when passing or shooting at opponents' pins. When a player acquires a ball, he may take only three steps before passing to a teammate or rolling the ball at a pin. However, players on the opposite team can intercept any passes or rolls at pins as long as they are not inside the area delineated by the shooting line. All children will be tempted to use their feet, but they may intercept a rolled ball with their hands only. Be sure to remind players that they may not go behind the designated shooting line unless they are going to retrieve a missed shot by the other team.

Teams may quickly adopt long passes as a strategy for moving the ball down the court quickly. Although this is a good strategy, it may exclude many children from playing. Consider allowing teams a certain number of long-range, full-court-type passes per round. Also, make sure students do not camp out on one side of the court the entire time; everyone should strike a balance between playing offense and defense.

Challenges Posed

Ask children to consider how a shooter may knock over more than one pin at a time, the best way to keep the other team from stealing the ball, the length of shot that has the highest probability of success, and how to guard the person with the ball. Children need to be aware of tactical issues, and some tactics require help from others. For example, children must learn that they need to pass the ball repeatedly to be successful in this game. Passing requires that the offense be spread out, and this requires the defense to spread out as well. Close-range shooting is more effective than long-range shooting, but it requires a more concerted effort from teammates.

Almost invariably, passing and shooting from close range seldom occur during the first few trials of this game. We suggest that you stop the game and point out to the class instances in which a team used multiple passes while spread out to shoot (but not necessarily make) a close-range shot. In fact, it is probably even more critical for you to do this when the shot is not successful because children usually equate success with making a shot, regardless of how it was achieved. Stopping to discuss a missed shot based on good decisions, and labeling the shot correct can underscore the notion that strategy is critical and will, more often than not, result in success.

Small Modifications and Moving On

Note whether children make good passes before they can shoot the ball. They will likely struggle with the three-step rule at first, but their performance will improve with time and reminders. Children should be able to complete multiple passes per ball possession and have regular chances to shoot before moving to the next game. Actually, a team should exhibit the ability to spread out during play rather than cluster around the ball (during offense or defense).

To modify the game, you could require a certain number of consecutive passes before a team shoots the ball, or require that everyone on a team touch the ball before a team member may take a shot.

Game Breakdown

Because the skills needed for Team Bowling are minimal, it is quite inclusive, which helps with groups of children with varying ability. Furthermore, equipment is readily available if needed.

Equipment

Needs based on a 30-student class:

- Two or more team handball balls (or other similar balls)
- Five to seven bowling pins per team (or similar targets, 30 maximum)

- 10 or more cones (tape or poly spots may also be used to delineate the shooting area)
- Pinnies or flag belts (for team identification)

Skills Needed

- Rolling and passing (a ball)
- Aiming at a target

Rules

1. Players may pass the ball in any manner, but must roll the ball when shooting at the pins.
2. A player holding the ball may take only three steps before passing to a teammate or rolling to (shooting at) a pin.
3. Players may intercept passes with their hands only.
4. Players must stay outside of the area designated by the shooting line during play unless they are going to retrieve a missed shot by the other team.
5. Out-of-bounds balls result in a turnover to the team without the ball, from the spot where the ball went out.

Questions

- Is it possible to knock over more than one pin at a time?
- How can you keep the other team from stealing the ball?
- Is it better to take a longer or closer shot? Why?
- Should everyone try to guard the person with the ball? Why or why not?

Super Team Bowling

Increasing the shooting distance and shrinking the size of the target create the additional challenges in Super Team Bowling. Although this game is quite similar to Team Bowling, children must now recognize when light or strong forces are needed and learn that not all situations require the same amount of force.

Teacher Essentials and Explanation Points

As the name of the game suggests, the basic format is largely the same as Team Bowling. However, in Super Team Bowling, children now face additional challenges around the shooting line. To facilitate these challenges, the shooting line should be several steps farther from the pins than in Team Bowling, and fewer pins should be arranged with more space (3 to 5 ft., or 1 to 1.5 m) between them (as an alternative, pins or targets of varying size can help you achieve this). Play areas remain largely the same. Be sure the children are aware of both the extended shooting area and the arrangement of the pins. Both are likely to increase the difficulty of the game. Passing is even more critical, because children must shoot at smaller targets from a longer distance. They will have to be aware of teammates who may be closer to the shooting zone and should pass the ball to them accordingly. All rules from Team Bowling still apply.

Challenges Posed

Children must move to open spaces to receive passes, and passers must realize that they may have to pass the ball backward to keep possession. Furthermore, children must be aware of open teammates, because the extended shooting distance and smaller, spaced-out targets require shots from varying angles.

The focus of Team Bowling was on learning the importance of passing; the challenge in Super Team Bowling is determining the types of passes that work best. The following questions should spur children's thought processes and help them decide which pass to use: "What does a good pass look like?" "When would an overhand pass not be the best way to pass?" "What about a bounce pass?" "How important is communicating with your teammates?" "What information should you be communicating, and how can you communicate it?"

You will, undoubtedly, need to focus on children's decision making regarding passing, particularly whether they are passing when it is best to do so and whether they are using the best type of pass for the situation. Once again, highlight strategies or moves they should copy as soon as you spot children using them. Stop the game and discuss a particularly good choice, and let the children who were involved describe it for their classmates.

Small Modifications and Moving On

Making three consecutive passes could be a game modification if children appear to be having trouble adapting to the shooting and target size challenges of Super Team Bowling. One modification could be to start without the three consecutive passes rule and gradually work up to it. To play well, children need to be adept at moving the ball both down the court and laterally around the shooting area. With the greater emphasis on passing in Super Team Bowling, children need a greater awareness as defenders; passers should be looking constantly for open teammates. Being open for a shot at the target is important in this game, because the greater shooting distance and smaller targets make each shot critical. Once children regularly exhibit mastery of the moves and strategies, move the class to the final game.

Game Breakdown

As you can see, the skills and equipment do not differ too much from those in Team Bowling. However, children do need to think differently when playing this game.

Equipment

Needs based on a 30-student class:

- Two or more team handball balls (or other similar balls)
- 20 or more bowling pins (or similar targets, 30 maximum)
- 10 or more cones
- Pinnies or flag belts (for team identification)

Skills Needed

- Rolling and passing (a ball)
- Aiming at a target

Rules

1. Players may pass the ball in any manner, but must roll the ball when shooting at the pins.
2. A player holding the ball may take only three steps before passing to a teammate or rolling to (shooting at) a pin.
3. Players may intercept passes with their hands only.
4. Players must stay outside of the area designated by the shooting line during play unless they are going to retrieve a missed shot by the other team.
5. Out-of-bounds balls result in a turnover to the team without the ball, from the spot where the ball went out.
6. Teams must make three consecutive passes before shooting.

Questions

- How do you make three passes without losing the ball?
- Do you need to be more careful with your shots than in Team Bowling? Why?
- Is communication between team members important? How so, and what should you be communicating?

Goalie Bowlie

Goalie Bowlie features all of the aspects of Super Team Bowling with the addition of a goalie for each team stationed in the shooting zone. The goalie attempts to block any shots bowled by the opposing team and may use her hands, feet, or body to do so. Pins should retain the same spacing used in Super Team Bowling as an additional challenge for the goalie.

Teacher Essentials and Explanation Points

Explain that this game is quite similar to Super Team Bowling in that the shooting line is still at an increased distance from the pins and the number of pins should be reduced with more space provided between them (3 to 5 ft., or 1 to 1.5 m). However, there is one exception: now there is a goalie to protect each team's pins. Emphasize that the addition of a goalie for each team makes scoring even more challenging. New rules for this game center on the goalie, who (1) may not exit the area delineated by the shooting line, (2) must pass the ball to a teammate standing on her own shooting line after blocking a bowled shot from an opponent, and (3) may use only her feet to block shots when one pin remains for either team. Retain pin spacing and any other modifications used in Super Team Bowling. Have players take turns being goalie after each round.

Challenges Posed

To help children consider tactical issues, explain how an attacking team can keep the goalie from blocking shots. Also, describe how to fake out a goalie with bowled shots, and help the children identify one way the attacking team can get more than one bowled shot per attack.

Having a goalie makes mounting a successful attack more difficult. As noted, children have to create chances for multiple shots at the targets, because a weak shot allows the goalie to give the ball directly to someone on his own team. The attacking team must try to recover any rebounds from bowled shots to provide increased stress on the goalie. Children are sure to find success in drawing the goalie to one side of the playing field or the other, allowing the attacker to bowl at targets farther from the goalie (e.g., draw him to a corner and then bowl across the shooting zone to targets on the opposite side).

Small Modifications and Moving On

None

Game Breakdown

One small addition to this game would be to use a special goalie shirt to distinguish the goalie from the rest of the team.

Equipment

Needs based on a 30-student class:

- Two or more team handball balls (or other similar balls)
- 20 or more bowling pins (or similar targets, 30 maximum)

- 10 or more cones
- Pinnies or flag belts (for team identification)

Skills Needed

- Rolling and passing (a ball)
- Aiming at a target

Rules

1. Players may pass the ball in any manner, but must roll the ball when shooting.
2. A player holding the ball may take only three steps before passing or shooting.
3. Teams must make three consecutive passes before shooting.
4. Players may intercept a pass with their hands only.
5. Players must stay outside of the designated shooting area during play.
6. A dropped, missed, or out-of-bounds pass results in a turnover for the team without the ball from the spot where the ball went out; a team's pass count returns to zero.
7. The goalie may not exit the shooting area.
8. The goalie must pass the ball to a teammate standing at her own shooting zone line after blocking a bowled shot from an opponent.
9. When only one pin remains in the goalie's pin area, she may use only her feet to block bowled shots.

Questions

- How does the attacking team deal with a goalie blocking its shots?
- Is it possible to fake out a goalie with bowled shots? How?
- How can the attacking team get more than one bowled shot per attack? (Think about getting a rebound that the goalie missed.)

Garbage Ball

A fourth game that illustrates the principle of mental control is Garbage Ball. This is an invasion game closely related to soccer. Invasion games allow children to work both as individuals and as members of a team while attacking and defending targets in a dynamic setting. Garbage Ball requires children to play both roles because they change positions after every goal.

Teacher Essentials and Explanation Points

Place students in teams of four to six in a way that balances skill levels as much as possible. Two teams play a short-sided game of soccer using trash cans or other comparable containers as goals. To score, a team must kick the ball along the ground and into the container. Teams may have a goalie who may block shots with his feet and body only, but they must keep at least two defenders on their own half of the play area at all times. This is a requirement that balances a team's attack and defense as in soccer. Attackers and defenders should swap roles after each goal. See figure 11.2 for the basic setup.

Special rules for the game that may be different from regulation soccer are as follows: (1) when a ball goes out of bounds, the team awarded possession in-bounds it by kicking it on the ground from the point at which the ball was ruled out; (2) players may shoot the ball from anywhere on the court or field, but no player may cherry-pick, because attackers can be no closer to the opponents' goal than the last defender; and (3) after any goal, attacking and defending players on each team swap positions.

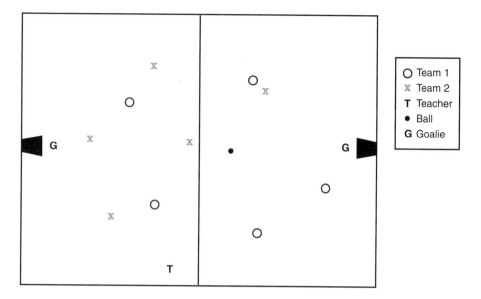

Figure 11.2   Diagram for Garbage Ball setup.

Challenges Posed

Numerous tactical issues will evolve during play. Help the children to think about (1) the best way to position attackers, (2) whether attackers should pass among themselves, (3) the optimal position for defenders, (4) whether one-on-one defense works better than a zone (area) defense, and (5) the importance of communication between positions and the information that should be communicated.

This game should force children to develop good offensive and defensive strategies. When asked how to succeed, children will likely say, "Teamwork." Ask for examples of teamwork behaviors. This will help them articulate cooperative and responsible game behaviors.

Goalies must focus on staying between the ball and the goal. Encourage goalies to find creative ways to block shots (e.g., seated or standing in different positions), and consider allowing team huddles after each goal or a series of goals so team members can discuss defensive strategies.

After about 10 minutes, identify obvious skill differences between the teams. If one team seems dominant because of player skill, redistribute players. If, however, teams appear evenly matched but one team still overwhelms the other, discuss with both teams why they believe one team is doing so well.

Small Modifications and Moving On

As a modification, use existing lines, markers, or cones to designate areas from which children could shoot to score more points. For example, you could place a line of cones near midfield and stipulate that a goal from behind the line is worth 3 points and simply hitting the trash can is worth 2 points. However, a goal into the trash can, but not from past the line of cones, is still worth the regular 2 points. Move on to the next game, Bountiful Ball, once children have had several chances to play both positions and have demonstrated that they understand basic strategies through team discussions.

Game Breakdown

If medium to large trash cans are not available, consider using plastic bins. They are usually inexpensive and can be purchased at local superstores.

Equipment

Needs based on a 30-student class:

- One soccer (or similar) ball per game, size 4 or 5
- Four trash cans (actual cans or buckets or other large containers)
- Colored pinnies for half the class
- 10 or more cones

Skills Needed

- Safe travel in general space
- Chasing, fleeing, dodging, kicking

Rules

1. The first pass of the game (and after all goals) must go to a teammate.
2. If the ball goes out of bounds, the team that did not kick it out gains possession. One player in-bounds the ball by kicking on the ground from where it went out.
3. Players may shoot the ball from anywhere on the court or field. Goals are worth 2 points.
4. Fouls (e.g., pushing, using hands, sliding) result in a turnover and a free kick from the place where the foul occurred.
5. Attackers can be no closer to the opponents' goal than the last defender.

Questions

- What is the best way to position attackers and defenders?
- Should attackers try to pass the ball? Why or why not?
- Should defenders guard a particular player? Why or why not?
- How should you kick the ball to get it to the target?

Bountiful Ball

In Bountiful Ball more than one ball is in play at once. This tests children's ability to focus on multiple targets at the same time. In addition, it results in a greater degree of involvement for all children compared to a game with only one ball. Allowing teams to alter the number of defensive and offensive players gives them the chance to explore solutions to dealing with an extra ball. Goals scored in the trash can earn 1 point.

Teacher Essentials and Explanation Points

As in Garbage Ball, place students in teams of four to six in a way that balances skill levels as much as possible. Two teams play a short-sided game of soccer using trash cans or other comparable containers as goals. To score, a team must kick a ball along the ground and into the container. Teams may have a goalie who may block shots with his feet and body only, but they must keep at least two defenders on their own half of the play area at all times. This is a requirement that balances a team's attack and defense as in soccer. Attackers and defenders should swap roles after each goal.

Special rules for the game that may be different from regulation soccer are as follows: (1) when a ball goes out of bounds, the team rewarded possession in-bounds it by kicking it on the ground from the point at which the ball was ruled out; (2) players may shoot balls from anywhere on the court or field, but no player may cherry-pick, because attackers can be no closer to the opponents' goal than the last defender; and (3) after any goal, attacking and defending players on each team swap positions.

Bountiful Ball differs from Garbage Ball in only one specific but important way: players have to contend with more than one ball. For the first two goals of the game, an extra ball is the only difference. After two goals, stop the game and explain that teams may now either remove or add defenders. Each team may have a goalie, as in the first game, but the use of a goalie is not a requirement. Choosing whether to have a goalie is a strategic choice that will either add to a team's attack or strengthen its defense. After two goals (regardless of which team makes them), allow each team to discuss the option. Players should continue to swap roles after each goal, as in the first game.

Challenges Posed

The challenge of this game lies in decision making and player awareness. Children must develop strategies for both offense and defense to accommodate the extra ball. They should realize that having more attackers makes scoring easier if the attackers can keep possession of both balls. More attackers means fewer defenders for a team, however, so keeping opponents from scoring could be difficult. Children must learn to balance the two positions.

Small Modifications and Moving On

As in Garbage Ball, you may also implement a required number of passes between teammates before shooting the ball. For example, a team may have to pass the ball three times between multiple players. Teams are welcome to pass the ball more than three times, although three is the minimum.

During a 10- to 12-minute play session, consciously focus on children's need to hold discussions and develop good strategies. You will need to intervene if the game devolves into boom ball, with children playing wildly with little thought or planning. In such a situation, stop the game and remind them about attacking and defending roles. Once they can balance offense and defense with an extra ball, they are ready for the game of Mega Garbage Ball.

In addition to modifying the scoring system, you might also require teams to make a certain number of consecutive passes before shooting the ball. Three is the minimum because it involves multiple players rather than just two. Under this condition players have to use the entire play space more effectively to move the ball and keep possession.

Game Breakdown

Be sure to have two balls for each game. Plastic containers could be substituted for trash cans.

Equipment

Needs based on a 30-student class:

- Two soccer (or similar) balls per game, size 4 or 5
- Four trash cans (actual cans or buckets or other large containers)
- Colored pinnies for half the class
- 10 or more cones

Skills Needed

- Safe travel in general space
- Chasing, fleeing, dodging, kicking

Rules

1. The first pass of the game (and after all goals) must go to a teammate.
2. If the ball goes out of bounds, the team that did not kick it out gains possession. One player in-bounds the ball by kicking on the ground from where it went out.
3. Players may shoot the ball from anywhere on the court or field. Goals are worth 1 point.

4. Fouls (e.g., pushing, using hands, sliding) result in a turnover and a free kick from the place where the foul occurred.

5. Attackers can be no closer to the opponents' goal than the last defender.

6. The goalie, if present, may use his hands or any other body part to block shots.

Questions

- How does having or not having a goalie help or hurt a team?
- Should a team have more attackers because there are two balls? Why or why not?

Mega Garbage Ball

Adding an extra scoring target for each team alters children's perception of the game in a way that is similar to adding another ball. To deal with an increased number of attackers and scoring opportunities, children's awareness of such threats and bonuses must increase. Furthermore, children will have an opportunity to create a variety of solutions for scoring and defending because of the additional space.

Children often have difficulty mastering the skills needed for dominating in Mega Garbage Ball. Because the game requires an awareness of multiple attackers and two scoring targets, they are continually engaged, both physically and mentally. Your focus should be on each team's defense. Because teams can now score on two goals, they will be more likely to abandon defensive strategies; thus, it could be helpful to place children in defensive positions if a team (or teams) begins to lose a balance between offense and defense.

Teacher Essentials and Explanation Points

Mega Garbage Ball is a combination of Garbage Ball and Bountiful Ball, but teams can now attack two goals with three balls. Teams need different colored pinnies, and each team defends its own goal, but attacks either of the two goals on the opposite half of the court. A team may not attack the goal directly beside its own. As in Bountiful Ball, a team must have at least one defender, but may have more, and it can choose to have a goalie. To give everyone a chance to play in a variety of positions, a player who scores must be the goalie until another player on the team scores. The only new rules for the game are that three balls are in play at a time and there is no out of bounds. Play never stops.

Challenges Posed

Children should be prompted to think about the challenges now presented by the use of three balls. Decisions need to be made regarding what to do when a team does not have (but wants) possession of a ball. If children are having difficulty with this decision, you could ask a prompting question such as, "Should teammates split up to go after different balls individually?" Sharing strategies of how to keep possession can benefit all players.

Having two goals at each end drastically changes the offensive and defensive aspects of the game. Teams often attempt to have a stronger offense at first, although such a strategy inevitably leads to many goals scored against them. Defenders are likely to become exasperated at first, so teams should take the time to develop a sound strategy for defending first, and then attacking.

Small Modifications and Moving On

None

Game Breakdown

Children are challenged by being able to attack two goals with three balls. Just be sure to keep reminding them that they are allowed to attack two goals with three balls.

Equipment

Needs based on a 30-student class:

- Three soccer (or similar) balls per game, size 4 or 5
- Four trash cans (actual cans or buckets or other large containers)
- Colored pinnies for half the class
- 10 or more cones

Skills Needed

- Safe travel in general space
- Chasing, fleeing, dodging, kicking

Rules

1. Only three balls are in play at a time.
2. The first pass of the game (and after all goals) must go to a teammate.
3. There is no out of bounds—play does not stop.
4. Players may shoot the ball from anywhere on the court or field. Goals are worth 1 point.
5. Fouls (e.g., pushing, using hands, sliding) result in a turnover and a free kick from the place where the foul occurred.
6. Attackers can be no closer to the opponents' goal than the last defender.

Questions

- What should a team do when not in possession of a ball?
- Should teammates split up to go after different balls individually?
- How could teammates work together to keep a ball?

Games Promoting Discovery

The principle of discovery is built into many games. At times, however, children discover strategies or tactics to use in a game by happenstance. Similarly, children's discoveries can lead to solutions that are not feasible or allowed by the rules. Your task is to provide an environment in which children can find new ways to achieve goals while staying within the game's parameters. Relying on games to tacitly provide children with chances to discover through trial and error decreases the probability that they will—you must create those chances with your choice of games and game alterations. The two games and their alterations presented in this section promote the principle of discovery.

Trash Can Polo

Trash Can Polo is derived from the traditional version of Pillow Polo, which is similar to floor hockey in that each team consists of five players and a goalie. The objective is to put the ball past the other team's goalie while preventing the opposing team from doing likewise. However, this game results in floor players experiencing the greatest amount of moderate-to-vigorous physical activity (MVPA) and mental engagement, and goalies experiencing much less. Furthermore, only one player at a time practices the manipulative skills needed. Our modifications of the traditional version, presented here, increase all participants' mental engagement and MVPA levels.

By simply eliminating the goalie position, Trash Can Polo increases MVPA and mental engagement. Replacing the typical goal with a small trash can turned on its side provides a target that does not need to be guarded by a player. A slightly smaller floor and a 3v3 format (three players on each team) force players to cover more of the play area and increase the number of touches they have. More touches and more space coverage increase both MVPA (more running) and the number and quality of strategic decisions (e.g., who to pass to, where to run, or who to defend against [two defenders mark an offensive player] when an opponent is open).

Teacher Essentials and Explanation Points

The objective of the game is to put the ball in the can while keeping the other team from doing the same. To accomplish this, passing to teammates in open space, dribbling, and playing are essential. To start the game, set up a trash can or other container on its side to represent a small goal (the game has no goalies). Group students into teams of five or six players. Explain that their goal is to shoot the ball into the can while keeping the other team from doing the same. Players pass the ball along the ground to open teammates using polo sticks.

Players may adopt varying strategies for striking the ball. Allow these, as long as they are safe. Also, for an out-of-bounds ball, make sure defenders spread out away from the in-bounding opponent.

Challenges Posed

This game prompts the kinds of questions elicited by invasion games. Address these directly and help the children discover the answers. Children need to address the following questions before moving on to other game versions:

- What is the best way to move the ball down the court?
- How does a player get open to receive a pass?
- How does a player move with the ball while also keeping track of where teammates are?
- What is the best way to position players on the court? Should there be more players on offense or defense?

Given that passing to teammates in open space, dribbling, and shooting are essential, observe the way children pass and move. The combination of not having a goalie and using a small trash can as the goal increases the complexity of the game because a rule change can now stipulate that a shot cannot be blocked or caught (i.e., what a goalie is typically allowed to do). Observe how the children protect their goal and highlight the approaches they use.

Small Modifications and Moving On

When you start to notice that the children are playing with less confusion, you can extend the game by modifying the boundaries slightly. Try dividing players into smaller teams (e.g., 3v3) and having them play on a smaller court. Doing so increases their level of MVPA and opportunities to respond (OTR) throughout a game, while also requiring them to plan careful attacking and defending strategies.

Game Breakdown

Trash Can Polo requires the use of a skill that many children have difficulty learning: striking with a long-handled implement. However, remind the children that the surface area of the polo stick gives them lots of room to hit the ball.

Equipment

Needs based on a 30-student class:

- Pillow polo (or foam-padded floor hockey) sticks for each player
- Four or more foam or pillow polo balls
- 15 or more cones
- Four trash cans or other large containers
- Pinnies or flag belts for team identification

Skills Needed

- Locomotor skills: sliding, running
- Manipulative skill: striking with a long-handled implement

Rules

1. Players may move the ball only on the ground (passing, catching, shooting) using polo sticks.
2. Neither team has a goalie.
3. If a ball goes out of bounds, the team that did not hit it out gets possession of the ball from that spot.
4. Fouls (e.g., pushing, tripping, high stick) result in a free hit from the foul spot.
5. Players may not raise sticks higher than knee height.

Questions

- What is the best way to move the ball down the court?
- How do you get open to receive a pass?
- Do you have to look for teammates? Why?
- Do you want more offense or defense for your team? Why?
- What makes catching the ball difficult, and how can you overcome this?

Four-Team Pillow Polo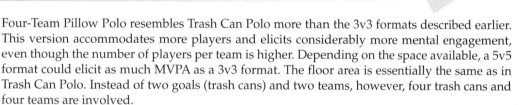

Four-Team Pillow Polo resembles Trash Can Polo more than the 3v3 formats described earlier. This version accommodates more players and elicits considerably more mental engagement, even though the number of players per team is higher. Depending on the space available, a 5v5 format could elicit as much MVPA as a 3v3 format. The floor area is essentially the same as in Trash Can Polo. Instead of two goals (trash cans) and two teams, however, four trash cans and four teams are involved.

To set up the game, place a trash can in each corner of the playing space. Number them 1 through 4, and have players use three balls rather than one. If you do not have 20 players to make up four teams of five players, the same game can be played with two teams of six or seven players. In that case, assign two goals (diametrically opposed) to each team and have them use just one ball. Players' MVPA and mental engagement are greater because the floor is larger and strategy dilemmas remain unchanged. See figure 11.3 for the setup.

Teacher Essentials and Explanation Points

Designate four teams of up to five players, and number them 1 through 4. They should wear pinnies that bear their team numbers. Each team defends a trash can or other container set in each of the play area's four corners; number the cans 1 through 4. Using three balls, teams try to score in the cans bearing their own numbers (e.g., team 1 scores in trash can 1). Winning depends on having a higher score than the other three teams, so defending other goals is just as important as scoring!

With more balls in play, game activity is furious and more player touches are possible. These tactical changes from the typical Trash Can Polo game greatly increase players' mental engagement. Although it seems that teams would need to just concentrate on scoring in their own trash cans, a team's score has to be higher than the other three teams' scores to win. Consequently, defending the other three goals is just as important as scoring points. This increases the importance of floor coverage and team tactics. On the surface, this version may not seem much different from Trash Can Polo; the added complexity comes from the players having to be concerned with stopping more than one team.

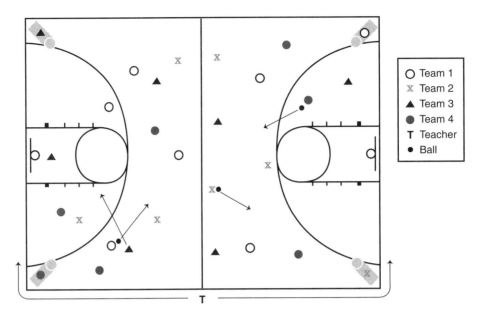

Figure 11.3 Setup for Four-Team Pillow Polo.

Challenges Posed

Perhaps more than any other version of this game, Four-Team Pillow Polo provides the most chances for the independent discovery of tactics and approaches. Because of the multitude of attackers and goals, players face the intensified challenge of keeping others from scoring while scoring themselves. Questions to spur children's thinking about the inherent challenges of this game include "How should you distribute your players on offense and defense?" "Which is more important: defending the opponents' goals or scoring on yours, and why?" and "How can your team draw opponents away from your goal?"

Small Modifications and Moving On

After two bouts of five to seven minutes, children's play should indicate that they understand the new rules and structure. You may have to stop play once or twice to highlight and discuss strategic situations before they settle into the new rules. Once all four teams are scoring evenly, the children are ready for the next version, 21 or Bust. Try returning play to two play areas featuring only two teams but make the teams slightly larger (e.g., 6v6 or 7v7). Teams still try to score on their own goal, although only one ball is in play.

Game Breakdown

As in Mega Garbage Ball, the notion of attacking multiple goals and defending their own will be somewhat foreign to children. Being able to identify the opposition and their teammates is vital—hence, the importance of pinnies.

Equipment

Needs based on a 30-student class:

- Pillow polo (or foam-padded floor hockey) sticks for each player
- Four or more foam or pillow polo balls
- 15 or more cones
- Four trash cans or other large containers
- Pinnies or flag belts for team identification

Skills Needed

- Locomotor skills: running, sliding
- Manipulative skill: striking with a long-handled implement

Rules

1. A team may have more than one ball in its possession at one time (although one player may not have more than one ball at a time).
2. If a team hits a ball out of bounds, the nearest player of another team receives possession of the ball.
3. Fouls (e.g., pushing, tripping, high stick) result in a free hit from the foul spot.
4. No team may have a dedicated goalie.

Questions

- How can you balance offense and defense?
- Is it more important to defend other goals or score on yours? Why?
- How can you draw opponents away from defending your goal?

21 or Bust

Combining the rules of Trash Can Polo and Four-Team Pillow Polo results in a third game called 21 or Bust, which can elicit even greater levels of physical activity, skill development, and mental engagement. As in the card and basketball games 21 and blackjack, 21 or Bust requires each team to score exactly 21 points before the other team does. In this game, a ball shot into the trash can is worth 2 points, and a shot that hits the trash can is worth 1 point. The rules could be extended to more closely resemble those of basketball if there is a line from which a shot can be taken. For instance, a ball neatly and cleanly shot into the trash can (perhaps after a required number of passes) could be worth 3 points. Stress that players do not have to shoot each time from a line or only after a number of passes, but both are options.

The added challenge of 21 or Bust is that this score must be achieved exactly; exceeding this score is penalized with a loss of points—called a bust. If a team with 20 points takes a shot and mistakenly puts the ball in the goal instead of just hitting the side of the goal, the team busts and its score falls back to 11 points. Offensively, teams now have an added consideration regarding which shots to take and where to take them from. This format also provides new defensive considerations. If a 1-point shot would end the game, the defense must try to defend the sides of the trash can and not the front. They might even try to force a shot into the can on a deflection so that the opposing team busts. To accommodate children with cognitive or learning disabilities, you can label the balls with numbers and having the value of a ball in the can be worth a set number of points. Seeing the numbers can help these children perform mathematic calculations as they keep score.

In 21 or Bust, not only are the skills and tactics important, but now children have to work with their teammates to decide what shots to take and what shots to force on the other team. In essence, a good tactic may be to let a team shoot the ball into the can if they have 20 points, because it will result in a bust. This keeps the game going.

Teacher Essentials and Explanation Points

The rules for 21 or Bust are largely similar to those of Trash Can Polo. Explain that teams earn 2 points by shooting the ball into the can and 1 point by hitting the outside of the can. The goal for all teams (you can decide on a two-team or four-team setup with no more than six players per team) is to score exactly 21 points before the other team(s). If a team scores more than 21 points, that team's score drops to 11 points. Only one ball is in play at a time. Play may become quite complex, because each team must keep track of its own score while also considering ways to force the other team(s) to bust. See figure 11.4 for an example of how to divide a play area to allow for multiple two-team games.

In addition to explaining the scoring rules, you should continually emphasize the concept of scoring in various ways. In other game versions (and in most traditional games), scoring happens only one way and all shots are worth the same number of points. Now that a goal in the can is worth 2 points and hitting the sides of the trash can is worth 1 point, children need to be aware of when to settle for 1 point and when to try for 2.

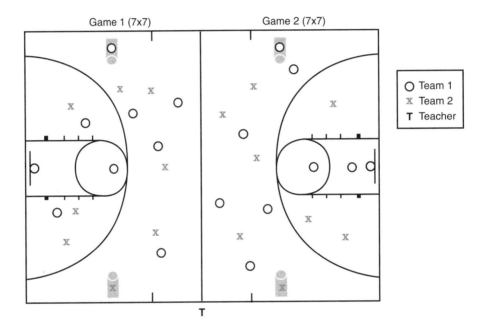

Figure 11.4   Setup for two simultaneous games of 21 or Bust, with two teams for each game.

Challenges Posed

Being continually aware of the score is essential for good strategic and tactical decision making in this game. The children have to do more than just keep up with who is winning. Team members must also communicate with each other so they can alter their defense to keep another team from scoring a particular type of goal while also determining which type of score they need on offense. Encourage children to devise their own systems for keeping track of scores and letting all their teammates know those scores.

As with most invasion games, teams must determine for themselves how many players to assign to defense and offense. A unique rule in 21 or Bust makes discovery more complex than in typical invasion games; that is, the game ends when a team acquires 21 points and no more. This affects how players' responsibilities are distributed and prioritized.

Small Modifications and Moving On

Possible modifications include a special 3-point shot taken from a particular area of the playing space. The 3-point goal counts only if, for example, the shot is from behind the marker or line and the ball goes into the can. Also, you may require a set number of consecutive passes before a team may attempt the special shot.

Game Breakdown

If this games seems chaotic, it is because it is chaotic. One thing to remember is that keeping track of scoring can be difficult. Reassure children that you are keeping track and that you will inform them of the score often—because it influences strategy.

Equipment

Needs based on a 30-student class:

- Pillow polo (or foam-padded floor hockey) sticks for each player
- Four or more foam or pillow polo balls
- 15 or more cones
- Four trash cans or other large containers
- Pinnies or flag belts for team identification

Skills Needed

- Locomotor skills: running, sliding
- Manipulative skill: striking with a long-handled implement

Rules

1. Players may move the ball only on the ground (passing, catching, shooting) using polo sticks.
2. No team may have a dedicated goalie.
3. If a ball goes out of bounds, the team that did not hit it out gets possession of the ball from that spot. The nearest player of another team receives possession of the ball.
4. Fouls (e.g., pushing, tripping, high stick) result in a free hit from the foul spot.
5. Players may not raise sticks higher than knee height.
6. Teams shoot 1- or 2-point shots as needed to earn 21 points.

Questions

- How many players should you have on offense, and how many on defense?
- How can you communicate your scoring needs (e.g., taking a 1- or 2-point shot)?
- How can you force the other team to bust?

Speedy Swappers

Adapted from Dowson 2009.

Speedy Swappers and its iterations are adapted from the well-known games of Crossover and Turn Tag (Dowson, 2009). Speedy Swappers and the more complex versions (Grid Runners and Doorway Tag, described next) are essentially chasing, fleeing, and dodging (CFD) games. CFD games are usually simple to teach and play, although they often provide a foundation for skills used in complex activities and most sports. If presented in a deliberate fashion and carefully designed, CFD games can be more than simply tag games; they actually provide plenty of physical and mental engagement.

Teacher Essentials and Explanation Points

This game requires five players, so set up as many play areas as necessary to accommodate all children. Place poly spots or cones at each corner of the play area(s). Four children stand at the corners and one stands in the middle. On your signal, children not in the middle must swap positions—two at a time—along the perimeter while the middle player tries to take over either open position. The goal is for the outer players to make five consecutive swaps. If they do, the middle player exchanges roles with an outer player. Reminding the children that only two players may swap at a time is essential. If they don't follow this rule, the game mechanics quickly break down, limiting player success. It might be instructive to show the players what happens when more than two players try to move at once because it illustrates why the two-at-a-time rule is essential to the game.

Challenges Posed

Unlike previous games that highlight the principle of discovery, in which teams had equal numbers of players, Speedy Swappers has one team of four children playing against a team of one. Furthermore, the four players are never together because each player must occupy a corner. This makes communication difficult, and the children will be confronted by this challenge in multiple ways. After playing one or two rounds, ask the children about the challenges they faced.

Small Modifications and Moving On

Before moving to the next version (Grid Runners), try increasing the play area size or the number of corners (this would be a good opportunity to discuss shapes such as squares and pentagons). This makes swapping positions more difficult.

After you have allowed time for practice and the players have tried various tactics, notice whether the outer players are continuously containing the middle player. If so, consider allowing diagonal swaps (in a square play area). Also, changing the mode of travel for all players (for example, skipping) or just the swappers may lead to new challenges that need new solutions.

Game Breakdown

Emphasize the importance of having only two players swap at once; the game mechanics break down when more than two try to swap at the same time.

Equipment

A 30-student class requires 10 or more cones or poly spots.

Skills Needed

Chasing, fleeing, dodging, dribbling (with hands)

Rules

1. Outer players must swap along the perimeter only—diagonal swaps are prohibited.
2. Only two outer players may swap positions at a time.
3. The middle player may count down from 5 to 0 if no runners are swapping positions. If the player reaches 0 then everyone must go.
4. Players must remain on their feet at all times.

Questions

- How do outer players decide to swap positions?
- Should outer players have a signal? Why or why not?
- Can the outer players confuse the middle player? How?
- Is the position of the middle player important? In what way?
- Where should the middle player stand to be most successful in stealing a spot from the outer players?

Grid Runners

Adapted from Dowson 2009.

Grid Runners differs from Speedy Swappers, but both involve CFD (chasing, fleeing, and dodging). CFD games are usually simple to teach and play, although they often provide a foundation for skills used in complex activities and most sports. Grid Runners is unique and provides plenty of physical and mental challenge!

Teacher Essentials and Explanation Points

Grid Runners requires enough players to create a grid of four rows of four children and to have one chaser and one fleeer (i.e., at least 18 players).

Explain that the children forming the grid face one direction holding hands and, on a signal (from you or a grid leader), turn to the left 90 degrees and rejoin hands. Grid players must lock hands or wrists after turning (see the modifications in the section Small Modifications and Moving On), and they must turn quickly and in unison (demonstrate a basketball pivot). The chaser and fleeer must contend with this ever-changing environment, and the chaser has only five grid turns to tag the fleeer. The runners may travel around or through the grid lanes. When the chaser tags the fleeer, or after five grid turns, runners swap with two grid players.

Challenges Posed

Grid Runners provides multiple cognitive challenges. Additionally, all players in the grid need to agree on a strategy for how fast and when to turn and implement it.

Small Modifications and Moving On

Grid players could perform simple physical activity tasks such as jumping jacks or stretches (feet spread and touching as long as the task creates the row/column effect. If the children are developmentally ready to combine motor and manipulative skills, having the runners dribble a basketball while playing provides an added challenge.

Game Breakdown

The good news about Speedy Swappers and Grid Runners is that almost no equipment is needed. Be ready for lots of starts and stops, but eventually, the children will get it.

Equipment

Needs based on a 30-student class:

- 10 or more cones or poly spots
- Two or three basketballs

Skills Needed

Chasing, fleeing, dodging, dribbling (with hands)

Rules

1. Grid players must lock hands or wrists after turning (see modifications).
2. Grid players must turn quickly, in unison, and to the left using a basketball pivot.
3. The runners may travel around or through the grid lanes.
4. When the chaser tags the fleeer, or after five grid turns, runners swap with two grid players.

Questions

- When should the grid players turn? How often?
- When should runners run around the grid and when should they run through it?
- Can the grid turns help or hurt the runners? How?

Doorway Tag

Adapted from Dowson 2009.

As in Grid Runners, for this game you will need enough players to create a grid of four rows of four children and to have one chaser and one fleeer (i.e., at least 18 players). The children forming the grid (grid players) face one direction holding hands and, on a signal (from you or a grid leader), turn to the left 90 degrees and rejoin hands. Grid players must lock hands or wrists after turning, and they must turn quickly, in unison using a basketball pivot. The chaser and fleeer must contend with this ever-changing environment.

Doorway Tag differs from Grid Runners in that the fleeer has to enter and exit the grid at specific spots, which increases the complexity quite a bit. Only after children have played and mastered Speedy Swappers and Grid Runners will Doorway Tag provide the mental challenge that is most appropriate.

Teacher Essentials and Explanation Points

Keeping the same layout and rules as Grid Runners, explain that the grid players' role remains largely the same in Doorway Tag. The biggest change is that the fleeer must enter the grid only at a specified point and is safe from the chaser only after exiting the grid at another specified point. To be safe, the fleeer exits between two particular grid players when those players are not holding hands (you may change the enter and exit locations after each round). The chaser may not guard the exit and must always make an effort to tag the fleeer. The fleeer has one minute to enter and exit the grid, during which there is no limit on the number of grid turns. When the chaser has tagged the fleeer, or after five grid turns, runners swap with two grid players.

Challenges Posed

Doorway Tag engages children in extrapolation and prediction behaviors in response to challenges that do not always have one correct answer. Leading questions that prompt this type of thinking include "Will it always be possible to go directly to the exit? Why or why not?" and "Should the chaser follow the fleeer's exact path through the grid? Why or why not?"

Small Modifications and Moving On

None

Game Breakdown

Of all the games in this text, Doorway Tag is perhaps the most complex. Do not introduce the dribbling modification until the children have learned the game well. When children have to worry about multiple things, both skill and strategy get short-changed.

Equipment

Needs based on a 30-student class:

- 10 or more cones or poly spots
- Two or three basketballs

Skills Needed

Chasing, fleeing, dodging, dribbling (with hands)

Rules

1. Grid players must lock hands or wrists after turning.
2. Grid players must turn quickly, in unison, and to the left using a basketball pivot.
3. The runners may travel around or through the grid lanes.
4. When the chaser has tagged the fleeer, or after five grid turns, runners swap with two grid players.
5. The chaser may not guard the exit and must always attempt to tag the fleeer.
6. The fleeer has one minute after entering the grid to exit it.
7. There is no limit on the number of grid turns within the one-minute period.
8. Players must remain on their feet at all times.

Questions

- Will it always be possible to go directly to the exit? Why or why not?
- Should the chaser follow the fleeer's exact path through the grid? Why or why not?

Implications for Educators

This chapter offers 18 physical activity games that challenge children's mental processing. Specifically, six games emphasize the principle of contextual interference; six, the principle of mental control; and six, the principle of discovery. Keep in mind that these are not the only games that can benefit children physically and cognitively. However, at this point it should be quite clear that the teacher is as important as any game in ensuring that children develop both cognitively and physically while enjoying playing games.

Glossary

abilities   Genetically linked physical and mental attributes that determine how quickly and how well particular skills can be learned.

accommodation   A process by which children attempt to modify what they know to reflect how the world really is.

acculturation   A process of cultural and psychological change.

acute exercise   Physical activity that produces temporary changes in children's physical arousal that affect thinking processes.

animistic thinking   Conferring human characteristics on physical, inanimate objects.

anti-imitation   A form of complex response inhibition in which children make gestures that are the opposite of the one made by the teacher.

applied research   Research focused on solving practical programs.

arousal modulation   A theory that children are innately driven to attain an optimal level of arousal.

assessment   The gathering of data to document student learning and teacher effectiveness.

assimilation   A process that directs children to establish an equilibrium, or balance, between their physical and mental worlds.

attachment disorders   Disorders characterized by difficulty bonding with parents and poor socialization behaviors.

attention   A state of focused awareness on some aspect of the environment and the ability to concentrate and maintain that focus.

attention shifting   When a change in the task requires disengaging attention from one cue and refocusing on a different cue.

autistic spectrum disorder   A neurodevelopmental disorder that impairs social skills, delays language development, results in repetitive behaviors and restricted interests, and impedes academic and social involvement.

automaticity   A type of processing that is fast and unconscious.

autotelic personality   The personality type of a person who is internally driven and exhibits a sense of purpose and curiosity.

basic research   Research focused on accumulating facts about humans and the world.

behavior shaping   A general term often used to describe how the application of reinforcement principles alters or modifies a learner's actions.

body mass index (BMI)   A mathematical method used to describe the relation between body weight and stature.

cerebellum   An area of the brain that connects with every major brain structure and plays an important role in movement control and learning new skills.

champion   A charismatic person who is a strong supporter of a particular innovation.

childhood anxiety   A state of worry, apprehension, or tension that often occurs in the absence of real or obvious danger.

childhood mood disorders   Disorders that include all types of depression and are sometimes referred to as affective disorders.

childhood self-esteem   How much children value themselves.

chronic exercise training   Repeated bouts of exercise over several weeks, months, or years that produce structural changes in the brain and improvements in physical fitness.

cognition   Any process that allows an organism to know and be aware.

cognitive immaturity hypothesis   The notion that the less developed state of children's nervous systems and their lack of experience make it difficult for them to perform higher-level cognitive tasks with the same efficiency as adolescents and adults.

complex response inhibition   The ability to hold a rule in mind, respond according to this rule, and inhibit another response (e.g., point to white when the teacher says "Grass" and to green when the teacher says "Snow").

complex working memory   The capacity to hold information in mind and to manipulate it.

conduct disorder   Excessive defiant or impulsive behavior.

conservation   The understanding that the amount or area of an object remains the same even though its shape is altered.

constant practice   Practice in which a single movement is performed repeatedly.

contextual interference A phenomenon in which a practice schedule results in less efficient performance but produces better long-term learning.

continuous feedback Feedback provided following every learning attempt.

cooperative learning An educational approach based on structuring positive interdependence among learners who work collectively toward a common goal.

cooperative play Organized play that involves acting out roles.

core-based motor teaching-learning A model of movement-based teaching and learning that offers numerous problem-solving situations that engage children in meaningful reflection and lead them to focus on practice and process rather than on a final outcome.

creativity The ability to produce work that is novel and useful as defined within a given social context.

critical periods Optimal times for the emergence of specific developmental processes and behaviors.

culture A system of beliefs about the way people interact within a segment of the population.

declarative memories Memories about events, facts, and concepts that require conscious awareness and attention to be stored and recalled.

deductive logic The ability to generate and test hypotheses about events.

delayed imitation Imitating a movement pattern, but after a time delay.

deliberate play Games and sports that are intrinsically motivating, provide immediate gratification, and maximize enjoyment.

deliberate practice Practice that is performed with the primary goal of improving skill and expertise. It is characterized by much mental effort and low levels of inherent enjoyment.

depression A disorder characterized in young children by pretending to be sick, refusing to go to school, clinging to a parent, or worrying that a parent may die. Older children may sulk, get into trouble at school, be negative, act grouchy, or feel misunderstood.

development Changes influenced by heredity, maturation, and experience.

developmental disability A pervasive disorder displayed during maturation.

dexterity the ability to find a solution for a problem using available physical and mental resources.

direct instruction method A method of teaching in which the instructor prescribes how students will accomplish a goal.

disequilibrium A sense of imbalance that forces children to reorganize and restructure their perceptions of nature.

divergent discovery A teaching style that employs open-ended tasks and encourages learners to discover multiple responses to each problem.

divided attention A mental process that helps people process and perform several activities at the same time.

early childhood The period of human life lasting from about 18 months to 6 years of age.

ecological models Models that emphasize how multiple factors determine people's health-promoting behaviors.

ecological psychology A theoretical approach to psychology that focuses on the interdependence of the individual and the environment.

egocentric The characteristic of being unable to view events from the perspective of other people.

embodied learning A theory that states that a dynamic interaction occurs among children's body movements, the sensory experiences obtained from the movements, and the context of the movements.

emotions Short-term positive or negative affective reactions to objects (either real or imagined).

enriching environment Any situation or condition that maximizes or enhances the development of a person's abilities.

equilibrium A steady state or balance between opposing forces.

error The difference between an expected outcome and the actual outcome.

eustress A state in which people are confident that they have the skills and resources necessary for meeting and overcoming potentially stressful situations.

executive function The capacity to think before acting, retain and manipulate information, reflect on the possible consequences of specific actions, and self-regulate behavior.

exercise A subset of physical activity consisting of planned, structured, repetitive bodily movements with the purpose of improving or maintaining one or more components of physical fitness or health.

exit slip A short written questionnaire (usually no more than three simple questions) used to determine whether children learned from and enjoyed an activity.

experiential motivation Motivation derived from the feelings generated while in the act of performing.

explicit learning   Learning that involves conscious attention and evaluation.

exploration   Focused investigation through which children gain familiarity with new objects or environments; may lead to play.

exploration and discovery method   A method of teaching in which students are given the opportunity to choose the method that best suits them to accomplish a goal.

extraverted   A description of people who tend to be outgoing, impulsive, and active because their general brain arousal is relatively low and as a result they seek stimulation.

extrinsic feedback   Information that cannot be obtained directly; it is provided by teachers and others who evaluate the learner's performance and movements.

extrinsic motivation   Behavior driven by external rewards from the environment (such as prizes, money, and praise).

feedback   Information that indicates something about the consequences of movements.

flexibility   Adjustments of movements as game conditions change.

flow   A psychological state experienced when one is caught up in the moment of playing or performing a skill.

fluency   The range of different solutions that can be applied.

forward chaining   Applying behavioral principles to learning to strengthen the connections between the steps of a complex skill.

fundamental movement skills   Patterns of movements that are the basis for learning complex motor skills. The three categories of fundamental movement patterns are locomotor actions (walking and running), nonlocomotor actions (bending, twisting, and balancing), and manipulative actions (knot tying, drawing).

games   Forms of competitive play characterized by established rules and set goals.

generalization   The transfer of learning from one task or situation to other tasks or situations.

generalized anxiety disorder (GAD)   A disorder characterized by worrying excessively about grades, family issues, friendships, and performance in school and sports.

goal setting   The process of targeting outcomes.

guidance   Any procedure that directs learners as they perform a task.

habits   Learned behavior patterns that are engrained and enduring.

hierarchy of needs   Maslow's theory of motivation that states that basic needs must be met before progress can be made toward self-actualization.

hippocampus   A structure located deep in the brain that plays a role in memory and learning.

homeostasis   The maintenance of equilibrium among body processes.

hyperkinetic disorder   An enduring disposition to behave in a restless, inattentive, distracted, and disorganized fashion.

implicit learning   Learning that produces habits that control movements in an almost reflexive fashion without conscious awareness.

instructions   Statements that describe how to do something.

interference control   The ability to select task-relevant information and filter out irrelevant, distracting information. This is difficult when the irrelevant information attracts attention more strongly than the relevant information does.

intermittent feedback   Feedback given on some, but not all, learning attempts.

intrinsic feedback   Feedback that originates from within the body during movement. Muscles, joints, skin, eyes, and ears send information to the brain that provides a sense of movement.

intrinsic motivation   Behavior driven by internal rewards (such as pleasure and enjoyment).

introverted   A description of people who tend to have relatively high levels of general brain arousal and avoid situations that are stimulating.

knowledge of performance   Information about the quality of a movement.

knowledge of results   Information about the degree to which a movement goal was met.

later childhood   The period of human life spanning between 6 and 12 years of age.

learned helplessness   Choosing to neither act nor attempt to meet the challenges that are part of skill-learning tasks because of a low expectancy of being able to solve problems on one's own.

learning   A process that results in relatively permanent and consistent change in behavior and is based on experience.

learning disorders   Disorders that make it difficult for children to listen, reason, and perform such academic skills as reading, writing, and solving mathematical problems.

life span developmental tasks   Tasks arising during certain periods of life that, if learned, contribute to happiness, success in later tasks, and societal approval.

locus of control   The belief about whether the outcomes of one's actions are due to internal or external factors.

macro factors   Factors that influence health behaviors on a global level, such as institutions and cultures.

maturation   A timetable of events related to growth and development that are genetically arranged and influenced little by environmental factors.

measurement sensitivity   The degree to which changes in performance can be assessed.

memory   Information about the environment that is stored for some period of time.

mental engagement   Energized, directed, and sustained action used to meet and overcome challenges and problems.

mental shifting   The ability to recognize changes in conditions that require a change in strategy and different behaviors.

mental skill hypothesis   A hypothesis that views executive function as a group of mental skills that are acquired gradually and influenced by practice.

metabolic equivalent units (METs)   A unit of measurement of physical energy cost that is computed as the ratio of metabolic rate to a reference metabolic rate.

metabolic syndrome   A combination of health measures such as body fat, blood pressure, and cholesterol that are combined and used to predict the onset of cardiovascular disease and type 2 diabetes.

meta-cognition   Children's awareness of what they know and how they can use it.

micro factors   Factors that influence health behaviors on a personal level, such as family, friends, and peers.

mnemonics   Strategies to improve memory and information recall.

modeling or observational learning   Learning by watching actions that are central to solving movement problems.

moods   General and pervasive negative or positive affective states that can influence thought and behavior.

motivation   A psychological or physiological state that energizes behavior to achieve a goal.

motive   A psychological state or physiological disposition that energizes behavior.

motor cortex   A strip of brain tissue that sends commands to control muscles involved in movements.

motor program   A set of commands from the brain that instructs the body to move in a specified way.

motricity   A biological property of the nervous system that oversees goal-directed actions.

movement effectiveness   The ability to achieve a particular goal.

movement efficiency   The degree of effort required to achieve a particular goal.

need   The object of a motive; it is the specific object (e.g., food, water, money), event (e.g., praise), or psychological state (e.g., well-being, happiness) that a person desires.

neurogenic reserve hypothesis   A hypothesis that states that combinations of physical activity and cognitive engagement are particularly important early in the life span because the reserve provides resources in later life.

obesogenic   Promoting excessive weight gain.

objectivity   A condition that results when two people conduct separate assessments on the same person and see the same results.

obsessive-compulsive disorder (OCD)   A disorder characterized by unwanted thoughts and feeling the need to perform rituals and routines that ease anxiety.

open-ended games   Games in which the starting point, the rules, and goals are explained, but not how to perform the game.

optimal challenge point   The hypothesis that skill learning is facilitated when the skill level of the performer, the complexity of the task, and the task environment are taken into consideration.

originality   The ability to generate unique and unusual products or solutions.

outcome expectations   The results that someone anticipates will happen.

outcome goals   Goals that focus on comparing performances—who is best, second best, and so on.

outcome variables   The changes in behavior caused by the intervention, or program, such as student game-play performance and skill development.

part practice   Practicing a sequence in segments until each is learned before progressively adding the parts together.

patterning therapy   A form of therapy that uses the passive movement of body limbs in sequences to simulate basic reflexes.

performance goals   Goals used to judge one's own progress (e.g., a personal best).

physical activity   Bodily movement produced by skeletal muscle contraction that requires energy expenditure.

play   Activity that is freely chosen and intrinsically motivating and pleasurable. Children can play by themselves (solitary play), adjacent to others (parallel play), or by interacting with others (cooperative play).

policy makers People whose opinions strongly influence the course of events at various societal levels.

positive psychology An area of study that focuses on aspects of life that are fulfilling and lead to obtaining optimal potential.

prefrontal cortex An area of the brain that consists of neural networks that make up the executive of the brain. It is involved in an awareness of current conditions, the retrieval of stored memories, and the formulation of action plans.

prescriptive feedback Information about how to improve on the next trial.

procedural memories Memories about how to do things (e.g., ride a bicycle, tie shoelaces, play a musical instrument) that can be stored and recalled without conscious effort.

process goals Goals that focus on the quality of movement patterns (e.g., keeping a good body position when kicking a ball).

process variables The elements of an intervention that lead to outcome variables, such as student engagement and teacher performance.

psychometrics A field of study that uses standardized tests to measure and classify abilities.

psychomotor abilities Enduring characteristics that influence the capacity to manipulate and control objects.

qualitative Narrative or categorical.

quantitative Numerical.

reliability An indicator of how well an assessment would produce the same data if it were given twice or more times in a relatively short period of time to the same person or people.

repetition without repetition A learning approach in which people do not repeat the same solution to a practiced motor task; rather, they solve the problem many times in various ways to identify the best solution(s).

response inhibition The ability to withhold actions or modify ongoing behaviors.

response shifting When a change in task conditions requires players to stop one movement and perform a different one.

reverse categorization A task that requires complex response inhibition. For instance, children sort big blocks into big buckets and small blocks into small buckets; then do the reverse.

rough-and-tumble play A social activity in which two or more children engage in pretend fighting, hitting, and wrestling.

rubric An evaluation matrix that describes varying levels of quality or achievement for a specific task.

scaffolding Support given by a teacher during the learning process.

schemas Conceptual rules that children use to link previously learned ways of viewing the world with potentially new ways of viewing it.

secular trends Alterations in the average pattern of growth or development in a population over several generations.

sedentary behavior Behavior that results in an energy expenditure equal to that of sleeping, sitting, lying down, or watching television.

selective attention A mental process used to both identify important information and block out information that, to the individual, is unimportant.

self-actualization A psychological state characterized by feelings of inner peace and harmony that is experienced when we attain our full potential, personal growth, and creative fulfillment.

self belief A general level of confidence in one's abilities or judgments.

self-efficacy The belief that one can perform adequately in a given situation.

sensitive period A period during which children are particularly receptive to certain environmental experiences.

separation anxiety disorder A disorder characterized by not wanting to go to school or social activities and not wanting to be separated from someone. It typically occurs between 18 months and 3 years of age.

significant others People important to children's well-being and self-concept.

simple response inhibition The ability to withhold or delay an automatic, habitual response (e.g., trading a smaller, but immediate reward for a larger, but delayed reward).

simple working memory The capacity to hold information in mind over a delayed period.

skill The ability to use knowledge effectively and readily in the execution of performance.

social responsibility The ability to interact cooperatively with others, inhibit antisocial behavior, and form close relationships, such as friendships.

sociodramatic play Social pretend play, common from around 3 years of age, in which children take on the roles of others (e.g., parents, siblings, teachers) in make-believe situations characterized by imaginary scenes.

sports   Forms of competitive physical activity.

stability   Movement precision that is achieved during game play.

stopping   A description of tasks in which an external stimulus signals the person to interrupt an already initiated motor response.

stress   A pattern of behavior in response to events that disturb equilibrium and tax the ability to cope.

sustained attention   A mental process that people use to ward off fatigue and help them focus on continuing to perform a task.

switching   Stopping what one is doing and acting in a totally different way.

task analysis   Identifying the key components of a game and then breaking the game down into a series of movements that are central to learning the game.

task orientation   A motivational disposition that leads people to focus on mastery through effort and persistence, doing their best, progressing over time, solving problems, and learning.

teachable moment   An unplanned opportunity in which a teacher has an ideal chance to offer insight to students.

theory of mind   A theory that explains how young children learn to take the perspectives of others.

time out (from reinforcement)   A method used to change the frequency of behaviors by the contingent withdrawal of the opportunity to obtain rewards or reinforcers.

toughening manipulations   Placing learners in challenging situations that evoke strong physiological responses.

traditional culture   Customs and practices handed down from one generation to the next.

trainability   How children respond to an exercise intervention at various stages of growth.

transfer   The degree to which learning in one setting is used in another setting.

translational research   The uptake, implementation, and sustainability of research findings within standard care.

triangulation   The process of cross-verifying data from two or more sources.

updating   Changing and manipulating information that is no longer relevant as new information becomes relevant to an ongoing task.

validity   The determination of whether an assessment truly measures what it is intended to measure.

varied practice   Successive practice trials in which problem-solving demands are changed (varied) across trials in no particular order.

working memory   The capacity to hold and manipulate information in consciousness.

Yerkes-Dodson Law   A law that describes the relationship between arousal and performance.

References

Allender, S., Cowburn, G., & Foster, C. (2006). Understanding participation in sport and physical activity among children and adults: a review of qualitative studies. *Health Education Research, 21*(6), 826-835.

Allensworth, D. D., & Kolbe, L. J. (1987). The comprehensive school health program: exploring an expanded concept. *Journal of School Health, 57,* 409-412.

Annesi, J. L. (2006). Relations of physical self-concept and self-efficacy with frequency of voluntary physical activity in preadolescents: Implications for after-school care programming. *Journal of Psychosomatic Research, 61,* 515-520.

Association for Supervision and Curriculum Development. (2007). The learning compact redefined: A call to action. Alexandria, VA: Author.

Audiffren, M. (2009). Acute exercise and psychological functions: a cognitive-energetic approach. In T. McMorris, P. D. Tomporowski & M. Audiffren (Eds.), *Exercise and cognitive function* (pp. 3-39). Chichester, United Kingdom: John Wiley & Sons.

Bailey, R. C., Olson, S. L., Pepper, S. L., Porszasz, J., Barstow, T. J., & Cooper, D. M. (1995). The level and tempo of children's physical activities: an observational study. *Medicine and Science in Sports and Exercise, 27,* 1033-1041.

Bandura, A. (1997). *Self-efficacy: The exercise of control.* New York, NY: Freeman.

Barnett, L. M., Van Beurden, E., Morgan, P. J., Brooks, L. O., & Beard, J. R. (2008). Does childhood motor skill proficiency predict adolescent fitness? *Medicine and Science in Sports and Exercise, 40,* 2137-2144.

Barnett, L. M., van Beurden, E., Morgan, P. J., Brooks, L. O., & Beard, J. R. (2009). Childhood motor skill proficiency as a predictor of adolescent physical activity. *Journal of Adolescent Health, 44,* 252-259.

Baumgartner, T. A., Jackson, A. S., Mahar, M. T., & Rowe, D. A. (2007). *Measurement for evaluation in physical education and exercise science* (8th ed.). New York, NY: McGraw-Hill.

Beighle, A., Morgan, C. F., Le Masurier, G., & Pangrazi, R. P. (2006). Children's physical activity during recess and outside of school. *Journal of School Health, 76,* 516-520. doi: 10.1111/j.1746-1561.2006.00151.x

Bertsch, J. (1983). *Le créativitè motrice. Son evaluation et son optimisation dans la pédagogie des situations motrices a l'ecole. [Motor creativity. Evaluation and optimization in the pedagogy of motor development. Test Handbook].* Paris, France: INSEP.

Bjerke, O., & Vereijken, B. (2007). Promoting motor skills in school children and adolescents. In J. Luikkonen, Y. V. Auweele, B. Vereijken, D. Alfermann & J. Theodorakis (Eds.), *Psychology for physical educators* (2nd ed., pp. 219-237). Champaign, IL: Human Kinetics.

Bjorklund, D. F., & Bering, J. M. (2002). The evolved child: Applying evolutionary development psychology to modern schooling. *Learning and Individual Differences, 12,* 347-373.

Bleich, S. N., Ku, R., & Wang, Y. C. (2011). Relative contribution of energy intake and energy expenditure to childhood obesity: a review of the literature and directions for future research. *International Journal of Obesity and Related Metabolic Disorders, 35,* 1-15.

BOKS.org. From http://www.bokskids.org/

Bjorklund, D. F., & Green, B. L. (1992). The adaptive nature of cognitive immaturity. *American Psychologist, 47,* 46-54.

Bransford, J., Brown, A. L., & Cocking, R. R. (1999). *How people learn: Brain, mind, experience, and school.* Washington, DC: National Academy Press.

Buckworth, J., Dishman, R. K., O'Connor, P. J., & Tomporowski, P. D. (2013). *Exercise Psychology* (2nd ed.). Champaign, IL: Human Kinetics.

Budde, H., Voelcker-Rehage, C., Pietrassyk-Kendziorra, S., Ribeiro, P., & Tidow, G. (2008). Acute coordinative exercise improves attentional performance in adolescents. *Neuroscience Letters, 441,* 219-223.

Burnette, D. (2011). School playground duty outsourced, *Minneapolis Star-Tribune.* Retrieved from http://www.startribune.com/printarticle/?id=121867879 (last updated: May 16, 2011)

Byon, K., Baker, T. A., Zhang, J. J., Berger, B. S., Sen, S., Min, S. D., & Mao, L. L. (2012). Relative influences of Multidimensional Parent Satisfaction Model on behavioral intentions. Paper presented at the *American Alliance of Health, Physical Education, Recreation, and Dance (AAHPERD)* Convention, Boston, MA.

California Department of Education. (2005). *A study of the relationship between physical fitness and academic achievement in California using 2004 test results.* Sacramento, CA: California Department of Education.

Carlson, S. A., Fulton, J. E., Lee, S. M., Maynard, L. M., Brown, D. R., Kohl, H. W., & Dietz, W. H. (2008). Physical education and academic achievement in elementary school: Data from the Early Childhood Longitudinal study. *American Journal of Public Health, 98,* 721-727.

Centers for Disease Control and Prevention. (2013). Goals of coordinated school health. From http://www.cdc.gov/healthyYouth/CSHP (last updated: February 27, 2013)

Chaddock, L., Erickson, K. I., Prakash, R. S., Kim, J. S., Voss, M. W., VanPatter, M., . . . Kramer, A. F. (2010). A neuroimaging investigation of the association between aerobic fitness, hippocampal volume, and memory performance in preadolescent children. *Brain Research, 1358,* 172-183.

Chaddock, L., Pontifex, M. B., Hillman, C. H., & Kramer, A. F. (2011). A review of the relation of aerobic fitness and physical activity to brain structure and function in children. *Journal of the International Neuropsychological Society, 17,* 1-11.

Cheffers, J. T. F., & Mancini, V. H. (1989). Cheffers' adaptation of the Flanders' Interaction Analysis System (CAFIAS). In P. W. Darst, Zakrajsek, D. B., & Mancini, V. H. (Ed.), *Analyzing Physical Education and Sport Instruction* (2ⁿᵈ ed.) (pp. 119-135). Champaign, IL: Human Kinetics.

Chomitz, V. R., Slinning, M. M., McGowan, R. J., Mitchell, S. E., Dawson, G. F., & Hacker, K. A. (2009). Is there a relationship between physical fitness and academic achievement? Positive results from public school children in the Northeastern United States. *Journal of School Health, 79,* 30-37.

Collins, M. A., & Amabile, T. M. (1999). Motivation and creativity. In R. J. Sternberg (Ed.), *Handbook of creativity* (pp. 297-312). New York, NY: Cambridge University Press.

Corbetta, D., & Vereijken, B. (1999). Understanding development and learning of motor coordination in sport: the contribution of dynamic systems theory. *International Journal of Sport Psychology, 30,* 507-530.

Cote, J., Baker, J., & Abernethy, B. (2007). Practice and play in the development of expertise. In R. Eklund & G. Tenenbaum (Eds.), *Handbook of sport psychology* (3rd ed., pp. 184-202). Hoboken, NJ: Wiley.

Creswell, J. W., & Clark, V. L. P. (2007). *Designing and conducting mixed methods research* Thousand Oaks, CA: Sage.

Csikszentmihalyi, M. (1978). Intrinsic rewards and emergent motivation. In M. R. Lepper & D. Greene (Eds.), *The hidden costs of rewards: New perspectives on the psychology of human motivation* (pp. 205-216). Hillsdale, NJ: Erlbaum.

Csikszentmihalyi, M. (1990). *Flow: The psychology of optimal experience.* New York, NY: Harper & Row.

Csikszentmihalyi, M. (2000). *Beyond boredom and anxiety.* San Francisco, CA: Jossey-Bass.

Csikszentmihalyi, M., & Bennett, H. S. (1971). An exploratory model of play. *American Anthropologist, 73,* 45-58.

Curlik, D. M., & Shors, T. J. (2012). Training your brain: do mental and physical (MAP) training enhance cognition through the process of neurogenesis in the hippocampus? *Neuropharmacology, 64,* 506-514.

Danish, S. J., Fomeris, T., Hodge, K., & Heke, I. (2004). Enhancing youth development throughout sport. *World Leisure Journal, 46,* 38-49.

Datar, A., Sturm, R., & Magnabosco, J. L. (2004). Childhood overweight and academic performance: national study of kindergartners and first-graders. *Obesity Research, 12,* 58-68.

Davis, C. L., & Cooper, S. (2011). Fitness, fatness, cognition, behavior, and academic achievement among overweight children: Do cross-sectional associations correspond to exercise trial outcomes? *Preventive Medicine, 52,* S65-S69.

Davis, C. L., Tomporowski, P. D., McDowell, J. E., Austin, B. P., Yanasak, N. E., Allison, J. D., . . . Miller, P. H. (2011). Exercise improves executive function and achievement and alters brain activation in overweight children: A randomized, controlled trial. *Health Psychology, 30,* 91-98.

Denzin, N. K., & Lincoln, Y. S. (1994). Entering the field of qualitative research. In N. K. Denzin & Y. S. Lincoln (Eds.), *Handbook of Qualitative Research* (pp. 1-17). Thousand Oaks, CA: Sage.

Diamond, A. (2013). Executive Functions. *Annual Review of Psychology, 64,* 135-168.

Diamond, A., & Lee, K. (2011). Interventions shown to aid executive function development in children 4 to 12 years old. *Science, 959,* 954-969.

Dienstbier, R. A. (1989). Arousal and physiological toughness: Implications for mental and physical health. *Psychological Review, 96,* 84-100.

Dienstmann, R. (2008). *Games for motor learning.* Champaign, IL: Human Kinetics.

Dishman, R. K., Heath, G. W., & Lee, I.-M. (2012). *Physical activity epidemiology* (2nd ed.). Champaign, IL: Human Kinetics.

Doman, G. (2005). *What to do about your brain-injured child.* New Hyde Park, NY: Square One Publishers.

Donnelly, J. E., Greene, J. L., Gibson, C. A., Smith, B. K., Washburn, R. A., Sullivan, D. K., . . . Williams, S. L. (2009). Physical Activity Across the Curriculum (PAAC): A randomized controlled trial to promote physical activity and diminish overweight and obesity in elementary school children. *Preventive Medicine, 49,* 336-341.

Dowson, A. (2009). *More fun and games.* Champaign, IL: Human Kinetics.

Dustman, R. E., & White, A. (2006). Efficacy of exercise on cognition in older adults: A reexamination of proposed mechanisms. In L. W. Poon, W. J. Chodzko-

Zajko & P. D. Tomporowski (Eds.), *Aging, exercise, and cognition: Active living, cognitive functioning, and aging* (Vol. 1, pp. 51-74). Champaign, IL: Human Kinetics.

Dwyer, G., Baur, L. A., & Hardy, L. L. (2009). The challenge of understanding and assessing physical activity in preschool-age children: Thinking beyond the framework of intensity, duration and frequency of activity. *Journal of Science and Medicine in Sport, 12*, 534-536.

Eisenberg, N., Valiente, C., & Eggum, N. D. (2010). Self-regulation and school readiness. *Early Education and Development, 21*, 681-898.

Eloranta, V., & Jakkola, T. (2007). Core-based motor teaching. In J. Luikkonen, Y. V. Auweele, B. Vereijken, D. Alfermann & J. Theodorakis (Eds.), *Psychology for physical educators* (Vol. 2nd, pp. 261-276). Champaign, IL: Human Kinetics.

Erickson, K. I., & Kramer, A. F. (2009). Aerobic exercise effects on cognitive and neural plasticity in older adults. *British Journal of Sports Medicine, 43*, 22-24.

Ericsson, K. A. (1996). The acquisition of expert performance: An introduction to some of the issues. In K. A. Ericsson (Ed.), *The road to excellence* (pp. 1-50). Mahwah, NJ: Erlbaum.

Estabrooks, P. A., & Glasgow, R. E. (2006). Translating effective clinic-based physical activity interventions into practice. *American Journal of Preventive Medicine, 31*, S45-S56.

Eysenck, H. J. (1967). *The biological basis of personality*. Springfield, IL: Thomas.

Eysenck, H. J., Nias, D. K., & Cox, D. N. (1982). Sport and personality. *Advances in Behaviour Research and Therapy, 4*, 1-56.

Faigenbaum, A. D., Farrell, A., Fabiano, M., Radler, T., Naclerio, F., Ratamess, N. A., . . . Myer, G. D. (2011). Effects of integrative neuromuscular training on fitness performance in children. *Pediatric Exercise Science, 23*, 573-584.

Faigenbaum, A. D., Stracciolini, A., & Myer, G. D. (2011). Exercise deficit disorder in youth: a hidden truth. *Acta Paediatrica, 100*, 1423-1425.

Faucette, N., Nugent, P., Sallis, J. F., & McKenzie, T. L. (2002). "I'd rather chew on aluminum foil." Overcoming classroom teachers' resistance to teaching physical education. *Journal of Teaching in Physical Education, 21*, 287-308.

Fitts, P., & Posner, M. I. (1967). *Human performance*. Belmont, CA: Brooks/Cole.

Fleishman, E. A., & Quaintance, M. K. (1984). *Taxonomies of human performance*. New York, NY: Academic Press.

Gabbard, C. P. (2004). *Lifelong motor development* (4th ed.). New York, NY: Pearson.

Gallahue, D. L., & Cleland, F. (2003). *Developmental physical education for all children* (4th ed.). Champaign, IL: Human Kinetics.

Garon, N., Bryson, S., & Smith, I. M. (2008). Executive function in preschoolers: A review using an integrative framework. *Psychological Bulletin, 134*, 31-60.

Gibbs, L., O'Connor, T., Waters, E., Booth, M., Walsh, O., Green, J. L., . . . Swinburn, B. (2008). Addressing the potential adverse effects of school-based BMI assessments on children's wellbeing. *International Journal of Pediatric Obesity, 3*, 52-57.

Ginsburg, K. R. (2007). The importance of play in promoting healthy child development and maintaining strong parent-child bonds. *Pediatrics, 119*, 182-191.

Glasgow, R. E., Klesges, L. M., Dzewaltowski, D. A., Bull, S. S., & Eastabrooks, P. (2004). The future of health behavior change research: What is needed to improve translation of research into health practice? *Annals of Behavioral Medicine, 27*, 3-12.

Goudas, M. (2010). Prologue: A review of life skills teaching in sport and physical education. *Hellenic Journal of Psychology, 7*, 241-258.

Graber, K., & Woods, A. M. (2013). *Physical education & activity for elementary classroom teachers*. New York, NY: McGraw-Hill.

Graham, G. (1995). Physical education through students' eyes and in students' voices: Implications for teachers and researchers. *Journal of Teaching in Physical Education, 14*, 478-482.

Graham, G., Holt/Hale, S. A., & Parker, M. (2013). *Children moving: A reflective approach to teaching physical education* (9th ed.). New York, NY: McGraw-Hill.

Griffey, D., & Housner, L. (1991). Differences between experienced and inexperienced teachers: Planning decisions, interactions, student engagement and instructional climate. *Research Quarterly for Exercise & Sport, 62*, 196-204.

Guadagnoli, M. A., & Lee, T. D. (2004). Challenge point: A framework for conceptualizing the effects of various practice conditions in motor learning. *Journal of Motor Behavior, 36*, 212-224.

Gunter, G. A., Kenny, R. F., & Vick, E. H. (2008). Taking educational games seriously: using the RETAIN model to design endogenous fantasy into standalone educational games. *Educational Technology Research & Development, 56*, 511-537.

Gutin, B. (2011). Diet vs exercise for the prevention of pediatric obesity: the role of exercise. *International Journal of Obesity and Related Metabolic Disorders, 35*, 29-32.

Gutin, B. (2013). How can we help people to develop lean and healthy bodies? A new perspective. *Research Quarterly for Exercise and Sport, 84*, 1-5.

Hastie, P., & Martin, E. (2006). *Teaching elementary physical education: Strategies for the classroom teacher.* San Francisco, CA: Benjamin Cummings.

Havighurst, R. J. (1972). *Developmental tasks and education* (3rd ed.). New York: David McKay.

Held, R. (1965). Plasticity in sensory-motor systems. *Scientific American, 213,* 84-94.

Hellison, D. R., & Templin, T. J. (1991). *A reflective approach to teaching physical education.* Champaign. IL: Human Kinetics.

Hertzog, C., Kramer, A. F., Wilson, R. S., & Lindenberger, U. (2009). Enrichment effects on adult cognitive development. Can the functional capacity of older adults be preserved and enhanced? *Psychological Science in the Public Interest, 9,* 1-65.

Hillman, C. H., Erickson, K. I., & Kramer, A. F. (2008). Be smart, exercise your heart: exercise effects on brain and cognition. *Nature Reviews Neuroscience, 9,* 58-65.

Hu, W. (2010). Forget goofing around: Recess has a new boss, *New York Times.* Retrieved from http://www.nytimes.com/2010/03/15/education/15recess.html?_r=1&pagewanted=print

Huges, F. P. (2010). *Children, play, and development.* Thousand Oaks, CA: Sage Publications.

Huizinga, M., Dolan, C. V., & Van der Molen, M. W. (2006). Age-related change in executive function: developmental trends and a latent variable analysis. *Neuropsychologia, 44,* 2017-2036.

Iacoboni, M. (2001). Playing tennis with the cerebellum. *Nature Neuroscience, 4,* 55-56.

Kazdin, A. E. (2013). *Behavior modification in applied settings.* Long Grove, IL: Waveland Publishers.

Kempermann, G. (2008). The neurogenic reserve hypothesis: what is adult hippocampal neurogenesis good for? *Trends in Neuroscience, 31,* 163-169.

Kirk, D. (2005). Physical education, youth sport and lifelong participation: the importance of early learning experiences. *European Physical Education Review, 11,* 239-255.

Kirk, D., & MacPhail, A. (2002). Teaching games for understanding and situated learning: Rethinking the Bunker-Thorpe model. *Journal of Teaching in Physical Education, 21,* 177-192.

Kobasa, S. C. (1979). Stressful life events, personality, and health: An inquiry into hardiness. *Journal of Personality and Social Psychology, 42,* 168-177.

Krafft, C. E., Schwarz, N. F., Chi, L., Weinberger, A. L., Schaeffer, D. J., Pierce, J. E., McDowell, J. E. (2014). An 8-month randomized controlled exercise trial alters brain activation during cognitive tasks in overweight children. *Obesity, 22,* 232-242.

Kramer, A. F., Hahn, S., McAuley, E., Cohen, N. J., Banich, M. T., Harrison, C., R., . . . Vakil, E. (2002). Exercise, aging, and cognition: Healthy body, healthy mind? In W. A. Rogers & A. D. Fisk (Eds.*),* *Human factors interventions for the health care of older adults* (pp. 91-120). Mahwah, NJ: Erlbaum.

Krukowski, R. A., Smith West, D., Philyaw Perez, A., Bursac, Z., Phillips, M. M., & Raczynski, J. M. (2009). Overweight children, weight-based teasing and academic performance. *International Journal of Pediatric Obesity, 4,* 274-280.

Kubesch, S., & Walk, L. (2009). Körperliches und kognitives Training exekutiver Funktionen in Kindergarten und Schule [Physical and cognitive training of executive functions in preschool and school children]. *Sportwissenschaft, 39,* 309-317.

Lafont, L., & Winnykamen, F. (1999). Co-operation and competition in children and adolescents. In Y. V. Auweele, T. Bakker, S. J. H. Biddle, M. Durand & R. Selier (Eds.), *Psychology for physical educators* (pp. 379-404). Champaign, IL: Human Kinetics.

Laguardia, A., & Pearl, A. (2009). Necessary educational reform for the 21st Century: The future of public schools in our democracy. *Urban Review, 41,* 352-368.

Lawson, H. A. (2009). Paradigms, exemplars and social change. *Sport, Education and Society, 14,* 97-119.

Lawson, H. A. (2012). Realizing the promise to young people: Kinesiology and new institutional designs for school and community programs. *Kinesiology Review, 1,* 76-90.

Lawson, M. A., & Lawson, H. A. (2013). New conceptual frameworks for student engagement research, policy, and practice. *Review of Educational Research.* Published online before print March 19, 2013, doi: 10.3102/0034654313480891

Livingston, C., & Borko, H. (1989). Expert-novice differences in teaching: A cognitive analysis and implications for teacher education. *Journal of Teacher Education, 40,* 36-42.

Lohrmann, D. K. (2010). A complementary ecological model of the coordinated school health program. *Journal of School Health, 80,* 1-9.

Magill, R. A., & Anderson, D. (2014). *Motor learning and control: Concepts and applications* (10th ed.). Boston: McGraw Hill.

Malina, R. M., Bouchard, C., & Bar-Or, O. (2004). *Growth, maturation, and physical activity* (2nd ed.). Champaign, IL: Human Kinetics.

Marshall, S. J., & Welk, G. J. (2008). Definitions and measurement. In A. L. Smith & S. J. H. Biddle (Eds.), *Youth physical activity and sedentary behavior* (pp. 3-29). Champaign, IL: Human Kinetics.

Martinez, S. M., Arredondo, E. M., Ayala, G. X., & Elder, J. P. (2008). Culturally appropriate research and interventions. In A. L. Smith & S. J. H. Biddle (Eds.), *Youth physical activity and sedentary behavior* (pp. 453-477). Champaign, IL: Human Kinetics.

McCullick, B., Metzler, M., Cicek, S., Jackson, J., & Vickers, B. (2008). Kids say the darndest things: PETE program assessment through the eyes of students. *Journal of Teaching in Physical Education, 27,* 4-20.

McKenzie, T. L., Sallis, J. F., & Nader, P. R. (1991). SOFIT: System for observing fitness instruction time. *Journal of Teaching in Physical Education, 11,* 195-205.

McLeroy, K. R., Bibeau, D., Steckler, A., & Glanz, K. (1988). An ecological perspective on health promotion programs. *Health Education Quarterly, 15,* 351-377.

Meinel, K., & Schnabel, G. (1998). *Bewegungslehre. Sportmotorik [Movement theory. Sports motility].* Berlin, Germany: Sportverlag Berlin.

Memmert, D. (2011). Sports and creativity. In M. A. Runco & S. R. Pritzker (Eds.), *Encyclopedia of Creativity* (2nd ed., Vol. 2, pp. 373-378). San Diego, CA: Academic Press.

Metzler, M. W. (2011). *Instructional models for physical education* (3rd ed.). Scottsdale, AZ: Holcomb Hathaway.

Mezzetti-Pantanelli, R., & Maiello, P. (2001). L'insegnante sufficientemente buono. Attività motoria per bambini dai tre agli otto anni. *[The sufficiently good teacher, Movement activities for children aged 3-8 years].* Rome, Italy: Brain Edizioni.

Milteer, R. M., Ginsburg, K. R., & Mulligan, D. A. (2012). The importance of play in promoting healthy child development and maintaining strong parent-child bond: Focus on children in poverty. *Pediatrics.* 129, e204-e213.

Mosston, M., & Ashworth, S. (2008). *Teaching physical education* (5th ed.). Pearson Publishers (on line http://www.spectrumofteachingstyles.org/pdfs/ebook/Teaching_Physical_Edu_1st_Online_old.pdf)

Moreau, D., & Conway, A. R. A. (2013). Cognitive enhancement: a comparative review of computerized and athletic training program. *International Review of Sport and Exercise Psychology, 6,* 155-183.

Motl, R. W., Birnbaum, A. S., Tykubik, M. Y., & Dishman, R. K. (2004). Naturally occurring changes in physical activity are inversely related to depressive symptoms during early adolescence. *Psychosomatic Medicine, 66,* 336-342.

National Association for Sport and Physical Education. (2003). *What constitutes a quality physical education program [Position statement].* Reston, VA: Author.

National Association for Sport and Physical Education. (2009). *Appropriate instructional practice guidelines for elementary school physical education* (3rd ed.). Reston, VA: Author.

National Association for Sport and Physical Education. (2011). *Physical education is critical to educating the whole child [Position statement].* Reston, VA: Author.

National Association for Sport and Physical Education. (2007). *What constitutes a highly qualified physical education teacher.* Reston, VA: American Alliance for Health, Physical Education, Recreation and Dance.

National Association for Sport and Physical Education and American Heart Association. (2012). *2012 Shape of the Nation Report: Status of Physical Education in the USA.* Reston, VA: American Alliance for Health, Physical Education, Recreation and Dance.

Nettlefold, L., McKay, H. A., Warburton, D. E. R., McGuire, K. A., & Bredin, S. S. D. (2011). The challenge of low physical activity during the school day: At recess, lunch, and in physical education. *Journal of Sports Medicine, 45,* 813-819.

Newcombe, N. S., & Frick, A. (2010). Early education for spatial intelligence: why, what, and how. *Mind, Brain and Education, 4,* 102-111.

Newell, A., & Rosenbloom, P. S. (1981). Mechanisms of skill acquisition and the law of practice. In J. Anderson, R. (Ed.), *Cognitive skills and their acquisition* (pp. 1-55). Hillsdale, NJ: Erlbaum.

O'Leary, K. C., Pontifex, M. B., Scudder, M. R., Brown, M. L., & Hillman, C. H. (2011). The effects of single bouts of aerobic exercise, exergaming, and video-game play on cognitive control. *Clinical Neurophysiology, 122,* 1518-1525.

Ogden, C. L., Carroll, M. D., Curtin, L. R., Lamb, M. M., & Flegal, K. M. (2010). Prevalence of high body mass index in US children and adolescents, 2007-2008. *Journal of the American Medical Association, 303,* 242-249.

Olds, T. S., Ridley, K., & Tomkinson, G. R. (2007). Declines in aerobic fitness: are they only due to increasing fatness? In G. R. Tomkinson & T. S. Olds (Eds.), *Pediatric Fitness: Secular Trends and Geographic Variability* (Vol. 50, pp. 226-240). Basel, Switzerland: Karger.

Papastergiou, M. (2009). Exploring the potential of computer and video games for health and physical education: A literature review. *Computers & Education, 53,* 603-622.

Parker, M. (1989). Academic learning time - physical education (ALT-PE), 1982 revision. In P. W. Darst,

Zakrajsek, D. B., & Mancini, V. H. (Eds.), *Analyzing physical education and sport instruction* (2nd ed.) (pp. 195-206). Champaign, IL: Human Kinetics.

Parkinson, B. (1995). Emotion. In B. Parkinson & A. M. Colman (Eds.), *Emotion and motivation* (pp. 1-21). New York: Longman.

Pate, R. R., O'Neill, J. R., & Lobelo, F. (2008). The evolving definition of "sedentary." *Exercise and Sport Science Reviews, 36*, 173-178.

Patton, M. Q. (2002). *Qualitative research & evaluation methods* (3rd ed.). Thousand Oaks, CA: Sage.

Pellegrini, A. D., & Bohn, C. M. (2005). The role of recess in children's cognitive performance and school adjustment. *Educational Researcher, 34*, 13-19.

Pesce, C. (2012). Shifting the focus from quantitative to qualitative exercise characteristics in exercise and cognition research. *Journal of Sport & Exercise Psychology, 34*, 766-786.

Pesce, C., Crova, C., Cereatti, L., Casella, R., & Bellucci, M. (2009). Physical activity and mental performance in preadolescents: Effects of acute exercise on free-recall memory. *Mental Health and Physical Activity, 2*, 16-22.

Pesce, C., Crova, C., Marchetti, M., Struzzolino, I., Masci, I., Vannozzi, G., & Forte, R. (2013). Searching for cognitively optimal challenge point in physical activity for children with typical and atypical motor development. *Mental Health and Physical Activity, 6*, 172-180.

Physical Activity Guidelines Advisory Committee. (2008). *Physical activity guidelines advisory committee report.* Washington, DC: U.S. Department of Health and Human Services. (last updated: April 8, 2014)

Preamble to the Constitution of the World Health Organization as adopted by the International Health Conference. (1946). New York.

Proctor, R. W., Reeve, E. G., & Weeks, D. J. (1990). A triphasic approach to the acquisition of response-selection skill. In G. H. Bower (Ed.) *The psychology of learning: Advances in research and theory* (pp. 207-240). New York, NY: Academic Press.

Rakoczy, H., Hamann, K., Warneken, F., & Tomasello, M. (2010). Bigger knows better: young children selectively learn rule games from adults rather than from peers. *British Journal of Developmental Psychology, 28*, 785-798.

Ridgers, N. D., Stratton, G., & Fairclough, S. J. (2005). Assessing physical activity during recess using accelerometry. *Preventive Medicine, 41*, 102-107.

Rink, J. E. (2010). *Teaching physical education for learning* (6th ed.). New York, NY: McGraw-Hill.

Roth, K., Ruf, K., Obinger, M., Mauer, S., Ahnert, J., Schneider, W., . . . Hebestreit, H. (2010). Is there a secular decline in motor skills in preschool children? *Scandinavian Journal of Medicine & Science in Sports, 20*, 670-678.

Rowland, T. W. (2005). *Children's exercise physiology.* Champaign, IL: Human Kinetics.

Rushall, B. S., & Siedentop, D. (1972). *The development and control of behavior in sport and physical education.* Philadelphia, PA: Lea & Febiger.

Sabbagh, M. A., Xu, F., Carlson, S. M., Moses, L. J., & Lee, K. (2006). The development of executive functioning and theory of mind. A Comparison of Chinese and U.S. Preschoolers *Psychological Science, 17*, 74-81.

Salvy, S.-J., Bowker, J. C., Germeroth, L., & Barkley, J. (2012). Influence of peers and friends on overweight/obese youth's physical activity. *Exercise & Sport Science Reviews, 40*, 127-132.

Schempp, P. G. (2003). *Teaching sport and physical activity: Insights on the road to excellence.* Champaign, IL: Human Kinetics.

Schmidt, R. A., & Wrisberg, C. A. (2008). *Motor learning and performance: A situation-based learning approach.* Champaign. IL: Human Kinetics.

Scibinetti, P., Tocci, N., & Pesce, C. (2011). Motor creativity and creative thinking in children: The diverging role of inhibition. *Creativity Research Journal, 23*, 262-272.

Seligman, M. E. P., & Csikszentmihalyi, M. (2000). Positive psychology: An introduction. *American Psychologist, 55*, 5-14.

Selye, H. (1974). *Stress without distress.* Philadelphia, PA: Lippincott.

Siedentop, D., & Tannehill, D. (2000). *Developing teaching skills in physical education* (4th ed.). Mountain View, CA: Mayfield.

Smith, E., Hay, P., Campbell, L., & Trollor, J. N. (2011). A review of the association between obesity and cognitive function across the lifespan: Implications for novel approaches to prevention and treatment. *Obesity Reviews, 12*, 740-755.

Smith, P. K., & Pellegrini, A. D. (2008). Learning through play. In R. E. Tremblay, R. G. Barr, R. D. V. Peters & M. Boivin (Eds.), *Encyclopedia on Early Childhood Development* (pp. 1-6). Montreal, Quebec, Canada: Centre of Excellence for Early Childhood Development. Available at: http://www.child-encyclopedia.com/documents/Smith-PellegriniANGxp.pdf. Accessed [August 4, 2014].

Society of Health and Physical Educators America. (2014). *National standards & grade-level outcomes for K-12 physical education.* Champaign, IL: Human Kinetics.

Solmon, M. A., & Lee, A. M. (2008). Research on social issues in elementary school physical education. *Elementary School Journal, 108*, 229-239.

Sparrow, S., & Zigler, E. (1978). Evaluation of a patterning treatment for retarded children. *Pediatrics, 62*, 137-150.

Sternberg, R. J. (2005). The triarchic theory of successful intelligence. In D. P. Flanagan & P. L. Harrison (Eds.), *Contemporary intellectual assessment: Theories, tests, and issues* (pp. 103-135). New York, NY: The Guilford Press.

Stockman, I. J. (2004a). Introduction: the clinical problem. In I. J. Stockman (Ed.), *Movement and action in learning and developmental: clinical implications for pervasive development disorders* (pp. 1-19). New York, NY: Elsevier.

Stockman, I. J. (2004b). *Movement and action in learning and development: Clinical implications for pervasive developmental disorders.* New York, NY: Elsevier.

Strong, W. B., Malina, R. M., Bumkie, C. J. R., Daniels, S. R., Dishman, R. K., Gutin, B., . . . Trudeau, F. (2005). Evidence based physical activity for school-age youth. *Journal of Pediatrics, 146*, 732-737.

Thelen, E. (2004). The central role of action in typical and atypical development: A dynamical systems perspective. In I. J. Stockman (Ed.), *Movement and action in learning and development: clinical implications for pervasive developmental disorders* (pp. 49-74). New York, NY: Elsevier.

Tocci, N., & Scibinetti, P. (2003). Essere creativi è utile? Studi sulla creatività motoria [Is being creative useful? Research on motor creativity]. *SdS – Rivista di Cultura Sportiva, 58-59*, 69-73.

Tocci, N., & Scibinetti, P. (2007). Essere creativi è utile. Indicazioni metodologiche per lo sviluppo della creatività motoria [Being creative is useful. Methods for promoting motor creativity development]. *SdS – Rivista di Cultura Sportiva, 72*, 53-71.

Tomkinson, G. R., & Olds, T. S. (2007). Secular changes in pediatric aerobic fitness test performance: The global picture. In G. R. Tomkinson & T. S. Olds (Eds.), *Pediatric Fitness: Secular Trends and Geographic Variability* (Vol. 50, pp. 46-66). Basel, Switzerland: Karger.

Tomporowski, P. D. (2003a). Cognitive and behavioral responses to acute exercise in youth: a review. *Pediatric Exercise Science, 15*, 348-359.

Tomporowski, P. D. (2003b). *The psychology of skill: A life-span approach.* Westport, CT: Praeger.

Tomporowski, P. D., McCullick, B. A., & Horvat, M. (2010). *Role of contextual interference and mental engagement on learning.* New York, NY: Nova Science Publishers, Inc.

Torrance, E. P. (1981). *Thinking creatively in action and movement.* Bensenville, IL: Scholastic Testing Service.

Tousignant, M., & Siedentop, D. (1983). A qualitative analysis of task structures in required secondary physical education classes. *Journal of Teaching in Physical Education, 3*, 47-57.

Tudor-Locke, C., Johnson, W. D., & Katzmarzyk, P. T. (2010). Accelerometer-determined steps per day in US children and youth. *Medicine & Science in Sports & Exercise, 42*, 2244-2250.

U.S. Department of Education. (2010). 21st Century Community Learning Centers descriptive study of program practices. Menlo Park, CA: Author.

van der Mars, H. (1989). Systematic observation: An introduction. In P. W. Darst, D. B. Zakrajsek & V. F. Mancini (Eds.), *Analyzing Physical Education and Sport Instruction* (2nd ed., pp. 3-17). Champaign, IL: Human Kinetics.

Voss, M. W., Nagamatsu, L. S., Liu-Ambrose, T., & Kramer, A. F. (2011). Exercise, brain and cognition across the lifespan. *Journal of Applied Physiology, 111*, 1505-1513.

Weis, R., & Cerankosky, B. C. (2010). Effects of video-game ownership on young boys' academic and behavioral functioning: A randomized, controlled study. *Psychological Science, 21*, 463-470. DOI:10.1177/0956797610362670.

Welk, G. J., Corbin, C. B., & Dale, D. (2000). *Research Quarterly for Exercise and Sport, 71*, S59-S73.

Wells, A., & Matthews, G. (1994). *Attention and emotion: A clinical perspective.* Hillsdale, NJ: Erlbaum.

Winner, E. (1996). The rage to master: The decisive role of talent in the visual arts. In K. I. Erickson (Ed.), *The road to excellence* (pp. 271-301). Mahwah, NJ: Erlbaum.

Woodlee, M. T., & Schallert, T. (2006). The impact of motor activity and inactivity on the brain. Implications for the prevention and treatment of nervous-system disorders. *Current Directions in Psychological Science, 15*, 203-206.

World Health Organization. (2005). *Child and adolescent mental health policies and plans.* (WHO reference number: WM 34 2005ME-1). Geneva, Switzerland: World Health Organization.

Yerkes, R. M., & Dodson, J. D. (1908). The relation of strength of stimulus to rapidity of habit formation. *Journal of Comparative Neurology and Psychology, 18*, 459-482.

Zigler, E., & Balla, D. (1982). Motivational and personality factors in the performance of the retarded. In E. Zigler & D. Balla (Eds.), *Mental retardation: The developmental-difference controversy* (pp. 9-26). Hillsdale, NJ: Erlbaum.

Zigler, E., & Styfco, S. J. (2004). *The head start debate.* Baltimore, MD: Paul H. Brooks.

Index

Note: The italicized *f* and *t* following page numbers refer to figures and tables, respectively.

About the Authors

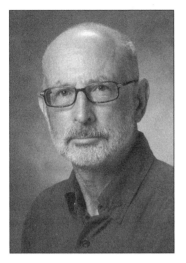

Phillip D. Tomporowski, PhD, is a professor of kinesiology at the University of Georgia. An experimental psychologist, Tomporowski has been involved in the study of learning and the effects of exercise on mental functions for four decades. He has authored, coauthored, or edited five books and contributed chapters to a dozen of other books. He is widely published in journals on cognitive function and exercise issues in children and has received numerous grants to conduct studies in these and related areas. Tomporowski is a sought-after speaker at symposia and conventions. He is a fellow of the American College of Sports Medicine and a member of the American Psychological Society. He enjoys participating and instructing in the martial arts and taking part in triathlons and obstacle races.

Bryan A. McCullick, PhD, is a professor of kinesiology at the University of Georgia. He is a former physical education teacher and has been a physical education teacher educator since 1997. He has given numerous keynote addresses at conferences related to physical education, physical activity, and teacher training. McCullick has coauthored two books, contributed numerous chapters in books, and written more than 40 journal articles. He has also received numerous grants to conduct research and received awards and recognitions, including winning the Mabel Lee Award from AAHPERD. McCullick is a fellow in the SHAPE America Research Consortium, has been associate editor for *Research Quarterly for Exercise and Sport* (*RQES*) and is on the *RQES* editorial board, was vice president of the *Association Internationale des Ecoles Superieures d'Education Physique (AIESEP)*, and has served on many other editorial boards. Among his joys are being a father and a husband, playing golf (poorly), and following the Alabama Crimson Tide and the Miami Dolphins.

Caterina Pesce, PhD, is a professor in the department of movement, human and health science at the Italian University Sport and Movement in Rome. She is a former physical education teacher with higher education in both sport science and experimental psychology. Since 2003 she has taught in higher education on physical activity for children. Her research focus has been on the effects of physical exercise on cognitive functioning. She coauthored a book on exercise and cognitive function and has authored or coauthored more than three dozen research publications in sport and exercise psychology and physical education. Pesce is a member of the Italian Society of Movement and Sport Sciences, associate editor for *Journal of Aging and Physical Activity,* a board member of the *Journal of Sport and Exercise Psychology,* and has been a board member of the Italian national program of motor literacy for elementary schools. She enjoys jogging and singing and, above all, being a mother.

241

You'll find other outstanding physical education resources at
www.HumanKinetics.com